Public Financing of Public Service Broadcasting and its Qualification as State Aid

Europäische Hochschulschriften

European University Studies

Publications Universitaires Européennes

Reihe II **Rechtswissenschaft**

Series II Law

Série II Droit

Band/Volume **5789**

Benjamin Linke

Public Financing of Public Service Broadcasting and its Qualification as State Aid

With Particular Regard to the Altmark Trans Jurisprudence

PL ACADEMIC RESEARCH

Bibliografische Information der Deutschen Nationalbibliothek
Die Deutsche Nationalbibliothek verzeichnet diese Publikation in der Deutschen Nationalbibliografie; detaillierte bibliografische Daten sind im Internet über http://dnb.d-nb.de abrufbar.

ISSN 0531-7312
ISBN 978-3-631-66568-8 (Print)
E-ISBN 978-3-653-05964-9 (E-Book)
DOI 10.3726/978-3-653-05964-9

PL Academic Research ist ein Imprint der Peter Lang GmbH.
Peter Lang – Frankfurt am Main · Bern · Bruxelles · New York · Oxford · Warszawa · Wien

Diese Publikation wurde begutachtet.

www.peterlang.com

Editorial

The scope for European Union (EU) intervention in the field of public service broadcasting has been extremely controversial, raising as it does the continuing competence of Member States to determine the scale and nature of public provision in the media sector. Member States first found themselves open to EU oversight through the application of the EU internal market rules, with cross border broadcasters challenging the advertising and content rules imposed in the country of reception on the basis that they restricted the free flow of services. These rules were often seen by the Commission and/or European Court of Justice as designed to protect the existing public service broadcasting systems from external competition.[1] As commercial operators began to gain a greater foothold in European markets the nature of the challenge shifted. Thus, complaints began to be brought not by broadcasters located outside the Member State concerned but by commercial operators established within the State itself who felt disadvantaged by the funding and operations of the incumbent public service broadcaster. Rather than rely on internal market rules the nature of the complaints shifted to the competition law field and, in particular, to the rules on state aid. At issue was the funding of public service broadcasters by the state, which, the commercial operators argued, enabled the public broadcasters to foreclose developing markets, undercut advertising rates and outbid the competition for attractive film and sports rights.

Given the potential social and political influence of public service broadcasting, State alarm at Commission oversight of this area was to be expected. The initial cases were fiercely fought over, culminating in the Member States asserting their ongoing competence in the field by means of a specific protocol attached to the Amsterdam Treaty, which provided that European Community law, with certain caveats, was to be 'without prejudice to the competence of Member States to provide for the funding of public service broadcasting insofar as such funding is granted to broadcasting organisations for the fulfilment of the public service remit as conferred, defined and organised by each Member State'. This provision has now been carried over to Protocol 29 of the Lisbon Treaty. Over time, too, the Commission clarified that its role was not as searching as some had suggested, with limited review of the substantive remit of public service broadcasters for manifest error.[2] In particular, the Commission has sought to encourage Member States themselves to establish procedural and

1 For an early example see case C-352/85, *Bond van Adverteerders and others v The Netherlands*, ECLI:EU:C:1988:196.

2 European Commission, Communication on the application of State aid rules to public service broadcasting, (2009) OJ 257/1, para.39.

accountability mechanisms designed to ensure that their public service broadcasters do not act anti-competitively and operate in a transparent manner.[3]

The development of the law has primarily been taken forward on the basis of, on the one hand, articles 107 and 108 of the Treaty on the Functioning of the European Union (TFEU), which establish the nature of state aid, potential derogations and notification requirements and, on the other, Article 106(2) TFEU, which establishes a derogation for services of general economic interest, interpreted to cover public service broadcasting. There has, however, been a continual line of argument that State funding for public service broadcasting should not be assessed under these provisions in that States are in reality paying for a service and are not therefore distorting competition. The possibility that funding could be seen as merely payment for a service was supported by the ruling of the European Court of Justice in the *Altmark* case, which established four criteria that, if met, take funding outwith the reach of the state aid provisions altogether.[4] A number of States subsequently sought to rely on *Altmark* in the broadcasting context but tended to founder on the fourth criterion, which requires them to show either that the funding was awarded on the basis of a competitive tender designed to minimise the risk of overpayment or that the compensation was determined on the basis of an analysis of the costs that a typical well run and adequately provided undertaking would have incurred in discharging the designated public service commitments, taking into account the relevant receipts and a reasonable profit for discharging those obligations.[5]

As a result, the *Altmark* route has tended to receive relatively little attention in the academic literature, the main focus of commentators being on the operation of article 106(2) TFEU. The present study addresses this gap by taking the *Altmark* case seriously, exploring in particular what would be required to comply with all four of the *Altmark* criteria in the broadcasting context. But before engaging with this issue, the study sets the scene by explaining how articles 107 and 106(2) TFEU have operated in the field. It covers the main Commission and judicial decisions, the specific guidance given by the Commission on the application of the state aid rules in its 2001 and 2009 public service broadcasting communications, and the surrounding academic commentary. In particular, the various lines of argument put forward by the various parties are critically assessed, with a helpful exploration of the legal force of the Amsterdam Protocol and who bears the burden of proof in applying Article 106(2) TFEU.

Certain of Dr. Linke's conclusions are undoubtedly controversial, notably that for aid to be legitimate the activities of public service broadcasters must be 'distinct

---

3 For an invaluable oversight see Donders, K., *Public Service Media and Policy in Europe* (Palgrave Macmillan, 2011).

4 Case C-280/00, *Altmark Trans GmbH and Regierungspräsidium Magdeburg v Nahverkehrsgesellschaft Altmark GmbH, and Oberbundesanwalt beim Bundesverwaltungsgericht* [2003] ECR I-07747.

5 Ibid. at para.95.

from the activities of commercial broadcasters and exhibit a higher public value' (p. 68 et seq.). A key question is then how one determines whether a programme or service is 'distinct' and how one assesses 'public value'. This is an argument that is currently raging in the UK as the future of the BBC is under scrutiny, with its Charter renewal scheduled for 2016.[6] The public service remit in the media context is, according to the Amsterdam Protocol, one that is tied to meeting the democratic, social and cultural needs of a particular society, as well as media pluralism. If States can no longer argue that a service meets such needs because the commercial sector offers something broadly similar then the freedom of the State to determine how key services in the media sector should be provided would be undermined and continually open to contestation. Yet, the freedom of the State to determine the economic mechanisms required to support the provision of public services is recognised in Article 14 TFEU and values such as universal access and affordability are specifically recognised as legitimate bases for the provision of services of general interest in Protocol 26 of the Lisbon Treaty. The provision of universal (both in geographic and content terms), free television and radio services has been one of the underlying rationales behind public service broadcasting in the UK, while in Germany public service broadcasting is seen as providing a basic, guaranteed service around which the private sector can build, not the other way round.[7]

Nor is the fact that commercial operators offer similar services a basis for concluding that the funding provided by the state for public service broadcasting is not necessary or proportionate. The relevant consideration here is whether the *public service* could still be provided without the state funding and whether the funding is no more than that needed to ensure that the specified service is provided. Moreover, it may be difficult to re-create a given public service once lost and there is no assurance that commercial operators will continue to provide a certain level or range of services at a certain price over time. This controversy over whether the level of public provision should be tied to the ambitions of the commercial sector will undoubtedly continue to run and the present study provides the reader with a thoughtful perspective from which to explore these issues.

How one answers this question also affects whether popular sport and entertainment programming are likely to be considered to fall within the public service remit and whether public service providers should be able to buy exclusive rights in relation to popular programme genres. In this context, Dr. Linke concludes that there is a strong argument in favour of including such rights within the public service broadcasting remit but that the requirement to provide a plural service may impose constraints on the extent to which public service operators can focus on such programming (p. 74 et seq.). The study also provides a helpful discussion of when

6 See DCMS, BBC Charter Review Public Consultation, 16 July-8 October 2015 at: https://www.gov.uk/government/uploads/system/uploads/attachment_data/file/445704/BBC_Charter_Review_Consultation_WEB.pdf.

7 BVerfGE 73, 118 1 BvR 1/84 4. Rundfunkurteil "Fourth Broadcasting Case".

newer forms of media content such as chat rooms, thematic digital channels, and user generated content can be included within the public service remit.

But the real contribution of this work to the existing literature lies in its exploration of the *Altmark* jurisprudence. As noted above, where the four *Altmark* criteria are met financial assistance falls outwith the state aid field. There is thus no obligation on Member States to notify such financial compensation to the Commission or for the Commission to keep such aid under regular review. As Dr. Linke notes, to date concrete instructions regarding how to conduct an analysis according to the fourth criterion, which requires either competitive tendering or proof that funding is limited to that which would be required by an efficient undertaking, are 'completely lacking' in this sector. He thus explores the opportunity for competitive tendering in the media field and how the 'efficiency' of a public service broadcaster can be assessed. In relation to the test of efficiency, for example, he notes that reliance could be placed either on benchmarking, using comparator companies that could be public or commercial depending on certain factors, or on an assessment of the efficiency of the particular public service broadcaster at issue. This would entail consideration of the prices paid for production, personnel, infrastructure, rights etc. and the way in which these resource are utilised in practice. Such an analysis would be exacting, requiring significant information and auditing, but, as Dr. Linke notes, it would also establish that the public service operator is well run and may help to confirm the legitimacy of licence fees or other funding mechanisms for the paying population. It is important to recognise, however, that this is not a procedure designed to reduce the scale of operation of the public service broadcaster, merely to test its efficiency in carrying out its allotted tasks.

Public Financing of Public Service Broadcasting and its Qualification as State Aid will be seen by many as a challenging thesis, particularly, one would expect, by the public service operators themselves. It raises important questions about how public service media can be validated in the future and opens up a line of legal enquiry that to date has received limited attention. Dr. Linke's study is one of the first to explore how *Altmark* in all its dimensions could operate in the media field and, given the importance of this issue for the media sector, is unlikely to be the last.

Dr. R. Craufurd Smith

Reader in Media Law, University of Edinburgh

Table of content

A. Introduction

Broadcasting is of particular importance in the modern structure of democracy. It helps building cultural identity, develops citizenship and has the potential of strengthening social cohesion.[1] Consequently, in the European tradition, broadcasting has become part of public services, i.e. infrastructural services supported by the state to meet public needs.[2] Such public service broadcasting (PSB) provides broadcasting services that are of higher quality and of more cultural value to the community than services provided by commercial broadcasters. To ensure the operation of PSB, Member States of the European Union have introduced various measures to support broadcasters.

Over the last two decades, the public aid provided to public service broadcasters has become more and more controversial. This has not always been the case. Up to the late 70s/beginning of the 80s, broadcasting was performed solely on a monopolistic or oligopolistic basis due to the limited technical possibilities,[3] and, as a result, this support did not have the potential to influence competition. By virtue of new transmission technologies, the market was opened up to private broadcasters, which did not receive public support.[4] Until the middle of the 80s all West European countries were seeing the introduction of private broadcasters that were solely financed by revenues earned from commercial activities (e.g. sale of advertisement space).[5] As public service broadcasters and commercial broadcasters were competing for the same license rights (e.g. sports, films), the same viewers and (at least partly) for the same advertisers and sponsors, public funding was seen more critically as it carried the potential to distort competition in the broadcasting market.[6] The situation aggravated as advertising revenues were falling by virtue of the significantly

1 *Katsirea*, Public Broadcasting and European Law, p. 323.

2 *Kübler*, in: *Fuchs/Schwintowski/Zimmer*, Festschrift für Ulrich Immenga zum 70. Geburtstag, p. 231.

3 *Schnaitter*, Möglichkeiten und Grenzen der Ausgestaltung des Programmauftrags der öffentlich-rechtlichen Rundfunkanstalten, p. 16. Cf. also *Niejahr*, in: *Montag/Säcker*, Münchener Kommentar zum Europäischen und Deutschen Wettbewerbsrecht (Kartellrecht) – Band 3, Sektoren para. 134; *Tigchelaar*, EStAL 2003, 169, 169 et seq.

4 Cf. *Commission*, Communication from the Commission on the application of State aid rules to public service broadcasting (OJ C 320/5 of 15.11.2001), para. 2.

5 Cf. *Schnaitter*, Möglichkeiten und Grenzen der Ausgestaltung des Programmauftrags der öffentlich-rechtlichen Rundfunkanstalten, pp. 16 et seq.

6 *Katsirea*, Public Broadcasting and European Law, pp. 323 et seq.

increased number of channels.[7] In particular, (possible) competitors of the favoured broadcasters saw considerable potential for market damage as the tasks of the public service broadcasters were broadly defined, thus enabling broadcasters to move both vertically and horizontally into neighbouring markets.[8]

European State aid law was soon discovered by competitors as an area of law that might preclude funding measures for public service broadcasters. Hence, in 1992, two Spanish commercial broadcasters filed the first State aid complaints regarding this matter.[9] Until then, precedents, or any other form of guidelines as to how to solve these cases, were completely lacking.[10] The Commission issued its first final decision in October 1996,[11] followed by decisions regarding the financing of the German channels '*Kinderkanal*' and '*Phoenix*'[12] and a decision concerning the British channel '*BBC News 24*'[13] in 1999. Additionally, in 2001, the Commission adopted a communication on PSB which provided guidelines for the Member States regarding the conditions under which the Commission would see public funding to be in line with the requirements of State aid law.[14] Since 2001, more than 20 decisions have been made based on the Communication.[15] In 2009 the Communication adopted in 2001 was superseded by new guidelines.[16]

---

7 *Katsirea*, Public Broadcasting and European Law, p. 324.

8 See *Depypere/Tigchelaar*, Competition Policy Newsletter 2004 (2), 19, 19 et seq. who mention the example of a cooking programme that leads to the publication of cookery books. Another example would be the launch of a website.

9 Cf. *Bartosch*, in: *Koenig/Bartosch/Braun*, EC Competition and Telecommunications Law, p. 164; *Katsirea*, Public Broadcasting and European Law, p. 324; *Tigchelaar*, EStAL 2003, 169, 170.

10 *Niejahr*, in: *Montag/Säcker*, Münchener Kommentar zum Europäischen und Deutschen Wettbewerbsrecht (Kartellrecht) – Band 3, Sektoren para. 134.

11 *Commission*, Decision of 02.10.1996, State aid No NN 141/95, *RTP*.

12 *Commission*, Decision of 24.02.1999, State aid No NN 70/1998, *Kinderkanal/Phoenix*.

13 *Commission*, Decision of 14.12.1999, State aid No NN 88/98, *BBC News 24*.

14 *Commission*, Communication from the Commission on the application of State aid rules to public service broadcasting (OJ C 320/5 of 15.11.2001).

15 *Commission*, Communication from the Commission on the application of State aid rules to public service broadcasting, (OJ C 257/1 of 27.10.2009), para. 4.

16 *Commission*, Communication from the Commission on the application of State aid rules to public service broadcasting, (OJ C 257/1 of 27.10.2009).

Despite the various decisions of the Commission,[17] and those of the *CFI*,[18] the question as to if and when public funding of public service broadcasters is to be qualified as illegal State aid has not yet been clarified.[19] In particular, a ruling of the European Court of Justice (*ECJ*) is still lacking.

In its *Altmark Trans*-ruling,[20] the *ECJ* (in a case concerning public transportation services) laid down specific criteria under which compensation for services of general economic interest (SGEI) should not be considered State aid in the sense of Art. 107(1) TFEU. These criteria are significant for the assessment of public funding for PSB, as PSB is part of the SGEI.[21] Nevertheless, the Commission frequently applies Art. 106(2) TFEU – a derogation from Art. 107(1) TFEU – as the decisive

---

17 *Commission*, Decision of 03.04.2002, State aid No NN 2/2002, *ZDF Medienpark*; Decision of 22.05.2002, State aid No N 631/2001, *BBC license fee*; Decision of 01.10.2003, State aid No N 37/2003, *BBC Digital Curriculum*; Decision of 15.10.2003, State aid No C 62/99, *RAI* (ad-hoc payments); Decision of 15.10.2003, State aid No C 85/2001, *RTP* (ad-hoc payments); Decision of 10.12.2003, State aid No C 60/99, *France 2 and 3* (ad-hoc payments); Decision of 19.05.2004, State aid No C 2/2003, *TV2*; Decision of 06.10.2004, State aid No N 313/2004, *TV2* (recapitalisation); Decision of 20.04.2005, State aid No E 8/2005, *RTVE*; Decision of 20.04.2005, State aid No E 10/2005, *France 2 and 3*; Decision of 20.04.2005, State aid No E 9/2005, *RAI*; Decision of 07.06.2005, State aid No N 54/2005, *Chaine française d'information international*; Decision of 22.03.2006, State aid No E 14/2005, *RTP*; Decision of 22.03.2006, State aid No N 638/2005, *Aide à la création de la chaîne corse Via Stella*; Decision of 22.06.2006, State aid No C 2/2004, *Ad-hoc financing measures of Dutch public service*; Decision of 04.07.2006, State aid No NN 31/2006, *RTP*; Decision of 07.03.2007, State aid No NN 8/2007, *RTVE*; Decision of 24.04.2007, State aid No E 3/2005, *Financing of public service broadcasters in Germany*; Decision of 27.02.2008, State aid No E 4/2005, *RTE* and *TNAG (TG4)*; Decision of 27.02.2008, State aid No E 8/2006, *VRT*; Decision of 16.07.2008, State aid No N 279/2008, *France Télévisions*; Decision of 04.08.2008, State aid No N287/08, *TV2/Denmark A/S* (rescue aid); Decision of 01.09.2009, State aid No C 27/2009, *France Télévisions*; Decision of 28.10.2009, State aid No E 2/2008, *ORF*; Decision of 03.12.2009, State aid No C 38/2009, *RTVE*; Decision of 26.01.2010, State aid No E5/2005, *Dutch public broadcasters*; Decision of 20.04.2011, State aid No C 2/2003, *TV2*; Decision of 20.04.2011, State aid No C 19/2009, *TV2* (restructuring); Decision of 20.12.2011, State aid No SA.33294, *RTP* (amendment of decision NN 31/2006); Decision of 20.12.2011, State aid No C 85/2001, *RTP* (years 1992–1998).

18 *CFI*, 10 May 2000, Case T-46/97, *SIC*; 26 June 2008, Case T442/03, *SIC*; 22 October 2008, joined Cases T-309/04, T-317/04, T-329/04 and T-336/04, *TV2*; 11 March 2009, Case T-345/05, *TF1*; *EGC*, 16 December 2010, Joined Cases T-231/06 and T-237/06, *ad hoc financing of Netherlands public service broadcasters* (on appeal, cf. C-104/11P).

19 See for example only *Degenhart*, K&R 2008, 214, 218 ICW fn. 41 and *Michel*, MMR 2005, 284, 285.

20 *ECJ*, 24 July 2003, Case C-280/00, *Altmark Trans*. Regarding the decision see the following in-depth analysis: *Linke*, Die Gewährleistung des Daseinsvorsorgeauftrags im öffentlichen Personennahverkehr, pp. 109 et seqq.

21 See below C. I. 1) a).

law, whereas the question whether the measures constitute State aid in the sense of Art. 107(1) TFEU is usually[22] answered in the affirmative.[23] This focus on Art. 106(2) TFEU is also illustrated in the aforementioned Communication of 2009, since these guidelines mention the *Altmark*-criteria, but do not give any further explanation as to their application to PSB.[24]

Rather than for compelling legal reasons, the shift towards Art. 106(2) TFEU is the result of difficulties in the application of the *Altmark*-ruling. Qualification of public funding as non-state aid, however, is accompanied by considerably more advantages for the beneficiary than a declaration that the measure is compatible with the internal market. According to Art. 108(3) TFEU, for example, Member States shall not introduce State aid without the prior approval of the Commission (the so-called standstill obligation). The approval-procedure, however, does not need to be carried out if the measure is not State aid. Since it is not yet common practice for the Member States to implement the procedure according to Art. 108(3) TFEU there are also significant risks to consider when solely relying on a compliance with Art. 106(2) TFEU. Beneficiaries not complying with Art. 107(1) TFEU could face serious proceedings in front of national courts. Contrary to the proceedings in front of the Commission, where compliance with Art. 106(2) TFEU prevents the recovery of State aid, national courts have to order the recovery of any benefit received as long as the Commission has not declared the measure compatible with the internal market.[25] Even if compatibility is declared, national courts are generally required to order the recovery of benefits arising from the infringement of Art. 108(3) TFEU and the consequent untimely granting of the aids (for example interests).[26] Moreover, a breach of Art. 108(3) TFEU obliges the national courts to prevent a future payment

22 An exception was the first decision, in which payments by the Portuguese State were not qualified as State aid: *Commission*, Decision of 02.10.1996, State aid No NN 141/95, *RTP*. Another exception was the Decision of 22.05.2002, State aid No N 631/2001, *BBC license fee*, in which the *Commission* followed the reasoning of the *ECJ's Ferring*-Jurisdiction, which has been specified through the *Altmark Trans*-ruling meanwhile (cf. *Linke*, Die Gewährleistung des Daseinsvorsorgeauftrags im öffentlichen Personennahverkehr, pp. 100 et seqq., 103). A very unique exception was the Decision of 03.04.2002, State aid No NN 2/2002, *ZDF Medienpark*.

23 This approach was confirmed by the *CFI*, 10 May 2000, Case T-46/97, *SIC*.

24 See also the criticism of *Bartosch*, EuZW 2009, 684, 685.

25 *Commission*, Commission notice on the enforcement of State aid law by national courts (OJ C 85/1 of 9.4.2009), paras. 30 et seqq., 34. See also *Bartosch*, in: *Koenig/Bartosch/Braun*, EC Competition and Telecommunications Law, pp. 209 et seqq.; *Niemeyer*, in: *Heidenhain*, European State Aid Law, § 44, paras. 24 et seqq.; *Soltész*, EuR 2012, 60, 62.

26 *Commission*, Commission notice on the enforcement of State aid law by national courts (OJ C 85/1 of 9.4.2009), paras. 37 et seq.; *Niemeyer*, in: *Heidenhain*, European State Aid Law, § 44, para. 32; *Tedoldi*, in: *Santa Maria*, Competition and State Aid, p. 265.

from taking place.[27] At last, every granting act (e.g. contract, administrative decision) is invalid as a result of the Member State's breach of Art. 108(3) TFEU.[28]

Due the aforementioned focus of the *Commission*, Art. 106(2) TFEU has been covered in much more detail in academic literature in contrast to the application of Art. 107(1) TFEU and the *Altmark*-judgment in relation to PSB. Although it has been argued that compliance with the criteria set out in the *Altmark*-judgment is impossible for public service broadcasters,[29] it is still not clarified as to if and when public funding for PSB might be qualified as non-State aid. An in-depth analysis of the possibility of compliance with the *Altmark*-judgment is lacking.

This work seeks to shed light on the demands of Art. 107(1) TFEU regarding public funding of PSB. Specific focus is placed on the *Altmark*-judgment, in particular, the frequently neglected 'fourth criterion'. Consequently, the work tries to enhance our understanding of the application of Art. 107(1) TFEU and contribute to the clarification of a still opaque area of law. Apart from Art. 107(1) TFEU, the work also looks at the effect of the Amsterdam Protocol (the content of the Amsterdam Protocol has now been carried over to Protocol 29 of the Lisbon Treaty), which is occasionally argued to have a significant impact on the application of the State aid rules to PSB. Although the work does not cover the exceptions according to Art. 106(2) and Art. 107(2–3) TFEU, it should be noted that the present analysis is also intended to enrich the discussion on the requirements of Art. 106(2) TFEU on PSB, as most of the requirements of the article are congruent with those of the *Altmark*-judgment.

Before delving into the examination of Art. 107(1) TFEU and its application to PSB, the work gives a brief overview of the significance of PSB and its financing.

---

27 *Commission*, Commission notice on the enforcement of State aid law by national courts (OJ C 85/1 of 9.4.2009), para. 28.

28 *Commission*, Commission notice on the enforcement of State aid law by national courts (OJ C 85/1 of 9.4.2009), para. 29; *Ritter/Braun*, European Competition Law – A Practitioner's Guide, pp. 1009 et seq.

29 See for example *Donders*, Public Service Media and Policy in Europe, pp. 65, 87; *Katsirea*, Public Broadcasting and European Law, p. 342. Cf. also *Mortensen*, EStAL 2008, 239, 244; Sumrada and Nohlen, 2005, p. 613. Mentioning the difficulties in complying with the criterion: *Depypere/Broche/Tigchelaar*, Competition Policy Newsletter 2004 (1), 71.

B. Public service broadcasting in the context of State aid

The media hold a key position in informing, educating and forming the opinion of the population. According to the Commission, '[t]here is no other service that at the same time has access to such a wide sector of the population, provides it with so much information and content, and by doing so conveys and influences both individual and public opinion.'[30]

Below, a short overview is given related to the definition of PSB (I.), its specific public value that distinguishes it from commercially operating broadcasting (II.) and the compensation which is granted by the Member States to maintain this public value (III.).

I. Definition

The term 'PSB' is not subject to any unanimously accepted legal definition, nor should it be understood in a rigid way. Although radio and television services are included, the scope of the term should not be limited to these services. Otherwise, albeit *functionally* they provide the same services as traditional broadcasting, technological improvements or changes (e.g. digitalisation of the programmes) could be unnecessarily excluded. This would cause severe difficulties for PSB to achieve its public service goal of reaching an ever increasing new-media-oriented audience.[31] Thus, the term 'PSB' – as understood in the present work – is technologically neutral and might also comprise new media services.[32]

Nevertheless, PSB is always connected to SGEI.[33] Therefore, the term used here refers to broadcasters who are subject to public service obligations. These public services show specific public value that distinguishes them from commercially successful broadcasting services.[34] The term 'public service broadcasters', however, does *not* imply that the broadcaster is publicly owned (so called public broadcasters), although this might the case.[35]

---

30 *Commission*, Communication from the Commission on the application of State aid rules to public service broadcasting, (OJ C 257/1 of 27.10.2009), para. 9.

31 *European Broadcasting Union*, Review of the Communication from the Commission on the application of State aid rules to public service broadcasting – EBU reply to the Commission's questionnaire, p. 7.

32 See also *Commission*, Communication from the Commission on the application of State aid rules to public service broadcasting, (OJ C 257/1 of 27.10.2009), para. 12; *Bravasso*, in: *Hancher/Ottervanger/Slot*, EU State Aids, para. 18–012.

33 See below C. I. 1) a).

34 In detail below C. I. 1) a) (1) and D. I. 1).

35 *Tigchelaar*, EStAL 2003, 169.

In summary, PSB can be defined as 'the transmission of programmes for general reception by the public through different broadcasting means by broadcasters for the fulfilment of the public service remit as organised, defined and conferred by the State'[36].

II. Public value

Although the line between PSB and commercial broadcasting is hard to draw case-by-case,[37] in the following section various (but not exclusive) examples of additional public value of PSB are demonstrated. The additional public value that PSB creates can thus vary greatly.[38]

First of all, public funding of broadcasters is intended to free the broadcasters from their dependence on advertisers, subscribers or other commercial interests.[39] Otherwise, that might impede an opinion-building process undisturbed by commercial considerations.[40] The independence from economic considerations enables broadcasters to buy and produce higher quality broadcasts (i.e. more expensive broadcasts than the open market would allow).[41] Hence, broadcasters are able to transmit different and broader ranges of productions than what commercial broadcasters would offer in their programme.[42] Consequently, innovative broadcasts or broadcasts arousing a lesser audience interest (e.g. educational broadcasts, political discussions, etc.) have a higher chance of being part of the programme.[43] This accounts also for advice- or entertainment-broadcasts.

The possibility of creating a programme different from the one allowed under market conditions gives the opportunity to create a higher public value in different directions. One would be the political and cultural self-portrayal of the State that mirrors the diversity of cultural trends and opinions, even if some views are not appealing to the average spectator.[44] In this respect, broadcasting can have an

---

36 *Tigchelaar*, EStAL 2003, 169.

37 See also *Bravasso*, in: *Hancher/Ottervanger/Slot*, EU State Aids, para. 18–001.

38 See *Harrison/Woods*, European Broadcasting Law and Policy, p. 291. Regarding the functions of broadcasting see fundamentally: *Bullinger*, AfP 4/1985, 257, 258 et seqq. Furthermore *High Level Group on Media Freedom and Pluralism*, A free and pluralistic media to sustain European democracy, pp. 10 et seqq.; *Reese*, Der Funktionsauftrag des öffentlich-rechtlichen Rundfunks vor dem Hintergrund der Digitalisierung, pp. 45 et seqq.

39 Cf. also *Bosman*, K&R 2012, 5, 6.

40 *Dörr*, in: *Detterbeck/Rozek/v. Coelln*, Recht als Medium der Staatlichkeit – Festschrift für Herbert Bethge zum 70. Geburtstag, pp. 451, 453.

41 Cf. *Donders*, Public Service Media and Policy in Europe, p. 31.

42 See *Fairbairn*, in: *Peacock*, Public Service Broadcasting Without the BBC?, p. 61.

43 Cf. also *Fairbairn*, in: *Peacock*, Public Service Broadcasting Without the BBC?, p. 66.

44 *Castendyk*, AfP 2008, 467, 469; *Schnaitter*, Möglichkeiten und Grenzen der Ausgestaltung des Programmauftrags der öffentlich-rechtlichen Rundfunkanstalten, pp. 135 et seq.

integrating impact as views and opinions are displayed in the framework of the full spectrum.[45] Considering all views and cultural differences of the population and putting them in the picture of the current cultural and political discussion might also help to close the gap between the population and state organs and enhance social cohesion.[46] Moreover, the portrayal, provision of information on and discussion about cultural heritage foster its preservation and motivate dialogue regarding culture in the future.[47] Not lastly, this comprises the transmission of usually more expensive and less mass-appealing domestic broadcasts, which are part of the national culture.[48] But PSB can also give objective overviews over international and European events, to support understanding and integration of non-national cultures. In conclusion, PSB can have a severe impact on the formation of the public opinion.

Ultimately, PSB not only creates a higher quality programme, but adds also to the range of offers on the broadcasting market (extended choice) and it could also increase audience accessibility to specific programmes.[49] In this respect, PSB can offer broadcasts that commercial broadcasters would not offer free of charge or under affordable conditions for everybody.[50] Hence, PSB can contribute to equal access to valuable and/or socially important broadcasting services for the population as a whole.

III. Compensation for public broadcasting services

The desirable independence from commercial considerations and the high quality of the programme generally cannot be reached without public support. Most European countries, therefore, grant broadcasters financial aid and other benefits. By 2001, about 15 billion Euros of public funds were already granted yearly to broadcasters in the Member States.[51]

---

45 *Donders*, Public Service Media and Policy in Europe, p. 50, writes about the unifying forces of television. See also *Fairbairn*, in: *Peacock*, Public Service Broadcasting Without the BBC?, p. 64.

46 *Katsirea*, Public Broadcasting and European Law, p. 323; *Schnaitter*, Möglichkeiten und Grenzen der Ausgestaltung des Programmauftrags der öffentlich-rechtlichen Rundfunkanstalten, p. 137.

47 Cf. *Commission*, Communication from the Commission on the application of State aid rules to public service broadcasting, (OJ C 257/1 of 27.10.2009), para. 10; *Fairbairn*, in: *Peacock*, Public Service Broadcasting Without the BBC?, p. 65; *Schnaitter*, Möglichkeiten und Grenzen der Ausgestaltung des Programmauftrags der öffentlich-rechtlichen Rundfunkanstalten, p. 137.

48 Cf. also *Fairbairn*, in: *Peacock*, Public Service Broadcasting Without the BBC?, pp. 61 et seqq.

49 Cf. *Commission*, Communication from the Commission on the application of State aid rules to public service broadcasting, (OJ C 257/1 of 27.10.2009), para. 10, 12; *Fairbairn*, in: *Peacock*, Public Service Broadcasting Without the BBC?, p. 64.

50 See also *Craufurd Smith*, LIEI 28 (1) [2001], 3, 17; *Donders*, Public Service Media and Policy in Europe, p. 31.

51 *Depypere/Tigchelaar*, Competition Policy Newsletter 2004 (2), 19.

These benefits are granted in different forms, as follows:

- direct financing by budget or levy[52]
- capital injections[53]
- debt cancellations or rescheduling of debts[54]
- debt assumptions[55]
- tax exemptions[56]
- loans[57]
- state guarantees[58]
- inappropriately low prices, or no price charged for the provision of facilities or other assets (e.g. operating licenses).[59]

---

52 *Commission*, Communication from the Commission on the application of State aid rules to public service broadcasting, (OJ C 257/1 of 27.10.2009), para. 21; *Bravasso*, in: *Hancher/Ottervanger/Slot*, EU State Aids, para. 18–002; *Craufurd Smith*, LIEI 28 (1) [2001], 3; *Frenz/Götzkes*, ZUM 2010, 563, 564; *Katsirea*, Public Broadcasting and European Law, p. 324; *Niejahr*, in: *Montag/Säcker*, Münchener Kommentar zum Europäischen und Deutschen Wettbewerbsrecht (Kartellrecht) – Band 3, Sektoren para. 143.

53 *Commission*, Communication from the Commission on the application of State aid rules to public service broadcasting, (OJ C 257/1 of 27.10.2009), para. 21; *Bravasso*, in: *Hancher/Ottervanger/Slot*, EU State Aids, para. 18–002; *Frenz/Götzkes*, ZUM 2010, 563, 564; *Katsirea*, Public Broadcasting and European Law, p. 324; *Niejahr*, in: *Montag/Säcker*, Münchener Kommentar zum Europäischen und Deutschen Wettbewerbsrecht (Kartellrecht) – Band 3, Sektoren para. 143.

54 *Commission*, Communication from the Commission on the application of State aid rules to public service broadcasting, (OJ C 257/1 of 27.10.2009), para. 21; *Bravasso*, in: *Hancher/Ottervanger/Slot*, EU State Aids, para. 18–002; *Craufurd Smith*, LIEI 28 (1) [2001], 3; *Frenz/Götzkes*, ZUM 2010, 563, 564; *Katsirea*, Public Broadcasting and European Law, p. 324; *Niejahr*, in: *Montag/Säcker*, Münchener Kommentar zum Europäischen und Deutschen Wettbewerbsrecht (Kartellrecht) – Band 3, Sektoren para. 143.

55 *Niejahr*, in: *Montag/Säcker*, Münchener Kommentar zum Europäischen und Deutschen Wettbewerbsrecht (Kartellrecht) – Band 3, Sektoren para. 143.

56 *Bravasso*, in: *Hancher/Ottervanger/Slot*, EU State Aids, para. 18–002; *Craufurd Smith*, LIEI 28 (1) [2001], 3; *Katsirea*, Public Broadcasting and European Law, p. 324; *Niejahr*, in: *Montag/Säcker*, Münchener Kommentar zum Europäischen und Deutschen Wettbewerbsrecht (Kartellrecht) – Band 3, Sektoren para. 143.

57 *Bravasso*, in: *Hancher/Ottervanger/Slot*, EU State Aids, para. 18–002; *Craufurd Smith*, LIEI 28 (1) [2001], 3; *Katsirea*, Public Broadcasting and European Law, p. 324.

58 *Bravasso*, in: *Hancher/Ottervanger/Slot*, EU State Aids, para. 18–002; *Craufurd Smith*, LIEI 28 (1) [2001], 3; *Niejahr*, in: *Montag/Säcker*, Münchener Kommentar zum Europäischen und Deutschen Wettbewerbsrecht (Kartellrecht) – Band 3, Sektoren para. 143.

59 *Craufurd Smith*, LIEI 28 (1) [2001], 3.

The forms are used cumulatively as well as separately.[60] Direct financing of PSB in particular is made up of means from the State budget or income from special levies (e.g. broadcasting fees).[61] In the case of the collection of levies, their structure depends on the Member State. In particular, the flow of funding can be different, as levies can be paid either directly from the consumer to the broadcaster, or first to the State and then (out of the budget) to the broadcaster. Also, the establishment of broadcasting fees varies depending on the Member State. They can be determined by law directly or within procedures and criteria defined by way of law.[62] Furthermore, the approval of such fees varies and may be declared by the parliament, the government or ministries.[63]

Lastly, the financing of public service broadcasters can be divided into two categories: single funding, i.e. financing solely based on public funding, and dual-funding, i.e. financing through public funds as well as commercial activities.[64]

The present analysis focuses on the direct financing of public service broadcasters (which comprises *ad hoc* capital injections). The other forms of public funding, in contrast, display certain particularities in respect of State aid law that are of general interest and not specifically connected to the character of PSB itself. Consequently, these issues are not considered here.

---

60 See the in-depth-analysis of the financing-forms in Europe: *Schwendinger*, Gemeinschaftsrechtliche Grenzen öffentlicher Rundfunkfinanzierung, pp. 58 et seqq. Cf. also *Tigchelaar*, EStAL 2003, 169.

61 *Frenz/Götzkes*, ZUM 2010, 563, 564.

62 *Schwendinger*, Gemeinschaftsrechtliche Grenzen öffentlicher Rundfunkfinanzierung, p. 60.

63 *Schwendinger*, Gemeinschaftsrechtliche Grenzen öffentlicher Rundfunkfinanzierung, p. 60.

64 *Commission*, Communication from the Commission on the application of State aid rules to public service broadcasting, (OJ C 257/1 of 27.10.2009), para. 57; *Depypere/Tigchelaar*, Competition Policy Newsletter 2004 (2), 19; *Schwendinger*, Gemeinschaftsrechtliche Grenzen öffentlicher Rundfunkfinanzierung, p. 77.

C. Requirements of State aid and their existence in public service broadcasting

Granting advantages to undertakings is not accepted without restraint in European law. The means granted to public service broadcasters for the discharge of public service obligations carry the potential of violating European State aid law. The applicable law is contained in Art. 107(1) TFEU, which defines State aid that is incompatible with the internal market and, therefore, generally inadmissible. Art. 107(2–3) and Art. 106(2) TFEU provide derogations from Art. 107(1) TFEU, in which Art. 106(2) TFEU refers specifically to SGEI.[65] These rules of European law always have precedence over domestic law.[66]

The Council's television directive[67] has no (direct) impact on State aid issues, as the framework, according to its recitals, does not affect the Member States' competence of financing broadcasting services.[68] The directive, therefore, is not part of the present work.

The recently adopted so-called *Almunia*-package[69], regarding the application of State aid law to SGEI, will presumably, if at all, have only a minor impact on

---

65 Both derogations, however, are not subject of the work presented here. Though, these rules have been covered by literature intensively. Cf. for example: *Antoniadis*, in: *Sánchez Rydelski*, The EC State Aid Regime – Distortive Effects of State Aid on Competition and Trade, pp. 606 et seqq. Regarding Art. 107(3) TFEU: *Ruttig*, Der Einfluß des EG-Beihilferechts auf die Gebührenfinanzierung der öffentlich-rechtlichen Rundfunkanstalten, pp. 189 et seqq.

66 See the fundamental decision: *ECJ*, 15 July 1964, Case C-6/64, *Flaminio Costa*.

67 Council Directive 89/552/EEC of 3 October 1989 on the coordination of certain provisions laid down by Law, Regulation or Administrative Action in Member States concerning the pursuit of television broadcasting activities (OJ L 298/23 of 17.10.1989). Amended through Directive 2007/65/EC of the European Parliament and of the Council of 11 December 2007 (OJ L 332/27 of 18.12.2007).

68 *Ehricke*, Die EG-rechtliche Beurteilung der Rundfunkfinanzierung, p. 50; *Krone*, Gebührenfinanzierter Rundfunk und Beihilferecht, p. 8; *Schwendinger*, Gemeinschaftsrechtliche Grenzen öffentlicher Rundfunkfinanzierung, p. 11. Of other opinion: *Dörr*, Die öffentlich-rechtliche Rundfunkfinanzierung und die Vorgaben des EG-Vertrages, p. 11.

69 The *Almunia*-Package clarifies key concepts related to State aid for services of general economic interest: *Commission*, Communication from the Commission on the application of the European Union State aid rules to compensation granted for the provision of services of general economic interest (OJ C 8/4 of 11.01.2012); Communication from the Commission – European Union framework for State aid in the form of public service compensation (2011) (OJ C 8/15 of 11.01.2012); Decision of 20 December 2011 on the application of Article 106(2) of the Treaty on the Functioning of the European Union to State aid in the form of public service compensation granted

PSB, most likely as interpretative guidelines. The Communication on the European framework for State aid, which is part of the *Almunia*-package, does not even apply to PSB.[70] The Commission's Decision[71] – which is also part of the package – could potentially apply, but the scope-requirements seem rather unlikely to be met by PSB, especially considering the amount of public funding broadcasters usually receive as public support (cf. Art. 2(1)(a) of the Decision).[72] Consequently, in the present work the *Almunia*-package will only be dealt with when the rules can be used to support the interpretation of the primary applicable acts to PSB.[73] A separate analysis of the *Almunia*-package will not be carried out.

A special regulatory act, however, might be seen in the Amsterdam Protocol regarding State aid for PSB. The Protocol is often used as a justification for public financing in this sector. The question whether the Amsterdam Protocol actually has an impact on a State-aid-assessment of PSB will be addressed at the end of this chapter (III.). Firstly, the requirements of State aid according to Art. 107(1) TFEU are evaluated regarding their application on PSB (I.). This examination is followed by the problematic practical question 'Who carries the burden of proof in case of a State aid procedure?' (II.).

I. Is public funding for public service broadcasting constituting State aid?

State aid in the sense of Art. 107(1) TFEU has several characteristics: a measure considered to be State aid must favour a certain undertaking or the production of

to certain undertakings entrusted with the operation of services of general economic interest (OJ L 7/3 of 11.01.2012); Regulation (EU) No 360/2012 of 25 April 2012 on the application of Articles 107 and 108 of the Treaty on the Functioning of the European Union to de minimis aid granted to undertakings providing services of general economic interest (OJ L 114/8 of 26.04.2012).

70 *Commission*, Communication from the Commission – European Union framework for State aid in the form of public service compensation (2011) (OJ C 8/15 of 11.01.2012), para. 8.

71 *Commission*, Decision of 20 December 2011 on the application of Article 106(2) of the Treaty on the Functioning of the European Union to State aid in the form of public service compensation granted to certain undertakings entrusted with the operation of services of general economic interest (OJ L 7/3 of 11.01.2012).

72 The same accounts for the application of the de minimis regulation (cf. Art. 2(2) therein): *Commission*, Regulation (EU) No 360/2012 of 25 April 2012 on the application of Articles 107 and 108 of the Treaty on the Functioning of the European Union to de minimis aid granted to undertakings providing services of general economic interest (OJ L 114/8 of 26.04.2012).

73 This accounts especially for the Communication from the Commission on the application of the European Union State aid rules to compensation granted for the provision of services of general economic interest (OJ C 8/4 of 11.01.2012).

certain goods (1) and has to be granted by the State or by means of State resources in any form whatsoever (2). The intervention, additionally, must distort or threaten to distort competition (3) and it must be liable to affect trade between Member States (4). Regarding the constituent elements of State aid, it is the effect and not the purpose which qualifies a measure as a relevant action under Art. 107(1) TFEU.[74] Hereinafter, the characteristics of Art. 107(1) TFEU are scrutinised regarding their application on PSB.

1) Favouring

A decisive element of State aid in the sense of Art. 107(1) TFEU is the favouring of a certain undertaking or the production of certain goods.[75] Therefore, the conferring of a selective benefit or advantage, which the undertaking would not have received in the normal course of business, is necessary.[76] The feature has to be interpreted broadly.[77]

The concept of an 'undertaking' covers any entity engaged in an economic activity.[78] The existence of an economic activity has to be determined regardless of the legal status of an entity, the way it is financed and whether it is profit-oriented or not.[79] Rather any activity consisting in offering goods and services on a given market is sufficient.[80] Public service broadcasters carry out such economic activities. Consequently, they have to be qualified as undertakings in the sense of Art. 107(1) TFEU.[81]

74 See also: *Hancher*, in: *Hancher/Ottervanger/Slot*, EU State Aids, para. 3–004.

75 Older opinions also demanded that favouring in the sense of Art. 107(1) TFEU has to be voluntarily and this requirement might not be met in case the State has to grant public funding for broadcasting mandatorily according to domestic fundamental rights (of this opinion: *Oppermann*, Deutsche Rundfunkgebühren und europäisches Beihilferecht, p. 43). This view, however, has no basis in the State aid dogmatic and is obsolete (cf. for example: *Krone*, Gebührenfinanzierter Rundfunk und Beihilferecht, pp. 82 et seq.; *Ruttig*, Der Einfluß des EG-Beihilferechts auf die Gebührenfinanzierung der öffentlich-rechtlichen Rundfunkanstalten, pp. 172 et seq.; *Schwendinger*, Gemeinschaftsrechtliche Grenzen öffentlicher Rundfunkfinanzierung, pp. 321 et seqq.; *Stulz-Herrnstadt*, Nationale Rundfunkfinanzierung und europäische Beihilfenaufsicht im Lichte des Amsterdamer Rundfunkprotokolls, p. 99).

76 *Hancher*, in: *Hancher/Ottervanger/Slot*, EU State Aids, para. 3–005.

77 *Linke*, Die Gewährleistung des Daseinsvorsorgeauftrags im öffentlichen Personennahverkehr, p. 98 with further references; *Thum*, NVwZ 2007, 521, 522.

78 *ECJ*, 19 February 2002, Case C-309/99, para. 46.

79 *Commission*, Decision of 01.10.2003, State aid No N 37/2003, *BBC Digital Curriculum*, para. 19; *Craufurd Smith*, LIEI 28 (1) [2001], 3, 8.

80 *EGC*, 16 December 2010, Joined Cases T-231/06 and T-237/06, *ad hoc financing of Netherlands public service broadcasters*, para. 92.

81 Cf. *EGC*, 16 December 2010, Joined Cases T-231/06 and T-237/06, *ad hoc financing of Netherlands public service broadcasters*, para. 96; *Commission*, Decision of 01.10.2003,

The question as to whether compensation payments for the provision of SGEI have to be qualified as a favouring in the sense of Art. 107(1) TFEU was controversial[82] until the publication of the *Altmark Trans*-ruling. Before that, decisions from the *ECJ* and from the *CFI* diverted.[83] The *ECJ* held in *ADBHU* that indemnities do not constitute State aid, but rather a consideration for the services performed.[84] The *ADBHU*-jurisprudence has been confirmed by the *ECJ* in *Ferring*.[85] The *CFI*, on the contrary, adopted the position that compensation for the provision of SGEI *per se* was to be considered State aid.[86] The latter jurisprudence was upheld in the judgment *SIC*, which concerned PSB.[87] With the *Altmark*-judgment, the *ECJ* eventually clarified that compensation does not necessarily have to be designated as State aid if several requirements are met. With the establishment of these requirements the *ECJ* specified the *Ferring*-judgment. According to this jurisprudence an advantage not only has to be granted to the undertaking, rather the advantage has to remain as a favouring in the sphere of the recipient. Such a favouring is missing, when the advantage has to be qualified as an appropriate consideration for the provision of

---

State aid No N 37/2003, *BBC Digital Curriculum*, para. 19; *Ehricke*, Die EG-rechtliche Beurteilung der Rundfunkfinanzierung, p. 50; *Hancher*, in: *Hancher/Ottervanger/Slot*, EU State Aids, para. 8–010; *Krausnick*, Das deutsche Rundfunksystem unter dem Einfluss des Europarechts, p. 135; *Krone*, Gebührenfinanzierter Rundfunk und Beihilferecht, p. 118; *Oppermann*, Deutsche Rundfunkgebühren und europäisches Beihilferecht, pp. 50 et seq.; *Schnaitter*, Möglichkeiten und Grenzen der Ausgestaltung des Programmauftrags der öffentlich-rechtlichen Rundfunkanstalten, p. 62; *Wittig-Terhardt*, in: *Classen/Dittmann/Fechner/Gassner/Kilian*, "In einem vereinten Europa dem Frieden der Welt zu dienen ..." – Liber amicorum Thomas Oppermann, pp. 727, 744.

82 See for example *Oppermann*, Deutsche Rundfunkgebühren und europäisches Beihilferecht, pp. 34 et seqq. and *Selmer/Gersdorf*, Die Finanzierung des Rundfunks in der Bundesrepublik Deutschland auf dem Prüfstand des EG-Beihilferegimes, p. 26 on one hand and *v. Wallenberg*, MMR 2004, 88, 89 et seq. on the other.

83 Concerning the development see: *Arhold*, in: *Montag/Säcker*, Münchener Kommentar zum Europäischen und Deutschen Wettbewerbsrecht (Kartellrecht) – Band 3, Art. 107 AEUV paras. 219 et seqq.; *Craufurd Smith*, LIEI 28 (1) [2001], 3, 8 et seqq.; *Linke*, Die Gewährleistung des Daseinsvorsorgeauftrags im öffentlichen Personennahverkehr, pp. 100 et seqq.; *Maillo*, in: *Amato/Ehlermann*, EC Competition Law – A Critical Assessment, pp. 613 et seqq.; *Quigley*, European State Aid Law And Policy, pp. 157 et seqq.; *Schwendinger*, Gemeinschaftsrechtliche Grenzen öffentlicher Rundfunkfinanzierung, pp. 210 et seqq.; *Winter*, CMLRev 41 [2004], 475, 496 et seq.

84 *ECJ*, 7 February 1985, Case 240/83, *ADBHU*, para. 18.

85 *ECJ*, 22 November 2001, Case C-53/00, *Ferring*, para. 26. Regarding this judgment see *Selmayr/Kamann*, K&R 2004, 49, 54; *Travers*, EStAL 2003, 387, 387 et seqq.

86 *CFI*, 27 February 1997, Case T-106/95, *FFSA*, paras. 168 et seqq. Regarding this judgment see *Travers*, EStAL 2003, 387, 387.

87 *CFI*, 10 May 2000, Case T-46/97, *SIC*, para. 84.

services or goods. Consequently, the value of performance and the consideration have to be compared economically.

The *Altmark*-test assesses the financing of SGEI exclusively. Consequently, a compensation for the provision of SGEI has to be assessed solely under the *Altmark*-criteria regarding the question whether State aid exists or not. A review under the so called Private Investor Test is not possible any more.[88] Especially, regarding that the test is rather suited for marketable products, it is also utterly impractical on SGEI.[89]

In the following (a)), the questions are raised: 'what are SGEI' ((1)), 'how is the definition of these services controlled by the Commission' and 'under which circumstances can PSB services be qualified as such services' ((3)). These questions are followed by the *Altmark*-criteria itself and their application on PSB (b)).

a) Public service broadcasting as a service of general economic interest (SGEI)

SGEI are mentioned in Art. 14[90] and Art. 106(2) TFEU. Neither article contains a full description of the concept, as there is no final definition available.

(1) Characteristics of services of general economic interest

The difference between a regular service and a service of general economic interest (SGEI) is based on the fact that a SGEI is, compared to other (commercial) activities,

---

88 *Bartosch*, EuZW 1999, 176, 178; *Braum-Schleicher*, Daseinsvorsorge und service public durch den öffentlich-rechtlichen Rundfunk, p. 82; *Linke*, Die Gewährleistung des Daseinsvorsorgeauftrags im öffentlichen Personennahverkehr, p. 131; *Jennert*, WRP 2003, 459, 464 et seq.; *Koenig*, EuZW 2001, 741, 744. Of other opinion: *Greissinger*, Vorgaben des EG-Vertrages für nationales Rundfunk- und Multimediarecht, pp. 166 et seq.; *Schwendinger*, Gemeinschaftsrechtliche Grenzen öffentlicher Rundfunkfinanzierung, pp. 283 et seqq. with further references.

89 Cf. *Bartosch*, EuZW 1999, 176, 178; *Braum-Schleicher*, Daseinsvorsorge und service public durch den öffentlich-rechtlichen Rundfunk, p. 82; *Linke*, Die Gewährleistung des Daseinsvorsorgeauftrags im öffentlichen Personennahverkehr, pp. 131 et seqq.

90 Art. 14 TFEU stresses the particular importance of services of general economic interest in the EU. The impact of the law on State aid law, however, is limited as it states that its provision is only applicable '[w]ithout prejudice to [...] Articles 93, 106 and 107 of this Treaty'. Therefore the rule is functioning as a manifestation of an objective, which in principle may have an interpretative effect on other laws. Due to the expressive restrictions considering Art. 106 and Art. 107 TFEU an impact on the legal assessment of public funding of public service broadcasting is negligible. Cf. also *Nitsche*, Broadcasting in the European Union: The Role of Public Interest in Competition Analysis, pp. 141 et seqq.

entrusted with particular tasks which exhibit 'special characteristics'.[91] The special characteristics relate to the virtue that these services carry for the public.

One special characteristic is that it must be 'addressed to citizens or be in the interest of society as a whole' (universality).[92] Otherwise, the service is not in the public interest but fosters private or particular ones.[93] The universality of the service does not demand that the service must respond to a need common to the whole population or be supplied throughout a territory.[94] Consequently, the services in question may only be used by a relatively limited group of users.[95] Furthermore, the universality criterion does not require the service to be free of charge, or to be offered without consideration of economic profitability.[96]

Additionally, SGEI have to be subject to public service obligations.[97] These public service obligations describe the duties an undertaking has been entrusted with by the State. Public service obligations may be seen as the specifications of a SGEI. *Mutatis mutandis*, the public service obligations are the specific duties of an undertaking that render the service from a commercial service to a SGEI. Those public service obligations are also the starting point for the calculation of an admissible compensation for an undertaking performing SGEI.[98] SGEI have the attribute that without the public service obligations the entrusted undertaking would not assume,

---

91 *ECJ*, 17 July 1997, Case C-242/95, *GT-Link*, para. 53; 18 June 1998, Case C-266/96, *Corsica Ferries*, para. 45; *Commission*, Communication from the Commission on the application of the European Union State aid rules to compensation granted for the provision of services of general economic interest (OJ C 8/4 of 11.01.2012), paras. 45, 47; *Grespan*, EStAL 2010, 79, 82; *Thyri/Jaeger*, wbl 2006, 197, 199.

92 *Commission*, Communication from the Commission on the application of the European Union State aid rules to compensation granted for the provision of services of general economic interest (OJ C 8/4 of 11.01.2012), para. 50. Cf. also *CFI*, 12 February 2008, Case T-289/03, *BUPA*, para. 172; *Arhold*, in: *Montag/Säcker*, Münchener Kommentar zum Europäischen und Deutschen Wettbewerbsrecht (Kartellrecht) – Band 3, Art. 107 AEUV para. 230; *Linke*, Die Gewährleistung des Daseinsvorsorgeauftrags im öffentlichen Personennahverkehr, pp. 37 et seqq. *Craufurd Smith*, LIEI 28 (1) [2001], 3, 13, stresses that the access to the service must be essential for a socially acceptable standard of living.

93 *Bartosch*, EU-Beihilfenrecht, Art. 86 Abs. 2 EGV, para. 5; *Ehricke*, Die EG-rechtliche Beurteilung der Rundfunkfinanzierung, pp. 67 et seq.; *Koenig/Kühling/Ritter*, EG-Beihilfenrecht, para. 31.

94 *CFI*, 12 February 2008, Case T-289/03, *BUPA*, para. 186.

95 *CFI*, 12 February 2008, Case T-289/03, *BUPA*, para. 187.

96 *CFI*, 12 February 2008, Case T-289/03, *BUPA*, para. 203.

97 *Craufurd Smith*, LIEI 28 (1) [2001], 3, 13; *Grespan*, EStAL 2010, 79, 82; *Harrison/Woods*, European Broadcasting Law and Policy, p. 294; *Schweitzer*, in: *Cremona*, Market Integration and Public Services in the European Union, pp. 11, 32. Cf. also *Bartosch*, EU-Beihilfenrecht, Art. 86 Abs. 2 EGV, para. 5 and Art. 87 Abs. 1, para 63.

98 See below D. III.

or would not assume to the same extent, or under the same conditions, the supply of the services due to its own commercial interests.[99]

Thus, an attribute of SGEI is usually that the service in question is different from those which are already provided, or can be provided satisfactorily and under conditions consistent with the public interest (as defined by the State) by undertakings operating under normal market conditions.[100] Differences in the services that are already provided under market circumstances might be seen, for example, in the price, objective quality characteristics, continuity and access to the service. Whether this attribute has to be demanded also in PSB is not undisputed and will be explored later on.

(2) Control standard of 'manifest error'

Member States have a wide discretion in defining which services can be seen as SGEI. This follows from the principle of subsidiarity according to Art. 5(2) TEU and takes into account the functioning of the services pursuant to Art. 14 TFEU.[101] The Commission is only able to check whether a Member State has made a 'manifest error' when defining the service as a SGEI.[102] With respect to this kind of terminological openness,

---

99 *CFI*, 12 February 2008, Case T-289/03, *BUPA*, para. 181; *Commission*, Communication from the Commission on the application of the European Union State aid rules to compensation granted for the provision of services of general economic interest (OJ C 8/4 of 11.01.2012), para. 47 with reference to the definition of public service obligations in the Regulation (EC) No 1370/2007 (Regulation (EC) No 1370/2007 of the European Parliament and of the Council of 23 October 2007 on public passenger transport services by rail and by road and repealing Council Regulations (EEC) Nos 1191/69 and 1107/70 (OJ L 315/1 of 03.12.2007)).

100 Explicit: *Nicolaides*, in: *Sánchez Rydelski*, The EC State Aid Regime – Distortive Effects of State Aid on Competition and Trade, p. 575. Cf. also *Commission*, Communication from the Commission on the application of the European Union State aid rules to compensation granted for the provision of services of general economic interest (OJ C 8/4 of 11.01.2012), para. 48; *Boysen/Neukirchen*, Europäisches Beihilferecht und mitgliedstaatliche Daseinsvorsorge, p. 151; *Grespan*, EStAL 2010, 79, 82; *Niels/Jenkins/Kavanagh*, Economics for Competition Lawyers, p. 409; *Santamato/Pesaresi*, Competition Policy Newsletter 2004 (1), 17, 21. Of other opinion: *Wiedemann*, EStAL 2004, 595, 599 et seq.

101 Cf. *Linke*, Die Gewährleistung des Daseinsvorsorgeauftrags im öffentlichen Personennahverkehr, p. 36. Further *CFI*, 12 February 2008, Case T-289/03, *BUPA*, para. 167. Cf. also *European Broadcasting Union*, Review of the Communication from the Commission on the application of State aid rules to public service broadcasting – EBU reply to the Commission's questionnaire, p. 11.

102 *CFI*, 22 October 2008, joined Cases T-309/04, T-317/04, T-329/04 and T-336/04, *TV2*, para. 101; 12 February 2008, Case T-289/03, *BUPA*, para. 166; *Commission*, Communication from the Commission on the application of the European Union State aid rules to compensation granted for the provision of services of general economic interest (OJ C 8/4 of 11.01.2012), para. 46; Decision of 14.12.1999, State aid No NN 88/98, *BBC News 24*, para. 47; Decision of 01.10.2003, State aid No N 37/2003, *BBC Digital Curriculum*,

a definitive definition of SGEI cannot be given.[103] It is, therefore, in the first place the responsibility of the State to decide whether services can be provided satisfactorily under market conditions or not. According to the Commission in PSB it was not for it to decide 'which programmes are to be provided and financed as a SGEI, nor to question the nature or the quality of a certain product'.[104] The Commission cites, however, advertising, e-commerce, teleshopping, the use of premium rate numbers in prize games and sponsoring or merchandising as specific examples of a manifest error.[105]

Where specific Union rules exist, the Member States' discretion is further bound by those rules.[106] Such rules exist in the form of the Amsterdam Protocol. The Protocol limits the scope of the Member States' prerogative to define PSB by requiring that the service has to foster democratic, social or cultural needs of the society or the need to preserve media pluralism.[107] The Commission therefore has the competence to check whether these objectives are not reasonably considered to be met by the definition adopted by the Member States. Nevertheless, this cannot be the only standard for the Commission in controlling the definition of the services. The Amsterdam Protocol only sets up minimum requirements the Member States' definition has to observe, but it does not exempt the service from compliance with the other characteristics of SGEI.[108]

(3) Does public service broadcasting meet the characteristics of the services of general economic interest in principle?

In principle, PSB has to be seen as a SGEI,[109] due to the provision of a programme pursuing democratic, social and cultural needs, as well as the need to preserve media

---

para. 40. Cf. also *Bartosch*, EU-Beihilfenrecht, Art. 87 Abs. 1 EGV, para. 62; *Grespan*, EStAL 2010, 79, 81; *Quigley*, European State Aid Law And Policy, p. 162.

103 Cf. *CFI*, 12 February 2008, Case T-289/03, *BUPA*, para. 165.

104 *Commission*, Communication from the Commission on the application of State aid rules to public service broadcasting, (OJ C 257/1 of 27.10.2009), para. 48.

105 *Commission*, Communication from the Commission on the application of State aid rules to public service broadcasting, (OJ C 257/1 of 27.10.2009), para. 48.

106 *Commission*, Communication from the Commission on the application of the European Union State aid rules to compensation granted for the provision of services of general economic interest (OJ C 8/4 of 11.01.2012), para. 46.

107 See below C. III. 2) a). Cf. also *Commission*, Communication from the Commission on the application of State aid rules to public service broadcasting, (OJ C 257/1 of 27.10.2009), para. 48.

108 See below C. III.

109 *CFI*, 26 June 2008, Case T-442/03, *SIC*, para. 153; *Bravasso*, in: *Hancher/Ottervanger/Slot*, EU State Aids, para. 18–002; *Ehricke*, Die EG-rechtliche Beurteilung der Rundfunkfinanzierung, p. 68; *Oppermann*, Deutsche Rundfunkgebühren und europäisches Beihilferecht, p. 37; *Ruttig*, Der Einfluß des EG-Beihilferechts auf die Gebührenfinanzierung der öffentlich-rechtlichen Rundfunkanstalten, p. 143; *Selmer/Gersdorf*, Die Finanzierung des Rundfunks in der Bundesrepublik Deutschland

pluralism for the whole population. In contrast to commercial broadcasters, market considerations are not made by public service broadcasters, which are entrusted with public service obligations. Albeit, the term 'economic' in 'SGEI' distinguishes from purely cultural or sovereign activities as well as from acts of ministration, PSB cannot be excluded from the category of SGEI simply because it fulfils cultural needs. Since the services have a significant effect on the advertising market (even without selling air-time to advertisers) and the market of license rights the services have to be seen as economic.[110] This applies even considering that broadcasting might be received by consumers without remuneration.

However, the general assumption that PSB has to be seen as a part of the SGEI does not answer the question addressed below,[111] namely whether *all* activities of a respective broadcaster may be subsumed as such services.

b) The Altmark Trans *jurisprudence*

The *Altmark*-ruling of the *ECJ*, as mentioned above, establishes the requirements for granted advantages to qualify as compensation for the discharge of SGEI and thus not considered to favour specific undertakings. The four *Altmark*-criteria, set out by the *ECJ*, are not clearly defined in EU law. Consequently, their application causes significant difficulties, not only related to PSB but also in all other fields of SGEI.[112] The criteria are the following:[113]

'first, the recipient undertaking is actually required to discharge public service obligations and those obligations have been clearly defined;

second, the parameters on the basis of which the compensation is calculated have been established beforehand in an objective and transparent manner;

third, the compensation does not exceed what is necessary to cover all or part of the costs incurred in discharging the public service obligations, taking into account the relevant receipts and a reasonable profit for discharging those obligations;

---

auf dem Prüfstand des EG-Beihilferegimes, p. 39; *Thum*, NVwZ 2007, 521, p. 522. Cf. also *Streinz*, in: *Stern*, Die Bedeutung des Europäischen Rechts für den nationalen Rundfunk, pp. 59, 71, who over and above that awards the public broadcasting services a special position among the services of general economic interest. Such a special position may, indeed, be acknowledged through the Amsterdam Protocol.

110 *CFI*, 26 June 2008, Case T-442/03, *SIC*, para. 153; *Ehricke*, Die EG-rechtliche Beurteilung der Rundfunkfinanzierung, p. 69. Of other opinion *Hesse*, AfP 2005, 499, 501, who sees the missing remuneration from viewers as an obstacle to qualify public service broadcasting as a service with economic aspects.

111 See D. I. 1).

112 Explicit: *Bartosch*, in: *Sánchez Rydelski*, The EC State Aid Regime – Distortive Effects of State Aid on Competition and Trade, p. 62: 'For practical purposes, it has to be acknowledged that the *Altmark*-criteria are, given the particularities of the Member States' compensation schemes, in almost all cases completely out of touch with reality'.

113 See *ECJ*, 24 July 2003, Case C-280/00, *Altmark Trans*, paras. 89 et seqq.

fourth, where the undertaking which is to discharge public service obligations is not chosen in a public procurement procedure, the level of compensation needed has been determined on the basis of an analysis of the costs which a typical undertaking, well run and adequately provided [...] so as to be able to meet the necessary public service requirements, would have incurred in discharging those obligations, taking into account the relevant receipts and a reasonable profit for discharging the obligations.'

Subsidies complying with the four criteria do not fall within Art. 107(1) TFEU, whereas those which do not comply with one or more of the criteria have to be regarded as a favouring in the sense of the article.[114] Whether PSB complies with the *Altmark*-criteria is elaborated in a separate chapter in detail below.[115]

2) Granted by Member States or through State resources

State aid has to be granted by a Member State or through State resources. Without doubt, the requirement is met whenever a Member State directly grants financial means out of the State budget.[116] But also, indirect state measures might meet the requirements of Art. 107(1) TFEU.

According to the common European jurisprudence, the criteria 'granted by a Member State' and 'through State resources' do not have to be separated strictly, but rather are used cumulatively. The *ECJ* takes the view that both attributes together clarify that State aid does not necessarily have to be granted directly by a Member State, but can also be granted through public or private bodies designated or established by the State.[117] Over time, the *ECJ* developed and specified two characteristics which indicate means that are 'granted by a Member State or through State resources': an existence of a burden on the State budget and imputability of the measure to the State.[118] It has to be noted, however, that the application of both attributes by the *ECJ* was very inconsistent in the past.[119] Therefore, it remains

114 *ECJ*, 24 July 2003, Case C-280/00, *Altmark Trans*, para. 94.

115 Cf. below D.

116 *Krone*, Gebührenfinanzierter Rundfunk und Beihilferecht, p. 164.

117 *ECJ*, 17 March 1993 – Joined Cases C-72/91 and C-73/91, *Sloman Neptun*, para. 19; 13 March 2001, C-379/98, *PreussenElektra*, para. 58; 15 July 2004, C-345/02, *Pearle*, para. 34. Cf. also *Ebner/Gambaro*, in: *Santa Maria*, Competition and State Aid, pp. 18 et seqq., 20; *Hancher*, EStAL 2003, 365, 369; *Koenig/Haratsch*, ZUM 2005, 275, 276; *Soltész*, in: *Montag/Säcker*, Münchener Kommentar zum Europäischen und Deutschen Wettbewerbsrecht (Kartellrecht) – Band 3, Art. 107 AEUV paras. 239 et seqq. Furthermore *Kühling/Koenig/Paul*, in *Streinz*, EUV/AEUV, Art. 107 AEUV para. 56; *Vesterdorf/Nielsen*, State Aid Law of the European Union, para. 1–032.

118 *ECJ*, 15 July 2004 – C-345/02, *Pearle*, para. 35. See also *Soltész*, in: *Montag/Säcker*, Münchener Kommentar zum Europäischen und Deutschen Wettbewerbsrecht (Kartellrecht) – Band 3, Art. 107 AEUV paras. 239 et seqq.

119 The requirement was introduced in the *van Tiggele*-ruling (*ECJ*, 24 January 1978, Case C-82/77, *van Tiggele*, para. 23) and resumed in the *Sloman Neptun*-ruling (*ECJ*, 17 March 1993, Joined Cases C-72/91 and C-73/91, *Sloman Neptun*, para. 21).

uncertain whether the court would strictly apply both characteristics in a decision on PSB.[120] Due to the court's varying decisions, it is highly controversial as to whether and when indirect grants, which are those that were (at least formally) never incorporated into the State budget, are State aid.

(1) Burden of State budget

The requirement of a burden on the State budget distinguishes State aid from other state interventions in the economy.[121] Without this criterion almost all interventions could be associated with State aid. Nevertheless, some authors give a very broad interpretation of Art. 107(1) TFEU and reject the requirement, whereby every advantage gained through the State's intervention is considered to be State aid.[122] The view puts forward the fact that Art. 107(1) TFEU distinguishes between the characteristics 'granted by a Member State' and 'through State resources' so that, in case of a direct measure of the State (e.g. an intervention in competition), an imputability to the state is already sufficient. Moreover, it is argued that all state interventions are able to distort competition, which would justify the application of Art. 107(1) TFEU.[123] According to this interpretation all fees that are directly transferred from private households to a broadcaster or a designated body associated with it have to be verified as State aid as long as they are imputable to the State.

However, the *ECJ* rightly has a more restrictive view on this matter. Although it has to be noted – as already indicated – that occasionally the court neglected the characteristic of a burden of State budget, the following decisions indicate that the requirement is still valid.[124]

(a) *PreussenElektra-ruling*

In the decision *PreussenElektra*,[125] the applicant (*PreussenElektra AG*), an electricity supplier, claimed a reimbursement of a sum it had formerly paid to the defendant

---

Not demanding a burden of the State budget for example: *ECJ*, 2 February 198, Joined Cases C-67/85, C-68/85 and C-70/85, *van der Kooy*, paras 32 et seqq. At least dubious is the demand for the characteristic in *Stardust Marine* (see below). See also the in-depth-analysis on the *ECJ*'s jurisdiction in this respect of *Krone*, Gebührenfinanzierter Rundfunk und Beihilferecht, pp. 167 et seqq.

120 Drawing the same conclusion: *Schipanski*, K&R 2006, 217, 218.

121 *Soltész*, in: *Montag/Säcker*, Münchener Kommentar zum Europäischen und Deutschen Wettbewerbsrecht (Kartellrecht) – Band 3, Art. 107 AEUV para. 240.

122 Opinion of AG *Darmon* from 17.03.1992 – Joined Cases C-72/91 and C-73/91, *Sloman Neptun*, paras. 41 et seqq. Cf. also *Arhold*, EStAL 2007, 151, 151 et seq.; *Bacon*, in: *Bacon*, European Community Law of State Aid, para. 2.91.

123 Cf. Opinion of AG *Darmon* from 17.03.1992 – Joined Cases C-72/91 and C-73/91, *Sloman Neptun*, paras. 41 et seqq.

124 Of the same opinion *Quigley*, European State Aid Law And Policy, p. 18.

125 *ECJ*, 13 March 2001, C-379/98, *PreussenElektra*. See also the reviews from *Koenig/Haratsch*, ZUM 2001, 537, 544; *Selmayr/Kamann*, K&R 2004, 49, 50 et seqq.

(*Schleswag AG*), a regional electricity supplier which bought its own electricity almost exclusively from *PreussenElektra*. The payments took place due to a law ('Stromeinspeisungsgesetz') that obliged the defendant to purchase electricity at fixed minimum prices from renewable sources produced within its area of supply. The law entitled the defendant to pass on economic losses caused by the aforesaid obligation to the upstream electricity supply undertaking (as the undertaking did not have the possibility to pass the costs on to the final consumers). *PreussenElektra* took the position that the rules on purchase and compensation constitute State aid in favour of the recipient of the payment.

Consequently, the court had to answer the question as to whether State aid covers 'national rules for the benefit of the recipient of the payment, under which the costs entailed are not met, either directly or indirectly, from the public budget but are borne by individual undertakings in a sector, which have a statutory obligation to purchase at fixed minimum prices [...]'[126].

In its decision the *ECJ* emphasised that 'only advantages granted directly or indirectly through State resources are to be considered aid within the meaning of Article 92(1)'[127] (now: Art. 107(1) TFEU). With reference to a number of precedents, it stated that the distinction made between 'aid granted by a Member State' and aid granted 'through State resources' does not signify that all advantages granted by a State, whether financed through State resources or not, constitute aid but was intended merely to bring within that definition both advantages which are granted directly by the State and those granted by a public or private body designated or established by the State.[128] Eventually, the *ECJ* did not see any indication for a transfer of State resources.[129] According to the court, the mere fact that the purchase obligation was imposed by statute and conferred an undeniable advantage on certain undertakings was not enough to confer upon it the character of State aid.[130]

In conclusion, the ruling records that a state's mere legislative intervention in the market does not constitute State aid as long as it is not accompanied by a burden on State resources.[131] However, the conclusion cannot be drawn that State aid is excluded whenever the financial burden of the State measure is carried solely by private entities.[132]

---

126 *ECJ*, 13 March 2001, C-379/98, *PreussenElektra*, para. 27.
127 *ECJ*, 13 March 2001, C-379/98, *PreussenElektra*, para. 58.
128 *ECJ*, 13 March 2001, C-379/98, *PreussenElektra*, para. 58.
129 Cf. *ECJ*, 13 March 2001, C-379/98, *PreussenElektra*, para. 59.
130 *ECJ*, 13 Match 2001, C-379/98, *PreussenElektra*, para. 61.
131 Of the same opinion for example *Hancher*, EStAL 2003, 365, 368.
132 Of other opinion: *Ehricke*, Die EG-rechtliche Beurteilung der Rundfunkfinanzierung, p. 101.

(b) *Essent-ruling*

In a similar but more recent case,[133] the *ECJ* had to delimit a measure from the *PreussenElektra*-jurisprudence. The applicant herein (*Essent Netwerk Noord BV*; hereinafter *Essent*) – an electricity net operator – was seeking payment of amounts in the main proceedings which it invoiced to *Aluminium Delfzijl BV* (hereinafter *Aldel*), a purchaser of electricity and transport services. *Essent* was entitled to these payments by a law that obliged customers of the services in question to pay a surcharge, which the net operator as the recipient in turn had to pay to a company designated by the legislature (hereinafter *SEP*). The purpose of the surcharge was defraying non-market-compatible costs which had arisen as a result of obligations incurred, or investments made, by *SEP* prior to the liberalisation of the electricity market. Whenever the amount transferred to *SEP* would exceed a specific sum, *SEP* was required to forward such surplus to the Minister. *Aldel* refused to pay the amounts on the ground that the law was contrary to State aid law.

Eventually, the *ECJ* qualified the means granted to *SEP* as State aid. The court emphasised that the amounts had their origin in the price surcharge imposed by the State, which qualified them as a charge.[134] Thus, the amounts had their origin in a State resource.[135] Due to the fact that *SEP* was not entitled to 'use the proceeds from the charge for purposes other than those provided by the Law'[136] (i.e. for the time being solely the managing of the collected means) and was monitored in carrying out its tasks, the amount remained under public control according to the *ECJ*. Consequently, the court stated that 'as long as that designated company did not appropriate to itself the amount [...], at the time when it was freely able to do so, that amount remained under public control and therefore available to the national authorities, which is sufficient for it to be categorised as State resources'[137].

Remarkable are the explications considering the question what distinguishes the case from the constellations of *Pearle*[138] and *PreussenElektra*. In *Pearle* monies had been collected by a professional body from its members for an advertisement campaign the members benefited from. The court stressed that these monies were therefore 'neither revenue for the State nor monies which remained under State control, by contrast to the amount received by *SEP*, which has its origin in a charge and can be used for no other purpose than that provided for by the Law'[139]. An additional argument, furthermore, was seen in the fact that the payment 'to the designated company had been the *subject of a decision by the legislature*' instead of being purely commercially motivated *without 'a policy determined by the authorities'* as in

---

133 *ECJ*, 17 July 2008, C-206/06, *Essent*.
134 Cf. *ECJ*, 17 July 2008, C-206/06, *Essent*, para. 66.
135 *ECJ*, 17 July 2008, C-206/06, *Essent*, para. 66.
136 *ECJ*, 17 July 2008, C-206/06, *Essent*, para. 69.
137 *ECJ*, 17 July 2008, C-206/06, *Essent*, para. 70.
138 See below C. I. 2) (2) (b).
139 *ECJ*, 17 July 2008, C-206/06, para. 72.

the *Pearle*-ruling.[140] The difference to the *PreussenElektra*-ruling was perceived in the circumstance that in *PreussenElektra* 'the undertakings had not been appointed by the State to manage a State resource, but were bound by an obligation to purchase by means of their own financial resources'[141]. Consequently, the difference was seen in the fact that the *ECJ* has qualified the monies as State resources beforehand.[142]

(c) *Reception of the Essent-ruling*

The *Essent*-ruling was applied in a Commission's decision in a case which concerned an obligation for electricity suppliers to purchase a percentage of their overall supply from a green electricity settlement centre (so called *OeMAG*) at a fixed price.[143] The Commission rejected the use of the *PreussenElektra*-jurisprudence as it was not comparable to the scheme in question. The Commission explained '[t]he PreussenElektra case was concerned with relations between private undertakings, without the involvement of any intermediate body, whereas the Green Electricity Act in Austria had given OeMAG the task of collecting and distributing the funds intended for the generation of green electricity'[144].

With reference to the *Essent*-ruling the Commission emphasised that is was decisive that a charge imposed upon private entities by an act of public authority and that *OeMAG* was not entitled to use the proceeds from the charge for purposes other than those provided for by the law. The existence of a 'charge' on electricity in turn was reasoned such that the law required 'electricity suppliers to purchase a certain volume of renewable electricity at a price above the market price'[145]. In particular the Commission reasoned that the level of the price was to be set annually by order of the Federal Minister for Economic Affairs and Labour (and thus by an act of public authority).[146] Control over the funds and use for a purpose designated by the law was answered in the affirmative due the fact that *OeMAG* could use the funds only

---

140 *ECJ*, 17 July 2008, C-206/06, *Essent*, para. 73. All accentuation by the author of the on hand work.

141 *ECJ*, 17 July 2008, C-206/06, *Essent*, para. 74.

142 Cf. *ECJ*, 17 July 2008, C-206/06, *Essent*, para. 66.

143 *Commission*, Decision of 8 March 2011 on State aid measure C 24/09 (ex N 446/08) – State aid for energy-intensive businesses under the Green Electricity Act in Austria (L 235/42 of 10.09.2011).

144 *Commission*, Decision of 8 March 2011 on State aid measure C 24/09 (ex N 446/08) – State aid for energy-intensive businesses under the Green Electricity Act in Austria (L 235/42 of 10.09.2011), para. 65.

145 *Commission*, Decision of 8 March 2011 on State aid measure C 24/09 (ex N 446/08) – State aid for energy-intensive businesses under the Green Electricity Act in Austria (L 235/42 of 10.09.2011), para. 68.

146 *Commission*, Decision of 8 March 2011 on State aid measure C 24/09 (ex N 446/08) – State aid for energy-intensive businesses under the Green Electricity Act in Austria (L 235/42 of 10.09.2011), para. 68.

for the purpose of purchasing renewable electricity.[147] Additionally, *OeMAG* at any time had to grant access to all documents concerning the account to the Federal Ministry of Economic Affairs and Labour or to the Austrian Court of Auditors.[148] Also ex post audits by the Court of Auditors were conducted.

(d) *Assessment*

The jurisdiction of the *ECJ* towards the requirement of a burden of State budget so far was not consistent.[149] Therefore, it is hard to tell whether this criterion is seen as replaceable.[150] The *Essent*-ruling at least shows that a formal transfer of the means into the State budget is not necessary to qualify favours as State aid.[151]

Taking a closer look at the precedents *PreussenElektra* and *Essent*, however, one might argue that – depending on the compensation-mechanism in question – *both* are not fully matching the situation of broadcasting fees that are transferred directly from private parties to the broadcasters, or to a designated body, established by the public sector to distribute the monies.

PreussenElektra, on the one hand, concerns solely the redistribution of resources between private bodies,[152] i.e. outside the public sphere. The parallel appears dubious regarding broadcasting fees whenever the public service broadcaster is a public

---

147 *Commission*, Decision of 8 March 2011 on State aid measure C 24/09 (ex N 446/08) – State aid for energy-intensive businesses under the Green Electricity Act in Austria (L 235/42 of 10.09.2011), para. 72.

148 *Commission*, Decision of 8 March 2011 on State aid measure C 24/09 (ex N 446/08) – State aid for energy-intensive businesses under the Green Electricity Act in Austria (L 235/42 of 10.09.2011), para. 72.

149 In the *Stardust Marine*-ruling the *ECJ* demanded the observation of the criterion (see below C. I. 2) (2) (a)).

150 *Krone*, Gebührenfinanzierter Rundfunk und Beihilferecht, p. 191.

151 See also *Commission*, Decision of 22.05.2002, State aid No N 631/2001, *BBC license fee*, para. 20: 'It can be added that, even if the revenue, after collection by the BBC, would stay within the BBC budget the aid character would not change, as the revenue remains under public control, and therefore available to the competent national authorities. This is sufficient for it to be categorised as state resources'. Furthermore *Selmayr/Kamann*, K&R 2004, 49, 51; *Thum*, NVwZ 2007, 521, 524; *Van de Casteele/Grespan*, in: *Mederer/Pesaresi/Van Hoof*, EU Competition Law – Volume IV – State Aid, para 2.13.

152 Cf. *ECJ*, 13 March 2001, C-379/98, *PreussenElektra*, para. 60. This is also the opinion of the *Commission*, see above C. I. 2) (1) (c).Also of the same opinion: *Grzeszick*, NVwZ 2008, 608, 612; *Laitenberger*, in: *Stern/Prütting*, Nationaler Rundfunk und Europäisches Gemeinschaftsrecht zwischen Kommunikationsfreiheit und Regulierung, pp. 31, 35; *Thum*, Einfachgesetzliche Präzisierung des verfassungsrechtlichen Funktionsauftrags des öffentlich-rechtlichen Rundfunks, p. 129. Rejecting this argument: *Bartosch*, in: *Koenig/Bartosch/Braun*, EC Competition and Telecommunications Law, p. 192.

broadcaster. In this case, the State transfers monies into a body established by the State. Therefore, one could argue that there is a transfer into the State's budget.

As the *Essent*-ruling showed, it is already sufficient to qualify monies being under *public control* and therefore available to the national authorities.[153] According to the Commission, such a control exists when a charge is imposed upon private entities by an act of public authority and the beneficiary is not entitled to use the proceeds from the charge for purposes other than those they were earmarked for.[154] The Commission also demanded a certain control of the accounts (i.e. audits) through the State.[155] On the other hand, the *Essent*-ruling also does not match the situation of broadcasting fees comprehensively in the case of public service broadcasters, which are direct recipients of the means and thus are not granted the monies via a manager or are, first of all, managers of the monies themselves.

The *Essent*-ruling, however, appears to be closer to the situation of a public broadcaster receiving broadcasting fees than *PreussenElektra*. As already described, the monies do not usually remain in the private sphere but are transferred to the public broadcasters, sometimes by means of administrative enforcement. This gives a clear indication that the means are part of a state budget rather than part of a private entity.[156] Moreover, broadcasting fees often are accompanied by a certain control of the State over the means in the sense of the *Essent*-ruling. Such a control might be derived from the earmarking of the means contrary to those in the *PreussenElektra*-ruling[157] and an additional control over the utilisation (for example, through the Court of Audit).[158]

It has also to be noted whether the State levies the monies through the adoption of a law. Although the imposition of levies through a law alone is not sufficient to answer the characteristic of a State resource in the affirmative according to the *PreussenElektra*-ruling,[159] at least the adopting of a law sets an additional indication

153 Cf. also *Thum*, Einfachgesetzliche Präzisierung des verfassungsrechtlichen Funktionsauftrags des öffentlich-rechtlichen Rundfunks, p. 129; *Selmayr/Kamann*, K&R 2004, 49, 52 et seq.

154 See above C. I. 2) (1) (c).

155 See above C. I. 2) (1) (c).

156 Of the same opinion: *CFI*, 22 October 2008, joined Cases T-309/04, T-317/04, T-329/04 and T-336/04, *TV2*, para. 158; *Grzeszick*, NVwZ 2008, 608, 612; *Selmayr/Kamann*, K&R 2004, 49, 52; *Storr*, K&R 2002, 464, 468.

157 In the case *PreussenElektra* the beneficiary – producers of electricity from renewable sources – could use the additional income for any purpose.

158 That this already might be enough to qualify the means as State aid shows *Commission*, Decision of 8 March 2011 on State aid measure C 24/09 (ex N 446/08) – State aid for energy-intensive businesses under the Green Electricity Act in Austria (L 235/42 of 10.09.2011), para. 68, 72. Cf. also *Tigchelaar*, EStAL 2003, 169, 173.

159 See above C. I. 2) (1) (a). Therefore, the existence of State aid rejecting: *Ehricke*, Die EG-rechtliche Beurteilung der Rundfunkfinanzierung, p. 104; *Krausnick*, Das deutsche Rundfunksystem unter dem Einfluss des Europarechts, p. 31.

for State control over the means.[160] A further argument arises when the State has a (constitutional) obligation to finance the broadcaster.[161] In this scenario, the State would have to finance the broadcaster anyway. The State budget, therefore, is intentionally unburdened by the measure. It cannot make a difference in this situation, whether the State transfers the monies first into its own budget and then to the broadcaster or the other way round. Otherwise, it would be possible for the State to circumvent State aid rules through formal restructuring.[162] Also, it is worth mentioning that broadcasting fees show a significant resemblance to parafiscal charges, which are seen as State resources.[163]

As a result, it can be noted that there are various ways of qualifying broadcasting fees paid directly from private entities to the broadcaster, or to a designated body associated with the broadcaster as a burden on the State budget.[164] Furthermore,

---

160 Of the same opinion: *CFI*, 22 October 2008, joined Cases T-309/04, T-317/04, T-329/04 and T-336/04, *TV2*, para. 158. Furthermore, see for example: *ECJ*, 17 July 2008, C-206/06, *Essent*, para. 66; *Commission*, Decision of 8 March 2011 on State aid measure C 24/09 (ex N 446/08) – State aid for energy-intensive businesses under the Green Electricity Act in Austria (L 235/42 of 10.09.2011), para. 68; Decision of 01.10.2003, State aid No N 37/2003, *BBC Digital Curriculum*, para. 21; Decision of 14.12.1999, State aid No NN 88/98, *BBC News 24*, para. 23; *Grzeszick*, NVwZ 2008, 608, 612; *Selmayr/Kamann*, K&R 2004, 49, 512. Further-going *Thum*, NVwZ 2007, 521, 524, who considers the exercising of regulatory control through law sufficient to fulfil the requirement in question. Of other opinion: *Streinz*, in: *Stern*, Die Bedeutung des Europäischen Rechts für den nationalen Rundfunk, pp. 59, 79.

161 *Degenhart*, AfP 2005, 493, 496; *Grzeszick*, NVwZ 2008, 608, 612; *Storr*, K&R 2002, 464, 468. Of other opinion: *Ehricke*, Die EG-rechtliche Beurteilung der Rundfunkfinanzierung, p. 105. To be rejected is the (older) opinion that the granting of State aid has to be voluntarily. Therefore, it cannot be argued that Art. 107(1) TFEU is not relevant in States in which constitutional law obliges States to support public service broadcasting. First of all, the voluntary is no characteristic of Art. 107(1) TFEU and, second of all, the constitutional obligation is voluntarily set by the State anyway. Of the same opinion: *Selmer/Gersdorf*, Die Finanzierung des Rundfunks in der Bundesrepublik Deutschland auf dem Prüfstand des EG-Beihilferegimes, p. 31.

162 *Braum-Schleicher*, Daseinsvorsorge und service public durch den öffentlich-rechtlichen Rundfunk, p. 101; *Degenhart*, AfP 2005, 493, 496; *Koenig/Kühling*, EuZW 2000, 197, 199. Cf. also *Selmer/Gersdorf*, Die Finanzierung des Rundfunks in der Bundesrepublik Deutschland auf dem Prüfstand des EG-Beihilferegimes, pp. 32 et seq.; *Thum*, NVwZ 2007, 521, 524.

163 Cf. *Braum-Schleicher*, Daseinsvorsorge und service public durch den öffentlich-rechtlichen Rundfunk, p. 100; *Selmayr/Kamann*, K&R 2004, 49, 52; *Storr*, K&R 2002, 464, 468; *Tigchelaar*, EStAL 2003, 169, 173. Of other opinion: *Ehricke*, Die EG-rechtliche Beurteilung der Rundfunkfinanzierung, pp. 106 et seqq.; *Oppermann*, Deutsche Rundfunkgebühren und europäisches Beihilferecht, p. 48.

164 Of the same opinion: *CFI*, 22 October 2008, Joined Cases T-309/04, T-317/04, T-329/04 and T-336/04, *TV2*, paras. 158 et seqq.; *Commission*, Decision of

the requirements of the *Essent*-ruling apply. There are various indications suggesting State control over the means as shown above. Not to be seen as a burden of the State budget according to the results found, however, would be a direct transfer of monies from privates to a private broadcaster. Questionable would be the same case, but with a stately obligation to support the private broadcaster, as the State would have to pay for the services anyway. Lastly, it should be given a thought that an exclusion of broadcasting fees from competition law is also hardly convincing regarding the magnitude of the funding and its impact on competition.[165]

(2) Imputability

According to the *ECJ* a further prerequisite for a measure to qualify as an advantage granted by a Member State is the imputability to the State.[166] Imputability cannot be inferred from the mere fact that the measure in question was taken by a public undertaking, even if the undertaking is controlled by the State.[167]

In the case of a direct transfer from the State to the broadcaster, however, imputability of the measure can be answered in the affirmative without question. Nevertheless, regarding the case of broadcasting fees, some authors challenge the

---

14.12.1999, State aid No NN 88/98, *BBC News 24*, para. 23; Decision of 22.05.2002, State aid No N 631/2001, *BBC license fee*, para. 20; Decision of 01.10.2003, State aid No N 37/2003, *BBC Digital Curriculum*, para. 21; *Döpkens*, ZUM 2009, 214, 215; *Dörr*, in: *Detterbeck/Rozek/v. Coelln*, Recht als Medium der Staatlichkeit – Festschrift für Herbert Bethge zum 70. Geburtstag, pp. 451, 458 et seq.; *Frenz/Götzkes*, ZUM 2010, 563, 564; *Geuer*, CR 2013, 156, 157; *Grzeszick*, NVwZ 2008, 608, 612; *Gundel*, ZUM 2008, 758, 763; *Katsirea*, Public Broadcasting and European Law, p. 336; *Koenigs*, ZEuS 2006, 135, 50 and 54; *Kruse*, ZHR 165 [2001], 567, 590; *Neun*, Öffentlich-rechtlicher Rundfunk: Grenzen des Wachstums, pp. 321 et seqq.; *Ruttig*, Der Einfluß des EG-Beihilferechts auf die Gebührenfinanzierung der öffentlich-rechtlichen Rundfunkanstalten, p. 172; *Selmer/Gersdorf*, Die Finanzierung des Rundfunks in der Bundesrepublik Deutschland auf dem Prüfstand des EG-Beihilferegimes, p. 33; *Thum*, Einfachgesetzliche Präzisierung des verfassungsrechtlichen Funktionsauftrags des öffentlich-rechtlichen Rundfunks, p. 131. See also the analysis of *Selmayr/Kamann*, K&R 2004, 49, 51 et seqq., in which the usage of State resources in the various Member States is assessed. Of other opinion: *Bartosch*, NVwZ 2001, 643, 645; *Braun*, in: *Castendyk/Dommering/Scheuer*, European Media Law, Article 87 EC, para. 53; *Eberle*, AfP 2001, 477, 480; *Ehricke*, Die EG-rechtliche Beurteilung der Rundfunkfinanzierung, pp. 98 et seq.; *Koenig/Haratsch*, ZUM 2005, 275, 276; *Krone*, Gebührenfinanzierter Rundfunk und Beihilferecht, p. 229; *Streinz*, in: *Stern*, Die Bedeutung des Europäischen Rechts für den nationalen Rundfunk, pp. 59, 79; *Stulz-Herrnstadt*, Nationale Rundfunkfinanzierung und europäische Beihilfenaufsicht im Lichte des Amsterdamer Rundfunkprotokolls, pp. 131 et seqq.

165 *Degenhart*, AfP 2005, 493, 494.

166 *ECJ*, 15 July 2004, C-345/02, *Pearle*, para. 35; *Quigley, European State Aid Law And Policy, p. 13.*

167 *CFI*, 26 June 2008, Case T442/03, *SIC*, paras. 94 et seqq.

existence of imputability when the fees are determined largely independently by the broadcasters or a designated public body.[168] A key argument is that the constitutions of the Member States might demand a degree of independence of public service broadcasters with a view to the calculation of the necessary funding.[169] Hence, the measure eventually is not imputable to the State.

The characteristic of 'imputability' has been shaped in particular through the *ECJ*-judgments *Stardust Marine* and *Pearle*. In the following, both decisions are examined regarding their impact on PSB.

(a) *Stardust Marine-ruling*

In the *Stardust Marine*-ruling[170] the *ECJ* had to assess supporting measures in favour of *Stardust Marine* (hereinafter *Stardust*) granted by companies that were partly owned and fully controlled by the French Republic. This was controversial, as it was questionable whether the means had to be regarded as coming from State resources, especially considering the public companies were using their own financial resources. Nonetheless, the *ECJ* answered the possibility of the use of State resources in the sense of Art. 87(1) EC (now: 107(1) TFEU) in the affirmative.

The court confirmed that Art. 87(1) EC 'covers all the financial means by which the public authorities may actually support undertakings, irrespective of whether or not those means are permanent assets of the public sector. Therefore, even if the sums corresponding to the measure in question are not permanently held by the Treasury, the fact that they constantly remain under public control, and therefore available to the competent national authorities, is sufficient for them to be categorised as State resources [...].'[171] The aforementioned requirement of mere (abstract) control over the measure, however, was not sufficient according to the *ECJ*. In particular it was not enough already that the measure was taken by a public undertaking.[172] Rather, the actual exercise of control had to be determined, to impute a measure taken by a public company to the State behind it.[173] To ascertain such actual exercise of control, however, it was enough inferring it 'from a set of indicators arising from the circumstances of the case and the context in which that measure was taken'.[174] These indicators were explicated by the court in detail.[175]

---

168 *Dörr*, Die öffentlich-rechtliche Rundfunkfinanzierung und die Vorgaben des EG-Vertrages, pp. 20 et seq.; *Ehricke*, Die EG-rechtliche Beurteilung der Rundfunkfinanzierung, p. 114.

169 *Ehricke*, Die EG-rechtliche Beurteilung der Rundfunkfinanzierung, p. 110. Cf. also *Koenigs*, ZEuS 2006, 135, 150.

170 *ECJ*, 16 May 2002, C-482/99, *Stardust Marine*.

171 *ECJ*, 16 May 2002, C-482/99, *Stardust Marine*, para. 37.

172 *ECJ*, 16 May 2002, C-482/99, *Stardust Marine*, para. 51.

173 *ECJ*, 16 May 2002, C-482/99, *Stardust Marine*, para. 52.

174 *ECJ*, 16 May 2002, C-482/99, *Stardust Marine*, para. 55.

175 Cf. *ECJ*, 16 May 2002, C-482/99, *Stardust Marine*, paras 55 et seqq.

(b) Pearle-*ruling*

In its *Pearle*-ruling[176] the *ECJ* rejected the imputability of a measure to the State. The appellants in the main proceedings – inter alia *Pearle BV* (hereinafter *Pearle*) – were trading in optical equipment and joined the so-called Board, a trade association governed by public law. At the request of a private opticians' association, of which the appellants in the main proceedings were then members, the Board imposed on its members, pursuant to a bye-law, a compulsory earmarked levy to finance a collective advertising campaign for opticians' businesses.[177] Subsequently, *Pearle* sought the annulment of the bye-law and repayment of the levy based on it.

The *ECJ* took the view that the levy could not be considered State aid in favour of the Board. Although the Board was a public body, the funding was not qualified as resources made available to the national authorities, so no burden on the State existed.[178] The court based its decision on the way that the monies were collected from its members, who benefited from the campaign by means of compulsory levies earmarked for the organisation of the advertising campaign.[179] Moreover, the *ECJ* argued that the initiative for the organisation and operation of that advertising campaign was that of the private association of opticians, and not that of the Board.[180] Therefore, the resources were collected for a purely commercial purpose that had nothing to do with a policy determined by the authorities.[181]

Eventually, the *Pearle*-ruling modified or rather complemented the *Stardust Marine*-jurisdiction from specified criteria to ascertain exercised control over the measure towards a criterion of initiative.[182]

(c) *Assessment*

The argument that a certain independence of the broadcasters, or respectively a designated body, disrupts the imputability to the State is not convincing.[183] The initiative behind the broadcasting fees is regularly taken solely by the State. Particularly in cases in which the State is already obliged to fund public services (e.g. by the constitution), broadcasting fees are used as a replacement for direct funding. What must also be taken into consideration is the often necessary final decision of the State over the means (e.g. through the adoption of a law), even when the State has only minor discretion regarding this decision in the context of its constitutional law.[184] In

176 *ECJ*, 15 July 2004, C-345/02, *Pearle*.
177 *ECJ*, 15 July 2004, C-345/02, *Pearle*, para. 15.
178 *ECJ*, 15 July 2004, C-345/02, *Pearle*, para. 36.
179 *ECJ*, 15 July 2004, C-345/02, *Pearle*, para. 36.
180 *ECJ*, 15 July 2004, C-345/02, *Pearle*, para. 37.
181 *ECJ*, 15 July 2004, C-345/02, *Pearle*, para. 37.
182 Promoting a modification: *Koenig/Busch*, GewArch 2011, 181, 182.
183 *Braum-Schleicher*, Daseinsvorsorge und service public durch den öffentlich-rechtlichen Rundfunk, p. 100.
184 *Katsirea*, Public Broadcasting and European Law, p. 336.

favour of this position points the fact that without the State's decision the levying of broadcasting fees would not be possible.[185] Furthermore, also the constitutional situation in a country generally is subject to change and therefore imputable to the State itself.[186] Therefore, the obligation of deciding the fee according to the broadcasters' needs cannot be an argument for excluding imputability. Moreover, it has to be remembered that the State usually also earmarks the means and controls the utilisation of them.[187] This also speaks in favour of an initiative through the State.

Bearing in mind the above-mentioned indicators that point to control by the State over the means, it is also remarkable that the *CFI* in its *SIC*-ruling named the following circumstances to be relevant regarding the imputability of a measure: the granting body's 'integration into the structures of the public administration, the nature of its activities and the exercise of the latter on the market in normal conditions of competition with private operators, the legal status of the undertaking (in the sense of it being subject to public law or ordinary company law), the intensity of the supervision exercised by the public authorities over the management of the undertaking, or any other indicator showing, in the particular case, an involvement by the public authorities in the adoption of a measure or the unlikelihood of their not being involved, having regard also to the compass of the measure, its content or the conditions which it contains [...].'[188] In conclusion, there are several indicators that impute the financial means to the State, even if particular bodies have discretion when adopting license fees.

Also, the requirements according to *Stardust Marine* and the subsequently *Pearle*-ruling are not extraordinarily high.[189] Above that, it is not necessary that use of the monies is determined in detail.[190] It is, rather, sufficient that the general granting of the means can be traced back to the State. In conclusion, broadcasting fees are generally imputable to the State.[191]

---

185 Cf. also *CFI*, 26 June 2008, Case T442/03, *SIC*, para. 98. Although it has been argued that the *Stardust Marine*-ruling shows that a mere imposition of levies is not sufficient (cf. *Ehricke*, Die EG-rechtliche Beurteilung der Rundfunkfinanzierung, p. 113), it has to be noted, firstly, that the obligation to pay broadcasting fees is not the only indication for imputability and, secondly, that the *Stardust Marine*-ruling has been completed by the rather applicable *Essent*-ruling (see above C. I. 2) (1) (b).).

186 In the same direction *Grzeszick*, NVwZ 2008, 608, 612. Cf. also *Degenhart*, AfP 2005, 493, 496.

187 Cf. *Katsirea,* Public Broadcasting and European Law, p. 334.

188 *CFI*, 26 June 2008, Case T442/03, *SIC*, para. 99.

189 According to *Schipanski*, K&R 2006, 217, 218, (the German) broadcasting fees would even meet the detailed criteria of the *Stardust Marine*-ruling. Of other opinion *Krone*, Gebührenfinanzierter Rundfunk und Beihilferecht, pp. 222 et seq.

190 Cf. *Kruse*, ZHR 165 [2001], 567, 589 et seq.

191 Of the same opinion: *Damm*, Gebührenprivileg und Beihilferecht, p. 113; *Geuer*, CR 2013, 156, 157; *Katsirea,* Public Broadcasting and European Law, p. 336; *Schipanski*, K&R 2006, 217, 218. Of other opinion: *Kirchhof*, Die Finanzierung des öffentlich-rechtlichen Rundfunks, p. 69; *Krone*, Gebührenfinanzierter Rundfunk

3) Distortion of or threat to distort competition

To fall within the scope of Art. 107(1) TFEU, State aid has to distort, or threaten to distort competition. The possibility of distortion presupposes competition on a certain market. Potential competitive relationships are sufficient already.[192]

A possible market can be seen in competition for advertising sales (advertising market).[193] Even if public service broadcasters do not sell advertising space, they compete for viewers or internet users (users/viewers market).[194] Although it may not be in all cases the primary objective of a public service broadcaster to address as many viewers as possible, the viewer rating generally gives the most valuable indication of a broadcaster's success. Their economic value depends primarily on the acceptance by the audience. Therefore, the competition for viewers is directly linked to all the economic interests of broadcasters. Public service broadcasters necessarily take part in this market. Even if the public service broadcaster does not participate in the advertising market, its programme attracts viewers and therefore is likely to distort competition within this important area for all commercial broadcasting activities.[195]

Furthermore, the market for the acquisition and sale of programme rights, as well as the personnel market, are markets on which the public service broadcasters compete with other demanders for offered rights, and specifically qualified persons.[196]

---

und Beihilferecht, p. 229; *Streinz*, in: *Stern*, Die Bedeutung des Europäischen Rechts für den nationalen Rundfunk, pp. 59, 79.

192 *Ehricke*, Die EG-rechtliche Beurteilung der Rundfunkfinanzierung, p. 120; *Katsirea*, Public Broadcasting and European Law, p. 344; *Koenig/Kühling*, EuZW 2000, 197, 200; *Selmer/Gersdorf*, Die Finanzierung des Rundfunks in der Bundesrepublik Deutschland auf dem Prüfstand des EG-Beihilferegimes, p. 46.

193 *Commission*, Decision of 24.04.2007, State aid No E 3/2005, *Financing of public service broadcasters in Germany*, para. 185; *Katsirea*, Public Broadcasting and European Law, p. 344; *Oppermann*, Deutsche Rundfunkgebühren und europäisches Beihilferecht, p. 62.

194 Cf. *Commission*, Decision of 20 September 1995 relating to a proceeding pursuant to Council Regulation (EEC) 4064/89 (OJ L 134/32 of 5.6.1996), paras. 25 et seq.; *Ehricke*, Die EG-rechtliche Beurteilung der Rundfunkfinanzierung, p. 120; *Katsirea*, Public Broadcasting and European Law, p. 343. Not qualifying the viewer's market as a separate market: *Bartosch*, in: *Koenig/Bartosch/Braun*, EC Competition and Telecommunications Law, pp. 196 et seq.; *Eberle*, in: *Geiss/Gerstenmaier/Winkler/Mailänder*, Festschrift für Karl Peter Mailänder zum 70. Geburtstag, pp. 497, 504.

195 Of the same opinion: *Braum-Schleicher*, Daseinsvorsorge und service public durch den öffentlich-rechtlichen Rundfunk, p. 108.

196 *Bartosch*, in: *Koenig/Bartosch/Braun*, EC Competition and Telecommunications Law, p. 198; *Ehricke*, Die EG-rechtliche Beurteilung der Rundfunkfinanzierung, p. 120; *Katsirea*, Public Broadcasting and European Law, p. 344; *Selmer/Gersdorf*, Die Finanzierung des Rundfunks in der Bundesrepublik Deutschland auf dem Prüfstand des EG-Beihilferegimes, p. 47.

All these relevant markets are threatened by distortion of competition through the public financing of public service broadcasters.[197] The means enable beneficiaries to strengthen their position in competition with other broadcasters.[198]

4) Affect trade between Member States

Aid granted is only incompatible with the internal market pursuant to Art. 107(1) TFEU in so far as it affects trade between Member States. A potential effect is sufficient.[199] The necessity of the adverse effect on trade serves the intention to establish boundaries between Community law and Member State law.[200]

Community trade is affected when aid granted by the State or through State resources strengthens the position of an undertaking compared with other undertakings competing in intra-Community trade.[201] The favouring of public service broadcasters strengthens their position in all kinds of competition. Nevertheless, it is necessary to have competition between undertakings of different Member States involving public service broadcasters. Such a competition could be seen in the acquisition and sale of programme rights, as this market is not limited solely to a national

---

197 *Commission*, Decision of 01.10.2003, State aid No N 37/2003, *BBC Digital Curriculum*, para. 24; Decision of 19.05.2004, State aid No C 2/2003, *TV2*, paras. 73 et seqq. Decision of 24.04.2007, State aid No E 3/2005, *Financing of public service broadcasters in Germany*, para. 183; *Ehricke*, Die EG-rechtliche Beurteilung der Rundfunkfinanzierung, p. 125; *Holmes/Houwen/Waite*, in: *Bacon*, European Community Law of State Aid, para. 13.13; *Katsirea*, Public Broadcasting and European Law, p. 344; *Koenig/Kühling*, EuZW 2000, 197, 200; *Koenigs*, ZEuS 2006, 135, 10; *Neun*, Öffentlich-rechtlicher Rundfunk: Grenzen des Wachstums, pp. 324 et seqq.; *Schipanski*, K&R 2006, 217, 222; *Selmer/Gersdorf*, Die Finanzierung des Rundfunks in der Bundesrepublik Deutschland auf dem Prüfstand des EG-Beihilferegimes, p. 49; *Storr*, K&R 2002, 464, 468; *Stulz-Herrnstadt*, Nationale Rundfunkfinanzierung und europäische Beihilfenaufsicht im Lichte des Amsterdamer Rundfunkprotokolls, p. 158; *Thum*, Einfachgesetzliche Präzisierung des verfassungsrechtlichen Funktionsauftrags des öffentlich-rechtlichen Rundfunks, p. 138. Of other opinion: *Eberle*, in: *Geiss/Gerstenmaier/Winkler/Mailänder*, Festschrift für Karl Peter Mailänder zum 70. Geburtstag, pp. 497, 504 et seqq.; *Krausnick*, Das deutsche Rundfunksystem unter dem Einfluss des Europarechts, p. 320.

198 Cf. *Commission*, Decision of 24.04.2007, State aid No E 3/2005, *Financing of public service broadcasters in Germany*, para. 184.

199 Cf. *Commission*, Decision of 22.05.2002, State aid No N 631/2001, *BBC license fee*, para. 22.

200 *Heidenhain*, in: *Heidenhain*, European State Aid Law, § 4, para. 78.

201 *ECJ*, 17 September 1980, Case C-730/79, *Philip Morris Holland*, para. 11; *Commission*, Communication from the Commission on the application of State aid rules to public service broadcasting, (OJ C 257/1 of 27.10.2009), para. 22; Decision of 20.04.2011, State aid No C 2/2003, *TV2*, para. 149; *Thum*, NVwZ 2007, 521, 525.

level.[202] Additionally, in the case of a public service broadcaster participating on the sales-market of advertising, broadcasters from different countries could compete for the same advertisers, as long as the language of the programme is the same.[203] In particular, online services have a global reach and advertisements are often offered either in different languages or do not necessarily depend on the language at all.[204] Eventually, it has to be considered that undertakings from one Member State could found or invest in broadcasting undertakings situated in other Members States.[205] In this situation, the market entry is hampered due to the existence of State-aided public service broadcasters. In all the aforesaid situations, competition (potentially) exists between undertakings from different Member States. This intra-Community trade could be affected by public funding of public service broadcasters. Thus, an adverse effect on trade between Member States generally is given.[206]

---

202 *Commission*, *Commission*, Decision of 22.05.2002, State aid No N 631/2001, *BBC license fee*, para. 22; Decision of 24.04.2007, State aid No E 3/2005, *Financing of public service broadcasters in Germany*, para. 182; Communication from the Commission on the application of State aid rules to public service broadcasting, (OJ C 257/1 of 27.10.2009), para. 22; *Bravasso*, in: *Hancher/Ottervanger/Slot*, EU State Aids, para. 18–002; *Frenz/Götzkes*, ZUM 2010, 563, 564.

203 *Commission*, Communication from the Commission on the application of State aid rules to public service broadcasting, (OJ C 257/1 of 27.10.2009), para. 22; *Bravasso*, in: *Hancher/Ottervanger/Slot*, EU State Aids, para. 18–002; *Frenz/Götzkes*, ZUM 2010, 563, 564.

204 *Frenz/Götzkes*, ZUM 2010, 563, 564.

205 *Commission*, *Commission*, Decision of 22.05.2002, State aid No N 631/2001, *BBC license fee*, para. 22; Decision of 01.10.2003, State aid No N 37/2003, *BBC Digital Curriculum*, para. 25; Decision of 24.04.2007, State aid No E 3/2005, *Financing of public service broadcasters in Germany*, para. 186; Communication from the Commission on the application of State aid rules to public service broadcasting, (OJ C 257/1 of 27.10.2009), para. 22; *Bravasso*, in: *Hancher/Ottervanger/Slot*, EU State Aids, para. 18–002.

206 *Commission*, Communication from the Commission on the application of State aid rules to public service broadcasting, (OJ C 257/1 of 27.10.2009), para. 22; *Commission*, Decision of 22.05.2002, State aid No N 631/2001, *BBC license fee*, para. 22; Decision of 01.10.2003, State aid No N 37/2003, *BBC Digital Curriculum*, para. 25; *Braum-Schleicher*, Daseinsvorsorge und service public durch den öffentlich-rechtlichen Rundfunk, pp. 112 et seqq.; *Bravasso*, in: *Hancher/Ottervanger/Slot*, EU State Aids, para. 18–002; *Frenz/Götzkes*, ZUM 2010, 563, 564; *Holmes/Houwen/Waite*, in: *Bacon*, European Community Law of State Aid, para. 13.13; *Katsirea*, Public Broadcasting and European Law, p. 344; *Koenig/Kühling*, EuZW 2000, 197, 200; *Koenigs*, ZEuS 2006, 135, 170; *Neun*, Öffentlich-rechtlicher Rundfunk: Grenzen des Wachstums, p. 326; *Schipanski*, K&R 2006, 217, 222; *Selmer/Gersdorf*, Die Finanzierung des Rundfunks in der Bundesrepublik Deutschland auf dem Prüfstand des EG-Beihilferegimes, p. 53; *Thum*, NVwZ 2007, 521, 525.

5) Intermediate conclusion

The analysis showed that compensation payments for PSB carry a strong potential to be qualified as State aid in the sense of Art. 107(1) TFEU. In particular, the often cited argument that broadcasting fees cannot be seen as being granted by the Member State or through State resources is not convincing even if the broadcasting fees are transferred directly from the viewers to the broadcasters. The answer to the question whether public funding of PSB constitutes also a favour in the sense of Art. 107(1) TFEU depends on the fulfilment of the *Altmark*-criteria and is – as already mentioned – subject to an analysis in a separate chapter below.

II. Burden of proof

It is questionable whether the Commission carries the burden of proof when it comes to a State aid procedure.

1) Art. 107(1) TFEU

It has been stated that the burden of proof regarding the existence/absence of the *Altmark*-criteria[207] (especially the fourth criterion) in a State aid procedure in front of the Commission has to be carried by the latter. This view for example was uttered in the procedure regarding the financing of the German public service broadcasters.[208] The Commission, however, was retaining its general decision-making practise[209] and objected the aforementioned opinion.[210] Other scholars see a partial inversion of the burden of proof caused through the Amsterdam Protocol, regarding the requirements of 107(1) TFEU and Art. 106(2).[211]

In favour of an obligation of the Commission to prove the absence of the *Altmark*-criteria is the fact that only if the *Altmark*-criteria are not met State aid can be answered in the affirmative. As it is the Commission's task to examine measures regarding the existing of State aid and release actions in the case of illegal State aid it comes natural to mind that the Commission has to prove a violation of Art. 107(1)

---

207 Regarding the criteria see below D.

208 *Commission*, Decision of 24.04.2007, State aid No E 3/2005, *Financing of public service broadcasters in Germany*, para. 83. Of the same opinion *Fuchs*, ZEuS 2007, 561, 596.

209 *Commission*, Decision of 01.10.2003, State aid No N 37/2003, *BBC Digital Curriculum*, para. 23; Decision of 25 January 2012 on the measure SA.14588 (C 20/09) implemented by Belgium in favour of De Post-La Poste (OJ L 170/1 of 29.06.2012), para. 194.

210 *Commission*, Decision of 24.04.2007, State aid No E 3/2005, *Financing of public service broadcasters in Germany*, para. 166.

211 E.g. *Stulz-Herrnstadt*, Nationale Rundfunkfinanzierung und europäische Beihilfenaufsicht im Lichte des Amsterdamer Rundfunkprotokolls, pp. 357 et seqq. Regarding this issue see the in-depth-investigation below C. III. 2) c).

TFEU (including the absence of the *Altmark*-criteria).[212] This assumption at most could only be opposed by the fact that the *Altmark*-criteria resemble an exception from the term State aid.[213] This is because generally any favouring may be seen as State aid, the *Altmark*-criteria, however, define under which an advantage has not to be qualified as a favouring in the sense of Art. 107(1) TFEU but as compensation for the discharge of public service obligations. Consequently, due that the burden of proof for exceptions/derogations lies on the Members States,[214] there are non-negligible indications that the Member State bears the burden of proof for the *Altmark*-criteria.

However, even if the burden of proof in this respect lays on the Commission, the Commission's options according to the Regulation[215] (EC) No 659/1999 (subsequently: procedural regulation) practically could 'shift' the burden to the Member States.[216] According to the *CFI* the 'apportionment of the burden of proof is subject to compliance with the procedural obligations imposed on the Commission and the Member State concerned in the course of the exercise by that institution of its powers to cause the Member State to provide it with all the necessary information'[217]. Pursuant to Art. 10, Art. 2(2) and Art. 5(1), (2) procedural regulation the Commission has the possibility to request information from the Member State. The Member State is obliged to provide all necessary information in order to enable the Commission to take a decision. This obligation follows out of Art. 4(3) TEU (formerly Art. 10 EC) already.[218] The information given by the Member State has to comprise all documentation, information and data necessary to carry out the review.[219] Where the Commission has fruitlessly ordered a Member State to provide the information

212 Of this opinion *Fuchs*, ZEuS 2007, 561, 597, but without paying further attention to the procedural regulation and the possibility to order information from the Member State. See also *Oldale/Piffaut*, in: *Bacon*, European Community Law of State Aid, para. 1.22. On the other hand *Arhold* (in: *Montag/Säcker*, Münchener Kommentar zum Europäischen und Deutschen Wettbewerbsrecht (Kartellrecht) – Band 3, Art. 107 AEUV para. 232) applies the rules for the burden of proof regarding Art. 106(2) TFEU (see next section) also to the first *Altmark*-criterion (without further dogmatic substantiation). The latter method might neglect the differences between rule and derogation.

213 In this direction *Commission*, Decision of 24.04.2007, State aid No E 3/2005, *Financing of public service broadcasters in Germany*, para. 166.

214 *CFI*, 12 September 2007, Case T68/03, *Olympiaki*, para. 34.

215 *Council*, Regulation (EC) No 659/1999 of 22 March 1999 laying down detailed rules for the application of Article 93 of the EC Treaty (OJ L 83/1 of 27.03.1999).

216 Cf. *CFI*, 12 September 2007, Case T68/03, *Olympiaki*, paras. 35 et seqq.

217 *CFI*, 12 September 2007, Case T68/03, *Olympiaki*, para. 35. See also *ECJ*, 6 April 2006, Case T-17/03, *Schmitz-Gotha Fahrzeugwerke*, para. 48.

218 Cf. *CFI*, 22 October 2008, joined Cases T-309/04, T-317/04, T-329/04 and T-336/04, *TV2*, para. 183; *CFI*, 12 September 2007, Case T68/03, *Olympiaki*, para. 36.

219 *CFI*, 12 September 2007, Case T68/03, *Olympiaki*, para. 36.

through an information injunction, it is entitled to adopt a decision on the basis of the information available (Art. 13(1)(3) procedural regulation). The Commission is not obliged to seek information from interested parties, if the Member State does not reply to the injunction.[220] If the delivered information is considered deficient by the Commission it has to explain sufficiently the reasons for the assessment and why the given information cannot be used as a basis for the final decision.[221]

In respect of the *Altmark*-criteria this means that the Commission is empowered to order all the information necessary to scrutinise whether the measure meets the *Altmark*-criteria. This comprises, for example, all information necessary to control whether the compensation an undertaking receives is determined on the basis of an analysis of the costs which a typical undertaking, well run and adequately provided so as to be able to meet the necessary public service requirements, would have incurred, in the sense of the fourth *Altmark*-criterion[222] (e.g. a benchmark-analysis). If the Member State does not provide the ordered information the Commission may assume that the respective *Altmark*-criterion is not met and therefore that a measure is State aid.[223] As a result it can be concluded that the procedural regulation imposes the responsibility to submit the necessary information to validate the compliance with the *Altmark*-criteria on the Member States. This does not cause an inversion of the burden of proof,[224] because the Commission still has to prove the existence of a granted advantage to an undertaking. Though, the procedural regulation shifts the risk for the attainment of the necessary information to proof the presence of Altmark-criteria to the Member State.

2) Art. 106(2) TFEU

Rather unambiguous, by contrast, is the allocation of the burden of proof in Art. 106(2) TFEU, as the provision is qualified as a derogation. The burden of proof, consequently, lies on the Member State.[225] It comprises the evidence for the existence

---

220 *Grespan*, in: *Mederer/Pesaresi/Van Hoof*, EU Competition Law – Volume IV – State Aid, para 3.152.

221 *Sinnaeve*, in: *Heidenhain*, European State Aid Law, § 32, para. 6.

222 *ECJ*, 24 July 2003, Case C-280/00, *Altmark Trans*, para. 93.

223 See *ECJ*, 24 July 2003, Case C-280/00, *Altmark Trans*, para. 94.

224 Cf. *CFI*, 12 September 2007, Case T68/03, *Olympiaki*, paras. 435 et seqq. Critical: *Michel*, MMR 2005, 284, 287.

225 *ECJ*, 23 October 1997, Case C-159/94, *Commission/French Republic*, para. 101; 17 May 2001, Case C-340/99, *TNT Traco*, para. 59; *CFI*, 22 October 2008, joined Cases T-309/04, T-317/04, T-329/04 and T-336/04, *TV2*, para. 183; *Commission*, Communication from the Commission on the application of State aid rules to public service broadcasting, (OJ C 257/1 of 27.10.2009), para. 39; *Bartosch*, EU-Beihilfenrecht – Kommentar, Art. 86 Abs. 2 EGV, para. 4; *Wolf*, in: *Montag/Säcker*, Münchener Kommentar zum Europäischen und Deutschen Wettbewerbsrecht (Kartellrecht) – Band 3, Art. 107 AEUV, para. 762.

of SGEI,[226] the clear and precise definition of public service obligations[227] and an entrustment with a public service remit[228]. Additionally, also the burden of proof regarding the requirement of proportionality in the sense of Art. 106(2) TFEU is carried by the Member State, including the question, whether the beneficiary of the measure has generated all achievable revenues and the expenses incurred were comprehensively necessary.[229] It is notable, however, that the *ECJ* has no high demands for the proof of the requirement of an obstruction of the performance, by stating 'that burden of proof cannot be so extensive as to require the Member State, when setting out in detail the reasons for which, in the event of elimination of the contested measures, the performance of the tasks of general economic interest under economically acceptable conditions would, in its view, be jeopardised, to go even further and prove, positively, that no other conceivable measure, which by definition would be hypothetical, could enable those tasks to be performed under the same conditions'[230].

All the same, it has to be noted that the burden of proof is inversed regarding the requirements of Art. 106(2)(2) TFEU. In this respect the Commission has to prove whether the development of trade has been affected to such an extent as would be contrary to the interests of the Union.[231]

III. Modification of the State aid-assessment through the Amsterdam Protocol?

In 1997, the Member States, pursuant to an initiative of the Belgian delegation,[232] agreed upon the so-called Amsterdam Protocol[233] concerning the financing of PSB in the Member States. According to Art. 51 TEU, protocols shall be an integrated part of the European Treaties.[234] The Amsterdam Protocol, therefore, constitutes an

---

226 *Wolf*, in: *Montag/Säcker*, Münchener Kommentar zum Europäischen und Deutschen Wettbewerbsrecht (Kartellrecht) – Band 3, Art. 107 AEUV, para. 762.
227 *Bartosch*, EU-Beihilfenrecht – Kommentar, Art. 86 Abs. 2 EGV, para. 6.
228 *CFI*, 12 February 2008, Case T-289/03, *BUPA*, para. 172.
229 *Bartosch*, EU-Beihilfenrecht – Kommentar, Art. 86 Abs. 2 EGV, para. 18. Considering the requirement see below C. III. 2) c).
230 *ECJ*, 23 October 1997, Case C-159/94, *Commission/French Republic*, para. 101.
231 *Bartosch*, EU-Beihilfenrecht – Kommentar, Art. 86 Abs. 2 EGV, para. 4; *Wolf*, in: *Montag/Säcker*, Münchener Kommentar zum Europäischen und Deutschen Wettbewerbsrecht (Kartellrecht) – Band 3, Art. 107 AEUV, para. 762.
232 *Krausnick*, Das deutsche Rundfunksystem unter dem Einfluss des Europarechts, p. 129. Furthermore *Streinz*, in: *Stern*, Die Bedeutung des Europäischen Rechts für den nationalen Rundfunk, pp. 59, 64, who is also mentioning Germany and Sweden as part of the initiating force.
233 OJ C 340/109 of 10/11/1997. Now carried over to Protocol 29 of the Lisbon Treaty.
234 *Ehricke*, Die EG-rechtliche Beurteilung der Rundfunkfinanzierung, p. 42; *Krone*, Gebührenfinanzierter Rundfunk und Beihilferecht, pp. 74 et seqq.; *Michel*, MMR

amendment of the TEU, the TFEU and related acts. Below, the Amsterdam is examined regarding its legal content and the effects it has on the State aid-assessment of PSB.

The Amsterdam Protocol substantially consists of two parts: an amendment of the TFEU concerning the financing of PSB and supporting reasons regarding the amendment. Considering the latter the Protocol states

> 'that the system of public broadcasting in the Member States is directly related to the democratic, social and cultural needs of each society and to the need to preserve media pluralism'. In view of the amendment, the Protocol specifies that the provisions of the Treaty establishing the European Community (now the TFEU) 'shall be without prejudice to the competence of Member States to provide for the funding of PSB'.

The Protocol requires that

> 'such funding is granted to broadcasting organisations for the fulfilment of the public service remit as conferred, defined and organised by each Member State, and insofar as such funding does not affect trading conditions and competition in the Community to an extent which would be contrary to the common interest, while the realisation of the remit of that public service shall be taken into account'.

The intention behind the Protocol was, as a reaction to the increasing number of State aid complaints, to secure the public funding of PSB.[235] It is therefore of little surprise that, despite its rather vague content, the act is often cited to justify public funding of PSB. In fact, assessments of the Protocol's impact range from almost unreserved justification of public financing to no impact at all. In the following section, the opposing views are explained and the impact of the Protocol itself will be explored.

Beforehand, it has to be acknowledged that as part of the European Treaties the Amsterdam Protocol is by any means legally binding. Its effects are concerning the financing of PSB under the TFEU, which comprises at least the financing of television or radio services. By contrast, it is questionable whether the Protocol is also applicable to the funding of internet services beside the traditional activities of broadcasters that were present at the time the Protocol was adopted (i.e. television and radio services. On the basis of the Commission's Communication on the application of State aid rules it can be concluded that the Commission regards online

2005, 284, 287; *Schnaitter*, Möglichkeiten und Grenzen der Ausgestaltung des Programmauftrags der öffentlich-rechtlichen Rundfunkanstalten, p. 24. For more information on the question whether the Amsterdam Protocol is considered to be a Protocol according to Art. 51 TEU: *Schwendinger*, Gemeinschaftsrechtliche Grenzen öffentlicher Rundfunkfinanzierung, p. 193.

235 *Krausnick*, Das deutsche Rundfunksystem unter dem Einfluss des Europarechts, p. 129; *Krone*, Gebührenfinanzierter Rundfunk und Beihilferecht, p. 70; *Streinz*, in: *Stern*, Die Bedeutung des Europäischen Rechts für den nationalen Rundfunk, pp. 59, 63.

services as covered by the Protocol, as the Communication declares that 'State aid to public service broadcasters may be used for distributing audiovisual services on all platforms provided that the material requirements of the Amsterdam Protocol are met'[236]. Considering the wording of the Protocol, which uses the open term 'PSB', this view deserves to be endorsed.[237] Nevertheless, this does not anticipate the question whether specific new media services are eligible to be part of a public service remit.[238]

1) Legal exception or derogation from Art. 107(1) TFEU?

The legal classification of the Protocol is controversial. Some voices claim that the Amsterdam Protocol dispenses fully from the application of the rules of the TFEU, especially the regulations concerning State aid (legal exception from the State aid rules).[239] According to this opinion, public funding compatible with the Amsterdam Protocol could not be considered as illegal State aid in the sense of Art. 107(1) TFEU, but would be assessed solely pursuant to its own provisions. Occasionally, the assertion can be found that the Protocol even determines the compliance of the financing of PSB with State aid law.[240] Considering the intention behind the Protocol, namely to secure the public funding of PSB, such an interpretation comes naturally to mind.

On the other hand, a rather seldom represented opinion interprets the Protocol to be a confirmation of the State-aid-quality of public financing of PSB.[241] This view, however, contradicts the intention behind the Protocol, namely to enable Member States to support broadcasters.

---

236 *Commission*, Communication from the Commission on the application of State aid rules to public service broadcasting, (OJ C 257/1 of 27.10.2009), para. 84.

237 Of same opinion: *Michel*, MMR 2005, 284, 287; *Niejahr*, in: *Montag/Säcker*, Münchener Kommentar zum Europäischen und Deutschen Wettbewerbsrecht (Kartellrecht) – Band 3, Sektoren para. 198; *Streinz*, in: *Stern*, Die Bedeutung des Europäischen Rechts für den nationalen Rundfunk, pp. 59, 84; *Wiedemann*, EStAL 2004, 595, 598. *Hesse*, AfP 2005, 499, 502 et seq., also argues that Art. 16 TEU (presumably meaning Art. 16 EC, now: Art. 14 TFEU) and Art. 11 Charter of Fundamental Rights of the European Union support the opinion of a dynamic remit which comprises new media services.

238 See below.

239 *Verwaltungsgericht Karlsruhe*, judgment of 28 September 2006 – Case 1 K 559/06, 1 K 559/06a, para. 25; *Eberle*, AfP 2001, 477; *Erkens*, Der öffentlich-rechtliche Rundfunk und exklusive Sportberichterstattung, p. 259; *Goerlich/Meier*, ZUM 2007, 889, 895; *Schnaitter*, Möglichkeiten und Grenzen der Ausgestaltung des Programmauftrags der öffentlich-rechtlichen Rundfunkanstalten, p. 70. Cf. also *Donders*, Public Service Media and Policy in Europe, p. 99 with further references.

240 *Fechner*, Medienrecht, 7. Kapitel para. 18. In the same direction: *Wittig-Terhardt*, in: *Classen/Dittmann/Fechner/Gassner/Kilian*, "In einem vereinten Europa dem Frieden der Welt zu dienen ..." – Liber amicorum Thomas Oppermann, pp. 727, 745.

241 *Damm*, Gebührenprivileg und Beihilferecht, p. 68.

A considerable number of scholars recognise the protocol to be a derogation from Art. 107(1) TFEU, similar to Art. 107(2–3) and Art. 106(2) or Art. 93 TFEU.[242] In accordance with this opinion, it would be possible to assess public financing of broadcasters as State aid according to Art. 107(1) TFEU, but such a measure could be qualified as justified solely under the provisions of the Protocol. Other possibly relevant derogations would not apply. In favour for this position it could be argued that the provisions of the Amsterdam Protocol resemble those of Art. 106(2) TFEU for which reason the Protocol, as the special rule, would prevail.

All of the aforementioned views, however, have to be rejected, wherefore PSB remains fully subject to the TFEU.[243] The view presented here is supported by the fact that the Amsterdam Protocol itself denotes the provisions in it as 'interpretative'. The wording already indicates that the Protocol takes effect only in connection with other provisions, namely the general State aid rules. Additionally, it has to be kept in mind that derogations from the general rules, as well as exceptions, exist very rarely in the TFEU (e.g. Art. 42 TFEU) and their conception as such (especially considering the wording) is generally clearly manifested.[244] Such an understanding of the Protocol (if it would have been hoped) could have been achieved very easily, for example through an amendment of Art. 107(1), (2) or (3) TFEU. From a systematic perspective an establishment like this would have been indicated.[245] In fact, the representatives of Germany on the Intergovernmental Conference fruitlessly tried to anchor a corresponding amendment of Art. 107(1) TFEU, which would have qualified financial means granted to public service broadcasters as free from

242 *Hesse*, AfP 2005, 499, 501, who wants to apply Art. 86(2) EC (now Art. 106(2) TFEU) only if the Amsterdam Protocol is not relevant.

243 Likewise: *Bravasso*, in: *Hancher/Ottervanger/Slot*, EU State Aids, para. 18–002; *Degenhart*, K&R 2008, 214, 218; *Donders*, Public Service Media and Policy in Europe, p. 99; *Krausnick*, Das deutsche Rundfunksystem unter dem Einfluss des Europarechts, p. 133; *Krone*, Gebührenfinanzierter Rundfunk und Beihilferecht, p. 75; *Nitsche*, Broadcasting in the European Union: The Role of Public Interest in Competition Analysis, p. 152; *Ruttig*, Der Einfluß des EG-Beihilferechts auf die Gebührenfinanzierung der öffentlich-rechtlichen Rundfunkanstalten, p. 135; *Schwarze*, ZUM 2000, 779, 796; *Schwendinger*, Gemeinschaftsrechtliche Grenzen öffentlicher Rundfunkfinanzierung, p. 195; *Streinz*, in: *Stern*, Die Bedeutung des Europäischen Rechts für den nationalen Rundfunk, pp. 59, 66. Implicitly: *CFI*, 22 October 2008, joined Cases T-309/04, T-317/04, T-329/04 and T-336/04, *TV2*, paras. 155 et seqq.

244 *Greissinger*, Vorgaben des EG-Vertrages für nationales Rundfunk- und Multimediarecht, p. 147. Whereas *Greissinger* highlights Art. 73 EC (now: Art. 93 TFEU) as a legal exception, while generally it is seen as a derogation similar to Art. 106(2) TFEU (cf. *Linke*, Die Gewährleistung des Daseinsvorsorgeauftrags im öffentlichen Personennahverkehr, pp. 139 et seqq., 145).

245 *Schwendinger*, Gemeinschaftsrechtliche Grenzen öffentlicher Rundfunkfinanzierung, p. 195.

the State aid regime.[246] This strongly indicates that an exception or derogation, or any other kind of exemption from the TFEU, was not the aim.

2) Impact of the Amsterdam Protocol

In the following, the question of the Protocol's impact on the State aid rules is explored. Although the Protocol might not be qualified as a derogation or an exception from these requirements, it certainly has legal implications.[247] To deny any consequences from the application of the Protocol would question the equality of the provisions of the Treaties of the EU,[248] since the amendment of the TFEU was implemented for a reason, namely to secure the public funding of the broadcasting services. This premise, however, is not a one-way street, for which reason the State aid law must also not be deprived of its substance.[249] In fact, it can be concluded from the wording that the Protocol concedes or acknowledges the Commission's competence to control the financing measures,[250] as funding is permitted only insofar as it 'does not affect trading conditions and competition in the Community to an extent which would be contrary to the common interest'. Otherwise, the restrictions would lack the possibility of enforcement, which could hardly have been intended. In favour of this position is the fact that the question, whether 'trading conditions' and 'competition in the Community' are affected, can only be answered if Art. 107 and Art. 106 TFEU are considered, as both articles protect competition and trade.[251] Their requirements, however, are controlled by the Commission.

The Protocol denotes its content as 'interpretative provisions'. The most significant impact of the Amsterdam Protocol, therefore, lies – as mentioned before – in its

---

246 Cf. *Streinz*, in: *Stern*, Die Bedeutung des Europäischen Rechts für den nationalen Rundfunk, pp. 59, 64. See also *Ruttig*, Der Einfluß des EG-Beihilferechts auf die Gebührenfinanzierung der öffentlich-rechtlichen Rundfunkanstalten, p. 135. Especially the United Kingdom, Spain and Luxembourg contested the proposal of the German delegation.

247 Of other opinion: Frey, ZUM 1999, 528, 541, who equates the requirements of the Protocol and those of Art. 86(2)(2) EC (now: Art. 106(2)(2) TFEU). Similar *Greissinger*, Vorgaben des EG-Vertrages für nationales Rundfunk- und Multimediarecht, p. 151 et seq.; *Laitenberger*, in: *Stern/Prütting*, Nationaler Rundfunk und Europäisches Gemeinschaftsrecht zwischen Kommunikationsfreiheit und Regulierung, pp. 31, 33.

248 *Degenhart*, AfP 2005, 493, 496.

249 *Degenhart*, AfP 2005, 493, 496. Cf. also *Katsirea*, Public Broadcasting and European Law, p. 326, who sees the effect of the Protocol particularly in the 'division of responsibility between the Member States and the Commission'.

250 *Streinz*, in: *Stern*, Die Bedeutung des Europäischen Rechts für den nationalen Rundfunk, pp. 59, 70; *v. Wallenberg*, MMR 2004, 88, 91.

251 *Schwendinger*, Gemeinschaftsrechtliche Grenzen öffentlicher Rundfunkfinanzierung, p. 195.

influence on the interpretation of the rules of the TFEU.[252] To the contrary, the Protocol cannot be seen as a final (positive or negative) decision regarding the legality of public financing.[253] How the Protocol influences the interpretation of Art. 106(2) and Art. 107(1) TFEU specifically will be the subject of the following sections.

Besides being an interpretative impact, however, the Amsterdam Protocol implicitly gives rise to the following three premises. First, the Amsterdam Protocol underlines that it is possible for the Member States to establish PSB (possibility of a 'dual system') and to grant advantages to public service broadcasters.[254] Due to the fact that the Protocol comprises any way of providing the funding of the organisations, the Protocol includes also indirect ways of funding, e.g. tax reductions or granting loans with low interest rates. Second, the permission to finance the relevant services implicitly includes a discretion for the Member States as to which form of financial measures is the most suitable to support the relevant undertaking.[255] Therefore, the Member States may finance PSB in any form they wish,[256] e.g. financing through single-funding or dual-funding;[257] through a State budget or a levy on specific undertakings or natural persons. Third, the Protocol states 'that the system of public broadcasting in the Member States is directly related to the democratic, social and cultural needs of each society and to the need to preserve media pluralism'. With

252 Likewise: *Craufurd Smith*, LIEI 28 (1) [2001], 3, 11; *Degenhart*, AfP 2005, 493, 496; *Ehricke*, Die EG-rechtliche Beurteilung der Rundfunkfinanzierung, pp. 42 et seqq.; *Krausnick*, Das deutsche Rundfunksystem unter dem Einfluss des Europarechts, p. 131; *Krone*, Gebührenfinanzierter Rundfunk und Beihilferecht, p. 75; *Schwarze*, ZUM 2000, 779, 796; *Schnaitter*, Möglichkeiten und Grenzen der Ausgestaltung des Programmauftrags der öffentlich-rechtlichen Rundfunkanstalten, p. 24; *Schwendinger*, Gemeinschaftsrechtliche Grenzen öffentlicher Rundfunkfinanzierung, p. 199; *Streinz*, in: *Stern*, Die Bedeutung des Europäischen Rechts für den nationalen Rundfunk, pp. 59, 66.

253 *Ehricke*, Die EG-rechtliche Beurteilung der Rundfunkfinanzierung, p. 43.

254 *Ehricke*, Die EG-rechtliche Beurteilung der Rundfunkfinanzierung, p. 43; *Hesse*, AfP 2005, 499, 501; *Krone*, Gebührenfinanzierter Rundfunk und Beihilferecht, p. 295; *Niejahr*, in: *Montag/Säcker*, Münchener Kommentar zum Europäischen und Deutschen Wettbewerbsrecht (Kartellrecht) – Band 3, Sektoren para. 137; *Schnaitter*, Möglichkeiten und Grenzen der Ausgestaltung des Programmauftrags der öffentlich-rechtlichen Rundfunkanstalten, p. 29.

255 Cf. *Commission*, Communication from the Commission on the application of State aid rules to public service broadcasting, (OJ C 257/1 of 27.10.2009), para. 58; *Streinz*, in: *Stern*, Die Bedeutung des Europäischen Rechts für den nationalen Rundfunk, pp. 59, 69.

256 Cf. *Niejahr*, in: *Montag/Säcker*, Münchener Kommentar zum Europäischen und Deutschen Wettbewerbsrecht (Kartellrecht) – Band 3, Sektoren para. 199. This does not anticipate the question how much Member States are allowed to grant or whether the benefits have to be qualified as State aids.

257 Considering theses terms see above B. III.

this the Protocol acknowledges that generally PSB may be seen as SGEI according to Art. 14 and Art. 106(2) TFEU.[258]

a) Impact on the definition of public service obligations

The Amsterdam Protocol has an interpretative impact on the rules of the TFEU. The question, however, is how far this reaches. For example, it could have an impact on the discretion of the Member States to define which activities of broadcasting undertakings are SGEI. The possibility of naming certain services as SGEI with broad latitude would give the Member States the option to justify financial support under the requirements of the *Altmark*-ruling as well as the exception of Art. 106(2) TFEU.

The extent of the Member States' discretion in this respect, however, is uncertain. Some authors claim that the Protocol demands an interpretation, such as a SGEI is any broadcast service a Member State designates as one.[259] Others plead merely for a wide discretion, where the remit of PSB can be defined in broad terms.[260] Nevertheless, the Commission has, according to the latter view, the ability to oppose manifest errors in the definition, though it remains unclear when such an occurrence is to have arisen.

The *Commission*, in its Communication, also limits its role to checking for manifest errors.[261] It was 'not for the Commission to decide which programmes are to be provided and financed as a SGEI, nor to question the nature or the quality of a certain product'.[262]

It has to be emphasised, however, that the Commission's restricted control competence (on a manifest error) is not a peculiarity of the PSB sector, but a general rule in the field of SGEI.[263] This ensues from the prerogative the Member States have to define SGEI. The Amsterdam Protocol does not broaden this prerogative of the Member States. The control standards of the Commission and the European courts ('manifest error') stay the same. Otherwise, the Protocol would further soften the

---

258 Cf. *CFI*, 26 June 2008, Case T442/03, *SIC*, para. 153; *Streinz*, in: *Stern*, Die Bedeutung des Europäischen Rechts für den nationalen Rundfunk, pp. 59, 76. This does not anticipate the question whether all the services of a public service broadcaster may fall under the services of general economic interest.

259 Cf. about that *Craufurd Smith*, LIEI 28 (1) [2001], 3, 14. In this direction for example *Krone*, Gebührenfinanzierter Rundfunk und Beihilferecht, pp. 295 et seqq., especially p. 299.

260 *Depypere/Tigchelaar*, Competition Policy Newsletter 2004 (2), 19; *Grespan*, EStAL 2010, 79, 80 et seq.; *Schipanski*, K&R 2006, 217, 218 et seq.

261 Of same opinion: *Streinz*, in: *Stern*, Die Bedeutung des Europäischen Rechts für den nationalen Rundfunk, pp. 59, 70.

262 *Commission*, Communication from the Commission on the application of State aid rules to public service broadcasting, (OJ C 257/1 of 27.10.2009), para. 48.

263 *CFI*, 12 February 2008, Case T-289/03, *BUPA*, paras. 167, 169; 15 June 2005, Case T-17/02, *Olsen*, para. 216; *Bartosch*, EU-Beihilfenrecht – Kommentar, Art. 86 Abs. 2 EGV, para. 5.

Commission's already thin general control-standard in State aid law. Being not even able to monitor manifest errors in the definition of the SGEI would render the control competence of the Commission almost irrelevant and, therefore, contradict the indirect acknowledgement of a remaining control competence of the Commission in the Protocol. This would not only expose the definition itself to arbitrariness, but affect the whole State aid control of the Commission. The third *Altmark*-requirement and Art. 106(2) TFEU – in particular the proportionality of the measure – is linked directly to the definition. The more a Member State defines services as SGEI the more the State is authorised to give an undertaking the necessary (financial) means to fulfil these services under the test of proportionality. The Commission would only have the competence to assess whether the undertaking has received more benefits than necessary to fulfil all the defined tasks and whether the public service remit is situated within the objectives of the supporting reasons of the Amsterdam Protocol.[264] Such limited control options would give rise to the potential of abuse on the part of the Member States.[265] Additionally, as the Protocol relates explicitly to the common interest, it has to be noted that this interest is also determined through the requirements of Art. 107 and Art. 106 TFEU and the monitoring of their compliance. Therefore, the services have to be defined in accordance with the respective requirements. Furthermore, it is noteworthy that the wording of the Protocol does not necessarily demand full latitude for the Member States to define PSB, as it states only that funding shall be 'granted to broadcasting organisations for the fulfilment of the public service remit as conferred, defined and organised by each Member State'. As a matter of fact, the wording of the Protocol is imprecise and, therefore, it appears rather questionable to draw far-reaching consequences from it.[266] As a result, the Amsterdam Protocol does not further limit the control competence of the Commission concerning the definition of SGEI in broadcasting.

Questionable is, however, whether the supporting reasons have any influence on the definition of PSB. The protocol was adopted 'CONSIDERING that the system of public broadcasting in the Member States is directly related to the democratic, social and cultural needs of each society and to the need to preserve media pluralism'. These supporting reasons are explaining why the lawgiver sees an eligibility of PSB

---

264 *Krone*, Gebührenfinanzierter Rundfunk und Beihilferecht, pp. 299 et seqq., on the other hand pleads that in view of the Protocol the Commission may only (!) control the existence of overcompensation, the fact that the funding is used for the fulfilment of the remit and whether the public service remit is situated within the objectives of the supporting reasons of the Amsterdam Protocol. He demands only a minimum of control competences for the Commission (p. 296). Likewise: *Stulz-Herrnstadt*, Nationale Rundfunkfinanzierung und europäische Beihilfenaufsicht im Lichte des Amsterdamer Rundfunkprotokolls, pp. 356 et seqq.

265 Cf. *Craufurd Smith*, LIEI 28 (1) [2001], 3, 14.

266 Cf. *Katsirea*, Public Broadcasting and European Law, p. 325, who designates the wording of the Protocol to be 'in an enough open-ended and imprecise manner so as to keep everybody satisfied'.

to be a SGEI worth to promote ('role of PSB'). Consequently, the Protocol suggests, which objectives a public service broadcaster has to follow, to be recognised as an undertaking performing SGEIs in the broadcasting sector.[267] Thus, it appears comprehensible to draw the conclusion from the wording that the Protocol imposes the *obligation* on the Member States to 'confer, define and organise' the public service remit, if they intend to favour broadcasters.[268] The provisions therefore restrict the competences of the Member States to define: a Member State goes beyond its definition-prerogative when the service in question does not foster democratic, social or cultural needs of the society or the need to preserve media pluralism. These premises have to be seen as minimum requirements regarding the definition of the public service remit.[269]

In summary, the Amsterdam Protocol does not modify the general competence of the Member States when defining SGEI, apart from the fact that the services have to support the objectives mentioned in the supporting reasons of the Protocol. It only acknowledges the general discretion Member States have in defining SGEI.[270] Therefore, the general premise of the manifest-error-standard remains untouched.

b) Impact on the question of proportionality of the measure

Still, the Amsterdam Protocol might have an impact on the assessment of overcompensation, or the proportionality of a measure pursuant to the third *Altmark*-criterion, and respectively Art. 106(2) TFEU.

An impact on Art. 107(1) TFEU, however, seems problematic considering the fact that the Protocol merely demands a competence of Member States to provide for funding in the PSB sector, and does not require the possibility of funding without the obligation to notify the measure to the Commission pursuant to Art. 108(3) TFEU. Thus, it appears to be enough that the Protocol only modifies the requirements of Art. 106(2) TFEU. With such an impact the competence of the Member States to

267 Cf. *Krone*, Gebührenfinanzierter Rundfunk und Beihilferecht, p. 294; *Laitenberger*, in: *Stern/Prütting*, Nationaler Rundfunk und Europäisches Gemeinschaftsrecht zwischen Kommunikationsfreiheit und Regulierung, pp. 31, 34; *Schnaitter*, Möglichkeiten und Grenzen der Ausgestaltung des Programmauftrags der öffentlich-rechtlichen Rundfunkanstalten, p. 31; *Stulz-Herrnstadt*, Nationale Rundfunkfinanzierung und europäische Beihilfenaufsicht im Lichte des Amsterdamer Rundfunkprotokolls, pp. 356 et seqq.

268 Of same opinion: *Greissinger*, Vorgaben des EG-Vertrages für nationales Rundfunk- und Multimediarecht, p. 149; *Reese*, Der Funktionsauftrag des öffentlich-rechtlichen Rundfunks vor dem Hintergrund der Digitalisierung, p. 169. Of other opinion: *Krausnick*, Das deutsche Rundfunksystem unter dem Einfluss des Europarechts, p. 134.

269 *Krone*, Gebührenfinanzierter Rundfunk und Beihilferecht, p. 294 ICW fn. 1051; *Stulz-Herrnstadt*, Nationale Rundfunkfinanzierung und europäische Beihilfenaufsicht im Lichte des Amsterdamer Rundfunkprotokolls, p. 361.

270 *Repa/Tosics/Dias/Bacchiega*, Competition Policy Newsletter 2009 (3), 10, 11.

provide for funding in PSB seems to be preserved, as a justification of the funding according to Art. 106(2) TFEU is always possible for the Member States. An effect on Art. 107(1) TFEU, however, is not necessarily indicated. In particular, because Art. 106(2) TFEU is the law with currently the least requirements to enable public funding for SGEI, it seems sufficient that it is the sole addressee of an adjustment of the requirements in the sense of the Protocol. An impact on other laws is (currently) not necessary to comply with the provisions of the Protocol. Consequently, the requirements of Art. 107(1) TFEU are not affected by the Amsterdam Protocol.[271]

Nevertheless, an influence on Art. 106(2) TFEU might arise from the emphasis on the desired realisation of the public service remit in the Protocol (contrary to the requirements in Art. 106(2) TFEU). According to several authors, the Protocol puts the realisation of the remit to the fore, wherefore a measure might only be seen as disproportionate, if it affects competition in the union to a major extent.[272] In the same direction a similar view regards public funding as proportionate, as long as it does not affect trading conditions and competition intolerably.[273] The less rigid limits of such an intolerably effect (respectively a major extended effect) on competition would be the crucial difference to the assessment in Art. 106(2)(2) TFEU.[274] A much more far-reaching approach has to be seen in the opinion that the proportionality-test in the Amsterdam Protocol supersedes the one of Art. 106(2) TFEU, whereas the Protocol was seeing the legality of the public funding as the rule, which can only be contradicted if the funding does not serve the realisation of the remit anymore.[275] This view limits the proportionality-test to the assessment whether the public funding is related to the tasks arising out of the public service remit.[276]

Having a closer look at the differences between the Amsterdam Protocol and the comparable rule of Art. 106(2) TFEU, it can be observed that the Protocol does

---

271 Likewise: *Stulz-Herrnstadt*, Nationale Rundfunkfinanzierung und europäische Beihilfenaufsicht im Lichte des Amsterdamer Rundfunkprotokolls, pp. 288 et seqq. Cf. also *Damm*, Gebührenprivileg und Beihilferecht, p. 168. Of other opinion: *Ehricke*, Die EG-rechtliche Beurteilung der Rundfunkfinanzierung, pp. 126 et seqq.; *Schnaitter*, Möglichkeiten und Grenzen der Ausgestaltung des Programmauftrags der öffentlich-rechtlichen Rundfunkanstalten, pp. 26 et seqq.

272 *Eberle*, in: *Geiss/Gerstenmaier/Winkler/Mailänder*, Festschrift für Karl Peter Mailänder zum 70. Geburtstag, pp. 497, 501. The author goes even further in *Eberle*, AfP 2001, 477, 480 (fulfilment of the remit has to be guaranteed regardless of the impact on competition).

273 *Krausnick*, Das deutsche Rundfunksystem unter dem Einfluss des Europarechts, p. 131; *Streinz*, in: *Stern*, Die Bedeutung des Europäischen Rechts für den nationalen Rundfunk, pp. 59, 67.

274 *Krausnick*, Das deutsche Rundfunksystem unter dem Einfluss des Europarechts, p. 131.

275 *Krone*, Gebührenfinanzierter Rundfunk und Beihilferecht, p. 297.

276 *Krone*, Gebührenfinanzierter Rundfunk und Beihilferecht, p. 297; *Stulz-Herrnstadt*, Nationale Rundfunkfinanzierung und europäische Beihilfenaufsicht im Lichte des Amsterdamer Rundfunkprotokolls, p. 346.

not contain an obstruction-clause similar to Art. 106(2)(1) TFEU, but it emphasises the realisation of the public service remit. Since the Protocol only constitutes an interpretative act, the absence of an obstruction-clause similar to Art. 106(2)(1) TFEU does not imply that the Protocol exempts from the observation of the respective clause in Art. 106(2)(1) TFEU, otherwise the protocol would have to be seen as an independently derogation with the same legal status as Art. 106(2) TFEU.

Furthermore, the provisions of the Protocol refer to trading conditions and competition in the Community. Whether *trading conditions* are affected contrary to the common interest is also being assessed in the evaluation of Art. 106(2)(2) TFEU, with a remarkably similar wording. On the contrary, the competition, and its infringement are regulated especially through the competition rules of the TFEU, whereas on hand Art. 106(2) and Art. 107(1) TFEU are generally relevant. Nevertheless, as showed above, a modification of Art. 107(1) TFEU is not necessary (to date at least) and therefore not indicated to comply with the provisions of the Protocol. The Protocol, however, highlights the possibility of the Member States to realise the public service remit at least in the framework of Art. 106(2) TFEU when assessing whether the public funding has reached an extent contrary to the common interest.

As a result, the Protocol demands recognition of a realisation of the remit in a 'more-than-usual-way'. This accounts both in the inspection of public funding under Art. 106(2)(2) TFEU and Art. 106(2)(1) TFEU as far as the proportionality of the funding (though not the definition of the remit)[277] is concerned. However, it has to be noted that the net-cost-principle-test in Art. 106(2) TFEU is already depending on the scope of the remit and therefore in the words of the Protocol on the 'realisation of the remit'. Thus, in this respect a further effect on this assessment is not necessary, as all necessary means to fulfil the remit are already possible to be granted. The aforesaid 'shift' must be applied, however, regarding the obstruction-test (for example regarding generated revenues)[278], the effect on the community interest[279] and also possible obligatory control mechanisms[280].[281] The assessment has to be made on a case-by-case basis.

c) *Impact on the burden of proof*

In the framework of a State aid procedure vis-a-vis the Commission or in front of one of the European courts, the burden of proof considering the fulfilment of the requirements of State aid law in principle lies on the Member State.[282] It is

---

277 See above C. III. 2) a).

278 Cf. *Klasse*, in: *Heidenhain*, European State Aid Law, § 28, paras. 119 et seqq.

279 Cf. *Klasse*, in: *Heidenhain*, European State Aid Law, § 28, paras. 123 et seqq.

280 Cf. *Bartosch*, EU-Beihilfenrecht, Art. 86 Abs. 2 EGV, paras. 15 et seqq.

281 Similar *Krone*, Gebührenfinanzierter Rundfunk und Beihilferecht, p. 297. The view of *Krone*, however, that the proportionality-test of the Protocol supersedes the one of the Art. 106(2) TFEU cannot be shared. This opinion contradicts the qualification of the Protocol as an interpretative rule.

282 See above C. II.

questionable whether this burden of proof can be upheld under the provisions on the Amsterdam Protocol. According to some scholars, the Protocol shifts the burden to the Commission in one respect, namely that services are unduly defined as part of the public service remit, in particular because the definition does not meet the requirements of the Amsterdam Protocol.[283] This conclusion is drawn from the assumption that, according to the Protocol, the Contracting Parties already considered PSB as being directly related to the democratic, social and cultural needs of each society and to the need to preserve media pluralism. In this case it was the burden of the Commission to prove the opposite. Nevertheless, because of the usage of the word 'insofar' in the main text of the Protocol the burden of proof has not been modified regarding other aspects of the legality of the financing.

Some voices say that an inversion of the burden of proof resides in the half sentence of the Protocol, which states 'while the realisation of the remit of that public service shall be taken into account'. This position argues in favour of a realisation of the public service remit, if it should be *doubtful* whether the funding does affect trading conditions and competition in the Community to an extent which would be contrary to the common interest.[284]

The latter view is not shared by the author. Regarding the requirements of Art. 106(2)2 TFEU, the Commission has the burden of proof already.[285] Considering Art. 107(1) TFEU, the Amsterdam Protocol has no impact, according to the view put forward here.[286] Lastly, the Protocol does not necessarily refer to the rules of burden of proof in its last half sentence. The impact of the formulation can be described more convincingly with an effect on the assessment of the proportionality of the measure rather than with an inversion of the burden of proof.[287]

The first mentioned view, however, may be shared. The Protocol states that PSB 'is' directly related to the mentioned relevant needs. The Contracting Parties, therefore, already set up a principle the Member States can refer to. Consequently, the Member States do not have to prove that the public service remit is situated in the objectives laid down in the Protocol. Regardless of this inversion of the burden of proof, the Member States still have to prove the *entrustment* of the beneficiary with public service *obligations* and the *clear definition* of these obligations. These aspects are not covered by the formulation in the Amsterdam Protocol which inverts the burden of proof.

---

283 *Krone*, Gebührenfinanzierter Rundfunk und Beihilferecht, pp. 302 et seqq.; *Schnaitter*, Möglichkeiten und Grenzen der Ausgestaltung des Programmauftrags der öffentlich-rechtlichen Rundfunkanstalten, p. 43; *Stulz-Herrnstadt*, Nationale Rundfunkfinanzierung und europäische Beihilfenaufsicht im Lichte des Amsterdamer Rundfunkprotokolls, p. 357.

284 *Krausnick*, ZUM 2007, 806, 813. Likewise *Eberle*, in: *Geiss/Gerstenmaier/Winkler/Mailänder*, Festschrift für Karl Peter Mailänder zum 70. Geburtstag, pp. 497, 501.

285 See above C. III. 2).

286 See above C. III. 2) b).

287 See above C. III. 2) b).

D. Does public funding of public service broadcasting comply with the Altmark-criteria?

So far, the analysis showed that there are no compelling reasons to qualify public funding in PSB as non-State aid. To not fall under Art. 107(1) TFEU, PSB has to fulfil the requirements of the *Altmark*-jurisprudence. In this case a favour in the sense of Art. 107(1) TFEU would be lacking. Below, we put under discussion the question whether, and under what circumstances do compensation payments comply with the four criteria from the *Altmark Trans*-jurisprudence.

I. 1st Criterion: Definition of and entrustment with public service obligations

The first *Altmark*-criterion demands that the recipient is actually required to discharge public service obligations and those obligations have to be clearly defined.[288] The importance of this requirement cannot be underestimated as the definition of the obligations sets the framework for the allocation of costs and revenues.[289] If the definition is too broad, almost any costs can be assigned to the public service obligations.

The requirement prevents Member States from compensating alleged public service obligations in hindsight (after the services have been executed).[290] Consequently, all public service obligations have to be defined in a comprehensive way beforehand. Compensation payments for services that are not part of the public service obligations at the time of service provision are not possible.

The first criterion resembles the first requirement of Art. 106(2) TFEU and has very likely been derived from it. This raises the question whether the first criterion demands exactly the same prerequisites as the first requirement of Art. 106(2) TFEU. Affirmatively answered it would be possible to consult judicial and other legal opinions on Art. 106(2) TFEU for the interpretation of the first *Altmark*-criterion. The

288 *ECJ*, 24 July 2003, Case C-280/00, *Altmark Trans*, paras. 89, 95.

289 Likewise *Hesse*, AfP 2005, 499, 501, who calls the formulation of the remit the crucial stipulation for the scope of public funding.

290 *Schwendinger*, Gemeinschaftsrechtliche Grenzen öffentlicher Rundfunkfinanzierung, p. 245; *Sinnaeve*, EStAL 2003, 351, 357.

predominant view in the literature[291] as well as with the Commission[292] is that the requirements of the first *Altmark*-criterion and the demanded entrustment with a clearly defined remit in Art. 106(2) TFEU are equivalent. Indeed, at first sight, the existing principles concerning the interpretation of Art. 106(2) TFEU should be equivalent to the criterion, as the *ECJ* developed it based on the requirements of Art. 106(2) TFEU. Nevertheless, it should be noted that the *Altmark*-criteria serve to qualify the definition of the term 'State aid' whereas Art. 106(2) TFEU sets out a derogation from Art. 107(1) TFEU (which should be interpreted narrowly). Consequently, the requirements are not coercively congruent.[293]

The following paragraphs discuss 'which activities of public service broadcasters may be defined as public service obligations' and raise the question 'what are the requirements in regard to the precision of the definition?'. Both questions should be *strictly separated* from each other,[294] since the competence to define something does not compellingly give the competence to define it ambiguous.

1) Public service obligations (or 'which activities can be part of the remit')

According to several authors, public service obligations are identical with SGEI.[295] This view is only shared partly, as public service obligations are a necessary element of SGEI, but not identical. Public service obligations are rather specific standards

291 *Bacon*, in: *Bacon*, European Community Law of State Aid, para. 2.68; *Bartosch*, EU-Beihilfenrecht, Art. 87 Abs. 1 EGV, para. 72; *Deuster*, Ausgleichszahlungen für Dienstleistungen von allgemeinem wirtschaftlichem Interesse, p. 157; *Ehricke*, Die EG-rechtliche Beurteilung der Rundfunkfinanzierung, p. 67; *Grespan*, EStAL 2010, 79, 88 et seq.; *Koenig*, BB 2003, 2185, 2186; *Koenigs*, ZEuS 2006, 135, 160; *Krone*, Gebührenfinanzierter Rundfunk und Beihilferecht, p. 129; *Quigley*, European State Aid Law And Policy, pp. 161 et seq.

292 *Commission*, Communication from the Commission on the application of the European Union State aid rules to compensation granted for the provision of services of general economic interest (OJ C 8/4 of 11.01.2012), para. 47. See also for example the German State aid procedure regarding the German broadcasting funding fees: *Commission*, Decision of 24.04.2007, State aid No E 3/2005, *Financing of public service broadcasters in Germany*, paras. 163, 165 ICW paras. 227, 236 and 268 et seqq.

293 Also with doubts: *Schwendinger*, Gemeinschaftsrechtliche Grenzen öffentlicher Rundfunkfinanzierung, pp. 245, 272. Furthermore cf. *Linke*, Die Gewährleistung des Daseinsvorsorgeauftrags im öffentlichen Personennahverkehr, pp. 110 et seqq. with further references.

294 *v. Wallenberg*, MMR 2004, 88, 90.

295 *Colucci*, in: *Mederer/Pesaresi/Van Hoof*, EU Competition Law – Volume IV – State Aid, para 4.2110; *Thum*, Einfachgesetzliche Präzisierung des verfassungsrechtlichen Funktionsauftrags des öffentlich-rechtlichen Rundfunks, p. 132. See also *CFI*, 12 February 2008, Case T-289/03, *BUPA*, para. 162.

for undertakings, when performing SGEI.[296] Accordingly, public service obligations have to be seen as a specification of SGEI. These obligations classify a service as a SGEI.[297]

Public service obligations are therefore requirements defined or determined by the State in order to ensure SGEI that an undertaking, if it were considering its own commercial interests, would not assume or would not assume to the same extent or under the same conditions without reward.[298] As shown above,[299] the Commission only controls the definition of SGEI, and consequently public service obligations, via the identification of manifest errors. The Member States, therefore, have the primarily competence to judge whether a service can be provided satisfactorily under market conditions or not, that is, whether an undertaking would undertake the same services to the same extent or under the same conditions in its own commercial interest.

In principle, questions relating to the quality of the programme of public service broadcasters are not part of the Commission's control competence.[300] The Commission may only check whether the activities of the public service broadcaster in general may be seen as SGEI. The Commission further monitors whether the defined public service obligations do not reasonably meet the democratic, social or cultural needs of the society or the need to preserve media pluralism according to the Amsterdam Protocol.

a) Public service obligations in public service broadcasting

Despite the uniform control standard of 'manifest error', in literature there are different perceptions of the Commission's competence to control the public service obligations. Several authors grant the Commission *only* the possibility to monitor

---

296 *Commission*, The Application of EU State Aid rules on Services of General Economic Interest since 2005 and the Outcome of the Public Consultation, SEC(2011) 397, 23.03.2011, p. 4. See also *ECJ*, 27 November 2003, Joined Cases C-34/01 to C-38/01, *Enirisorse*, para. 33.

297 See also above C. I. 1) a) (1).

298 Cf. *Commission*, Communication from the Commission on the application of the European Union State aid rules to compensation granted for the provision of services of general economic interest (OJ C 8/4 of 11.01.2012), para. 47, with reference to the definition of public service obligations under the Regulation (EC) No 1370/2007 (Regulation (EC) No 1370/2007 of the European Parliament and of the Council of 23 October 2007 on public passenger transport services by rail and by road and repealing Council Regulations (EEC) Nos 1191/69 and 1107/70 (OJ L 315/1 of 03.12.2007)). See Art. 2(e) thereof (considering this law cf. *Linke*, Die Gewährleistung des Daseinsvorsorgeauftrags im öffentlichen Personennahverkehr, pp. 185 et seqq.).

299 See above C. I. 1) a) (2).

300 *Commission*, Communication from the Commission on the application of State aid rules to public service broadcasting, (OJ C 257/1 of 27.10.2009), para. 48.

whether activities of public service broadcasters could not reasonably be considered to meet the democratic, social and cultural needs of the society.[301] This conclusion is hardly surprising since the Commission itself cites such a control standard as legit.[302] However, if such a monitoring standard were to be seen as right, the Commission's power of review would tend to zero.

For example, the very concept of 'culture' cannot serve as a significant limitation of the Member States' competence to define services since already by 1952, the anthropologists *Kroeber and Kluckhohn* gathered more than 150 different definitions of culture.[303] Since culture in its widest sense comprises everything a human being forms, it is hardly conceivable that an activity does not fulfil some cultural needs of a society. One might even argue that a legal concept of culture does not exist at all.[304] As a matter of fact, the Commission itself, despite the aforementioned self-restraining control standard, does not apply the respective standard as the sole benchmark.[305] Rather a comparison with commercial activities on the market is the ordinary control aspect regarding the existence of SGEI.[306] Supporting this approach is the fact that the Amsterdam Protocol does not limit the Commission's control standard of monitoring manifest errors to the simple question of whether activities of public service broadcasters could not reasonably be considered to meet the democratic, social and cultural needs of each society.[307] In principle, the general control standard for SGEI remains rather the same with PSB. This applies in particular for the comparison of a performed activity with the supply already provided by the market. Consequently, the activities[308] of the public service broadcaster have to be

---

301 *European Broadcasting Union*, Review of the Communication from the Commission on the application of State aid rules to public service broadcasting – EBU reply to the Commission's questionnaire, p. 12; *Bravasso*, in: *Hancher/Ottervanger/Slot*, EU State Aids, para. 18–003; *Katsirea*, Public Broadcasting and European Law, p. 348.

302 Cf. for instance: *Commission*, Decision of 24.04.2007, State aid No E 3/2005, *Financing of public service broadcasters in Germany*, para. 220.

303 *Kroeber/Kluckhohn*, Culture: a critical review of concepts and definitions, passim.

304 *Eifert*, in: *Hahn/Vesting*, Beck'scher Kommentar zum Rundfunkrecht, § 11 RStV, para. 57.

305 See next paragraph. The *Commission*, however, did that in earlier decisions, see for example: *Commission*, Decision of 22.05.2002, State aid No N 631/2001, *BBC license fee*, para. 34. Nevertheless, this kind of monitoring cannot be considered sufficient.

306 See above C. I. 1) a) (1).

307 See above C. III. 2) a).

308 In assessing, such an activity of the broadcaster doesn't have to be a single or a group of broadcasts, but the activity of the broadcaster as a whole. A comparison of single parts of the programme (instead of the programme as a whole) with commercially provided services would undermine the Member States' power to define the SGEI (see also: *CFI*, 22 October 2008, joined Cases T-309/04, T-317/04, T-329/04 and T-336/04, *TV2*, para. 123). Also arguing for the possibility of a 'full-service' programme: *Gundel*, ZUM 2008, 758, 764.

distinct from the activities of commercial broadcasters and exhibit a higher public value (so called 'test of distinctiveness').[309]

Therefore, the opposing stance,[310] that the failure of the market to provide certain services cannot be a criterion to qualify SGEI regarding broadcasting, has to be rejected. Also, the Commission uses various other delimiting criteria for SGEI (respectively public service obligations) in broadcasting. The criteria, however, are not always applied consistently.[311] In its German decision, the Commission focused firstly on the significance of the services for the public opinion-forming process and the specific contribution to the fulfilment of democratic, social and cultural needs.[312] The distinct public value, which the services offer in this regard, is determined by the Commission through a comparison with similar or identical services already offered by the market.[313]

(1) Segregation from commercial broadcasters?

The additional public value, that distinguishes PSB from commercial broadcasting, might be seen in various aspects as long as they are directly related to the democratic, social and cultural needs of each society and to the need to preserve media pluralism.[314] For example, the provision of a service free of advertisements.[315] Accordingly, the distinctiveness of a public service from those offered by the market does not necessarily have to be evaluated through a comparison between the programmes of public service broadcasters and commercial broadcasters, as behind the transmission of the same programme might be completely different motives, which exhibit

---

309 Cf. *Commission*, Decision of 14.12.1999, State aid No NN 88/98, *BBC News 24*, para. 53, where the Commission takes into account that specific features of the service in question could not be found in services provided by private broadcasters. See also *Craufurd Smith*, LIEI 28 (1) [2001], 3, 15.

310 Cf. *Bartosch*, EuZW 2009, 684, 687; *Braun*, in: *Castendyk/Dommering/Scheuer*, European Media Law, Article 87 EC, para. 49; *Hesse*, AfP 2005, 499, 503; *Schnaitter*, Möglichkeiten und Grenzen der Ausgestaltung des Programmauftrags der öffentlich-rechtlichen Rundfunkanstalten, p. 42; *Wiedemann*, EStAL 2004, 595, 599. *Michel*, MMR 2005, 284, 287, calls the market-failure-test an inadmissible and improper benchmark.

311 Cf. *Craufurd Smith*, LIEI 28 (1) [2001], 3, 15 et seq.

312 *Commission*, Decision of 24.04.2007, State aid No E 3/2005, *Financing of public service broadcasters in Germany*, para. 232.

313 *Commission*, Decision of 24.04.2007, State aid No E 3/2005, *Financing of public service broadcasters in Germany*, para. 233. Therein the Commission was monitoring the eligibility of online-services. Also taking the offers of the market into consideration: *Commission*, Decision of 14.12.1999, State aid No NN 88/98, *BBC News 24*, para. 49.

314 See above C. III. 2) a).

315 *Commission*, Decision of 14.12.1999, State aid No NN 88/98, *BBC News 24*, paras. 52 et seq.

the special characteristic of the public service. According to the *CFI*, it is possible, though, that PSB may comprise potentially profitable television programmes, too.[316] Particularly, the definition of SGEI is related to the satisfaction of general needs and not to the method of financing.[317] Even when parts of the programme have the sole purpose of entertainment, it might create an additional public value.[318] For example, the same sports broadcast could be a commercial service provided by a commercial broadcaster or, on the contrary, a public service broadcast when the intention behind the transmission is to create a higher public value.[319] Nevertheless, the Member State has to explain the additional public value created through the supported activities.[320]

(2) New conditions applied by the Commission?

With regard to online services, the Commission required in recent acts a distinct relation to the television programmes of the public service broadcaster, as otherwise the significance of the services for the public opinion-forming process would be negligible.[321] Additionally, in relation to online chat-rooms, the Commission stated that such services do not necessarily reflect the specific function or the specific editorial arrangement of public service broadcasters.[322]

At first sight, these 'new' conditions (for online services) hardly appear to be inferable from the general criteria for SGEI, particularly considering that the services in question actually had an effect on the public opinion forming process (e.g. through the possibility for the public of discussing subjects in the chat-rooms), although maybe a negligible one. From the demands it can be inferred that activities of a public service broadcaster should not only stimulate the public opinion forming process (or other objectives of the Amsterdam Protocol) by whatever means, but the activities must be coined (directly or indirectly) by editorially processed content. This demand seems to be consistent with the Amsterdam Protocol, which reaffirms

---

316 *CFI*, 22 October 2008, joined Cases T-309/04, T-317/04, T-329/04 and T-336/04, *TV2*, para. 113. See also the opposing opinion of the applicant in para. 90.

317 *CFI*, 22 October 2008, joined Cases T-309/04, T-317/04, T-329/04 and T-336/04, *TV2*, para. 108. Cf. also *Commission*, Communication from the Commission on the application of State aid rules to public service broadcasting, (OJ C 257/1 of 27.10.2009), para. 49.

318 See below D. I. 1) b).

319 See below D. I. 1) c) for a further analysis of the public value of specific sorts of services.

320 See for possible explanations D. I. 1) b) and c).

321 *Commission*, Decision of 24.04.2007, State aid No E 3/2005, *Financing of public service broadcasters in Germany*, para. 233. About that *Donders*, Public Service Media and Policy in Europe, pp. 101 et seq.

322 *Commission*, Decision of 24.04.2007, State aid No E 3/2005, *Financing of public service broadcasters in Germany*, para. 233.

the responsibility of the Member States to define the PSB services,[323] as the Protocol has set its sight on PSB from the date of its adoption. Although this does not prevent Member States from offering services other than television and radio,[324] still there has to be a similarity to the traditional activities of a public service broadcaster, namely edited audio, visual or audiovisual content (including edited texts). Otherwise the content of the term 'PSB' in the sense of the Protocol is depreciated, eventually it would be tantamount to 'everything that a broadcaster would like to do and that is defined in the remit'. Consistently, the Commission demands a relation of online chat-rooms to the programme of the broadcaster. A simple provision of chat-rooms is not permitted. Furthermore, with regard to the Commission's demand for a more than negligible significance of the services for the public opinion forming process, it can be concluded that the Commission tolerates any additional public value that is offered in comparison to other commercial activities. Therefore, the additional public value must not be negligible. Otherwise, it is the case of a manifest error.

In summary, besides the general criteria, which include a test of distinctiveness, the Commission scrutinises whether the distinctiveness is negligible and whether the activities take the form of edited audio, visual or audiovisual services.[325]

b) Application of the criterion

The above mentioned test of distinctiveness has to be applied on a case-by-case basis. Considering the criterion of universality,[326] however, it can be concluded that it is generally met in PSB, as it is addressed to the whole population in the receiving area of the programme and tries to meet the democratic, social and cultural needs of each society or the need to preserve media pluralism. The interests behind PSB are therefore generally universal and not private or particular ones. In particular, the universality-criterion does not demand that the service responds to the needs common to the whole population or is supplied throughout a territory. Consequently, local or regional PSB services do not violate the universality criterion.[327] Due to the fact that universality does not require the service to be free of charge or to be offered without consideration of economic profitability, in principle it is possible to offer pay-tv services to a certain extent or to generate revenues through advertising or sponsoring.[328]

The Commission has further designated various activities as not being compatible with the definition of SGEI. For example the Commission qualified e-commerce

---

323 Of other opinion *Ehricke*, Die EG-rechtliche Beurteilung der Rundfunkfinanzierung, p. 78; Michel, MMR 2005, 284, 287, who argues that the new criteria have neither a foundation in primary nor in secondary European law.

324 See above B. I and below D. I. 1) c).

325 Against new criteria: *Wiedemann*, EStAL 2004, 595, 601 et seq.

326 See above C. I. 1) a) (1).

327 Of other opinion: *Hesse*, AfP 2005, 499, 505.

328 Likewise *Bartosch*, EuZW 2009, 684, 686.

(the selling of goods and services over the Internet), advertisement, sponsoring and merchandising as such activities.[329] In principal, services that are subject to payment, such as pay-tv or pay-per-view[330] as well as teleshopping offerings or the use of premium rate numbers in prize games,[331] have a tendency not to be categorised as PSB. According to the Commission, however, a manifest error must not be seen in a change of the broadcasting platform, as long as the content is going to be distributed under the same circumstances as conventional broadcasting.[332] Consequently, the definition of so called mobile services as SGEI should not be seen as a manifest error.[333] Although, it would go beyond the limits to sell broadcasting content to telecommunication providers.[334] The same principle must apply for the production of programmes for consideration on condition that the productions are not created for own purposes but only to be sold to third parties.

This brings into question whether the Commission's approach endangers the possibility of the broadcasters to obtain revenues through the sale of advertising space.[335] As pointed out above, the Commission expressly classifies advertising and sponsoring as commercial activities.[336] This position, however, may not be understood in a way that the selling of advertisement or sponsoring regarding a programme being subject to public service obligations cannot be part of the SGEI. Rather the 'advertisement' and 'sponsoring' are an independent activity outside the public service obligations, which is still part of the SGEI.[337] Any contrary conclusion would lead to a contradiction in the Commission's and the *CFI*'s view, as they expressly allow dual funding, including 'the sale of advertising space or programmes and the offering of services against payment'.[338]

---

329 *Commission*, Communication from the Commission on the application of State aid rules to public service broadcasting, (OJ C 257/1 of 27.10.2009), para. 48. See also the German decision: *Commission*, Decision of 24.04.2007, State aid No E 3/2005, *Financing of public service broadcasters in Germany*, para. 239.

330 *Commission*, Decision of 24.04.2007, State aid No E 3/2005, *Financing of public service broadcasters in Germany*, para. 239.

331 *Commission*, Communication from the Commission on the application of State aid rules to public service broadcasting, (OJ C 257/1 of 27.10.2009), para. 48.

332 *Commission*, Decision of 24.04.2007, State aid No E 3/2005, *Financing of public service broadcasters in Germany*, para. 240. See also *Commission*, Decision of 14.12.1999, State aid No NN 88/98, *BBC News 24*, para. 57.

333 Of same opinion *Hesse*, AfP 2005, 499, 506.

334 *Commission*, Decision of 24.04.2007, State aid No E 3/2005, *Financing of public service broadcasters in Germany*, para. 240.

335 This way *Katsirea*, Public Broadcasting and European Law, pp. 348 et seq.; *Pelny*, ZUM 2005, 22, 28.

336 See C. I. 1) a) (2).

337 Regarding the difference see above C. I. 1) a) (1).

338 *Commission*, Communication from the Commission on the application of State aid rules to public service broadcasting, (OJ C 257/1 of 27.10.2009), para. 57. See also

c) *Special areas of public service obligations*

In the following sections, various significant activities of public service broadcasters are scrutinised with a view to assessing their eligibility to be a part of the SGEI.

(1) Sport events or entertainment programmes

It is debatable whether sport events or entertainment broadcasts in principle can be part of a public service remit. The Commission has the competency to monitor manifest errors in this respect.[339]

A quick analysis of the requirements of SGEI on sport transmissions and other entertainment shows will show that the criterion of universality is met in principle. The services do not have to respond to a need common to the whole population; on the contrary, they may only be used by a relatively limited group of users. Even a consideration or the levying of charges for that service would not contradict the criterion.

More controversial is the specific additional public value that such services provide compared to the services provided by other market participants. Sport events as well as movies and other entertainment broadcasts catch the attention of a considerable amount of the population.[340] Consequently, the transmission of these events or programmes is in high demand among the broadcasting companies. The market for the acquisition of respective rights is very competitive.[341] Thus, the provision to the public of these programmes does not necessarily need the intervention of public service broadcasters. Consequently, commercial broadcasters and several authors have criticised the usage of sport events, entertainment movies and shows in PSB under the banner of SGEI. This accusation would be justified if sport- and entertainment-shows provided by public service broadcasters would not display any additional public value in the sense of the Amsterdam Protocol distinct from the one commercial broadcasters would offer.

Additional public value might reside in the populations' enhanced perception of public service broadcasters throughout the population. A significant market share in this sense raises the broadcaster's chances of reaching the population, not only with the sport or entertainment programme itself but also with other programmes

---

CFI, 26 June 2008, Case T442/03, *SIC*, paras. 201 et seqq.; 22 October 2008, joined Cases T-309/04, T-317/04, T-329/04 and T-336/04, *TV2*, para. 113.

339 Of other opinion: *Eberle*, in: *Geiss/Gerstenmaier/Winkler/Mailänder*, Festschrift für Karl Peter Mailänder zum 70. Geburtstag, pp. 497, 505 et seq., who regards the Commission's criticism on sport events and online services in the public service remit out of their competencies.

340 Cf. for example *Craufurd Smith/Böttcher*, European Public Law 8 (1) [2002], 107, 107 et seq.

341 *European Broadcasting Union*, Review of the Communication from the Commission on the application of State aid rules to public service broadcasting – EBU reply to the Commission's questionnaire, p. 31.

which pursue public values other than those provided by commercial broadcasters. The additional public value of the sports or entertainment programme in this sense, therefore, is an indirect one, as it enforces the effects of the programme as a whole,[342] therefore including transmissions designated to fulfil democratic, social and cultural needs or the need to preserve media pluralism. In the same direction points the argument that viewers of a sport event or an entertainment programme might stay with the channel after the programme has ended, thus the viewer might also watch the subsequent programme on the channel, which is designated to pursue the objectives in the Amsterdam Protocol (e.g. a documentary or an educational programme).[343]

The major argument, though, why entertainment programmes may be part of the public service obligations, is that they are able to create their own public value. Such an additional public value can be seen in the integrating function as well as the function for identification and good example.[344] Sport events definitely carry such benefits as they promote good team and sports spirit, and encourage physical (health-promoting) activities. They have, therefore, significant social, educational and further cultural functions.[345] This is recognised by European Parliament as well as by the Council.[346] Entertainment programmes may also be an effective way of addressing and conveying information.[347] In this respect the direct additional public value may be debatable on a case-by-case basis. However, it has to be borne in mind, that the Commission may only judge an activity unsuitable to be part of a public service remit in the case of a manifest error. This assessment may not be implemented on a single broadcast but only on the programme as a whole. Therefore

---

342 Of same opinion: *Eberle*, in: *Geiss/Gerstenmaier/Winkler/Mailänder*, Festschrift für Karl Peter Mailänder zum 70. Geburtstag, pp. 497, 500; *Ehricke*, Die EG-rechtliche Beurteilung der Rundfunkfinanzierung, p, 81; *Fairbairn*, in: *Peacock*, Public Service Broadcasting Without the BBC?, p. 64. Cf. also *Commission*, Communication from the Commission on the application of State aid rules to public service broadcasting, (OJ C 257/1 of 27.10.2009), para. 12; *Castendyk*, AfP 2008, 467, 469 et seq.; *Donders*, Public Service Media and Policy in Europe, p. 1.

343 Cf. considering the deadweight-effect: *Castendyk*, AfP 2008, 467, 469 ICW fn. 34.

344 Opinion of the German public service broadcaster 'ARD': ARD-Leitlinien und Programmschwerpunkte 2009/2010, in: ARD-Jahrbuch 2008, pp. 480, 481. See also: *Craufurd Smith/Böttcher*, European Public Law 8 (1) [2002], 107, 112.

345 *European Broadcasting Union*, Review of the Communication from the Commission on the application of State aid rules to public service broadcasting – EBU reply to the Commission's questionnaire, p. 31. See also *Craufurd Smith/Böttcher*, European Public Law 8 (1) [2002], 107, 111 et seq.; *Erkens*, Der öffentlich-rechtliche Rundfunk und exklusive Sportberichterstattung, pp. 13 et seq.

346 Decision No 291/2003/EC of the European Parliament and of the Council of 6 February 2003 establishing the European Year of Education through Sport 2004 (OJ L 43/1 of 18.2.2003), passim. Cf. for example para. 11 thereof: 'Education through sport should promote personal identity and development for girls and boys'.

347 *Craufurd Smith*, LIEI 28 (1) [2001], 3, 17, with examples.

the Commission might not criticise single shows, but only the entertainment-part of the overall programme.

Considering the aforementioned importance of sport events, and thus the importance of the population receiving these programmes,[348] another additional public value effect might be the framework of the accessibility of these services.[349] If a public service broadcaster intends to offer the services remuneration-free compared to commercial providers, or under higher qualitative aspects (for example, without the transmission of advertisements), then this might be seen as an additional public value the public service broadcasters offers.

In conclusion, the transmission of sport events or entertainment programmes can be part of the public service obligations.[350]

It has to be noted, however, that public service broadcasters are not permitted to transmit sport events and other entertainment shows arbitrarily as part of SGEI. According to the Amsterdam Protocol, PSB pursues the need to preserve media pluralism. The fulfilment of this need demands a balanced programme-concept. Therefore, public service broadcasters cannot give sport shows or purely entertainment programmes a share of the entire programme which would be excessive and call a balanced concept into question.[351] The Commission's competence to criticise such behaviour is – as shown before – limited to manifest errors. In its decision-making practice, the Commission accepted an overall share of sports as being part of the public service broadcaster's programme activities that did not exceed on

---

348 The importance of accessibility in this context is stressed by the *European Broadcasting Union*, Review of the Communication from the Commission on the application of State aid rules to public service broadcasting – EBU reply to the Commission's questionnaire, p. 31.

349 The same applies for entertainment shows, if their accessibility is important considering the democratic, social and cultural needs and the need to preserve media pluralism.

350 Likewise: *CFI*, 26 June 2008, Case T442/03, *SIC*, para. 201 (possibility of 'full-spectrum programming'); *Commission*, Decision of 24.04.2007, State aid No E 3/2005, *Financing of public service broadcasters in Germany*, paras. 242, 291; *European Broadcasting Union*, Review of the Communication from the Commission on the application of State aid rules to public service broadcasting – EBU reply to the Commission's questionnaire, pp. 31 et seqq.; *Craufurd Smith*, LIEI 28 (1) [2001], 3, 17; *Ehricke*, Die EG-rechtliche Beurteilung der Rundfunkfinanzierung, p. 81; *Laitenberger*, in: *Stern/Prütting*, Nationaler Rundfunk und Europäisches Gemeinschaftsrecht zwischen Kommunikationsfreiheit und Regulierung, pp. 31, 34; *Michel*, MMR 2005, 284, 287; *Thyri/Jaeger*, wbl 2006, 197, 200. Of other opinion: *Pelny*, ZUM 2005, 22, 28.

351 *Thyri/Jaeger*, wbl 2006, 197, 200, also argue for a balanced deployment of sports broadcasts. Cf. furthermore the decision-making practice of the Commission: *Commission*, Decision of 24.04.2007, State aid No E 3/2005, *Financing of public service broadcasters in Germany*, paras. 292 et seqq.

average 10% of the broadcasting time.[352] However, the Commission stated in the same paragraph that 'the mere share of sports compared to the overall programme cannot as such be regarded as a competition concern, considering that this share not only includes major and mass attractive sports events but also other sports which attract less audience and are therefore of less or no interest for private competitors'. These latter (less mass-attractive) sport events have by any means a positive impact on the need to preserve media pluralism as the public service broadcasters report over activities a commercial broadcaster would not transmit. Nevertheless, the mentioned 10% share could serve as a mere indicator for an admissible proportion, though not more.

It is also problematic as to whether public service broadcasters are allowed to buy *exclusive* rights regarding the transmission of sport events, or also entertainment-broadcasts that would hypothetically be provided by the market. In this respect, an issue occurs solely when the holder of the rights is not willing to sell the rights to more than one interested party.[353] If the rights are not sold exclusively, however, the purchase through a public service broadcaster is not more problematic than the before described transmission of sought-after sport events or entertainment-programmes. The argument against the possibility of purchasing exclusive rights is that a waiver to participate in the tender would infringe competition the least, as competitors would have the possibility to buy the sought-after rights. This way, the programmes (and their possible public value) would be disseminated anyway. The issue is intensified as public service broadcasters often have high financial means to outbid their private competitors and therefore have the possibility to close their access to the respective market. On the other hand the possibility to buy exclusive rights fortifies the market position of the public service broadcaster. Consequently, whenever the public value of sports events or entertainment broadcasts is intended to be an amplifier of the effects of the programme as a whole (through the reaching of a wider audience), exclusive rights will further assist this goal.[354] Therefore it is doubtful whether the Commission could observe a manifest error in the purchase of exclusive rights. Additionally, the issue of closing the market for the purchase of specific rights dogmatically seems better situated in the application of the antitrust rules than in State aid law.[355] Thus, the acquisition of exclusive rights is admissible

352 *Commission*, Decision of 24.04.2007, State aid No E 3/2005, *Financing of public service broadcasters in Germany*, para. 292.

353 Usually, however, the proceeds of the right holder are higher when he sells exclusive rights to the interested parties.

354 *Commission*, Decision of 24.04.2007, State aid No E 3/2005, *Financing of public service broadcasters in Germany*, para. 284.

355 Cf. also *European Broadcasting Union*, Review of the Communication from the Commission on the application of State aid rules to public service broadcasting – EBU reply to the Commission's questionnaire, p. 32.

under the application of the State aid rules.[356] An alternative question might be whether public service broadcasters have to sublicense rights they are not exploiting. This question is relevant in the framework of the fourth Altmark criterion[357] and Art. 106(2) TFEU.

(2) New media services

The use of the Internet and online services is now common among the vast majority of the population. This structural change also affects public service broadcasters, as now the Internet-users utilise the Internet to enjoy the same or comparable services to those traditionally provided by television or radio. Consequently, public service broadcasters shift their attention from their traditional offerings to new media services, to keep up with the trend. The expectations of the internet-consumers are comparable to those towards the traditional media services. Two thirds of the media-users also expect an independent online-offer with original content comparable to the traditional services.[358] Despite these expectations it has to be borne in mind that almost all of the Internet services, potentially offered by a public service broadcaster, are (at least, in similar form) already offered by a commercial provider. Consequently, the question is raised as to whether new media services may be seen as SGEI.[359] This question has to be scrutinised by the Commission under the benchmark of a manifest error.[360]

The criterion of universality can be answered in the affirmative. More questionable is the distinctiveness of the services from the services already offered by the market.[361] As shown before, a manifest error may not be seen in a change of the broadcasting media platform.[362] Therefore, in principle the possibility for public service broadcasters to use new media platforms exists.[363] Nevertheless, when considering online services – due to the boundaries of the Amsterdam Protocol – there

356 *Commission*, Decision of 24.04.2007, State aid No E 3/2005, *Financing of public service broadcasters in Germany*, para. 284; *European Broadcasting Union*, Review of the Communication from the Commission on the application of State aid rules to public service broadcasting – EBU reply to the Commission's questionnaire, pp. 31 et seq.; *Michel*, MMR 2005, 284, 287.

357 See below D. IV.

358 *Michel*, MMR 2005, 284, 285.

359 Cf. the extensive references considering this debate from *Castendyk*, AfP 2008, 467.

360 Of other opinion *Eberle*, in: *Geiss/Gerstenmaier/Winkler/Mailänder*, Festschrift für Karl Peter Mailänder zum 70. Geburtstag, pp. 497, 505.

361 Cf. for possible justifications in view of the 'market-failure'-test: *Armstrong/Weeds*, in: *Seabright/Hagen*, The Economic Regulation of Broadcasting Markets, pp. 81, 114.

362 See above D. I. 1) b).

363 *Commission*, Communication from the Commission on the application of State aid rules to public service broadcasting, (OJ C 257/1 of 27.10.2009), para. 81;

has to be either a noticeable relation of the online-services to the traditional television or radio programme of the broadcaster or the original online-content has to reflect the specific task of the public service broadcasters.[364] The assessment has to be made on a case-by-case basis. Opposing this restriction with the argument that unlimited possibilities to create online services are necessary to create a serious market-position for public service broadcasters because the respective broadcasters would otherwise lose the access to a more and more internet orientated audience is not convincing.[365] Although, the broader the online offers of a broadcaster, the higher the chances that it reaches the Internet participants and may fulfil its public service remit; yet, the fulfilment of the public needs still has to be effected through the offering of high quality audio or audiovisual content formed by a broadcaster. Otherwise, when the prominence of the broadcaster or any additional value through the service would be the only legitimate demand, public service broadcasters could participate with their license fees in any activity, which has an effect on the public opinion (e.g. sponsoring of sportsmen), or offer anything with public value behind it (e.g. distribute a newspaper). That was not the intention behind the Amsterdam Protocol. This conclusion does not exclude entertaining elements from the online services,[366] but excludes elements that are *not* provided as audio or audiovisual services or respective annexes and ancillary services to these activities (such an annex-service could be for example texts that are directly related to the aforementioned services).

The aforementioned demand of a connection to the ordinary audio or audiovisual activities generally excludes, for example, the provision of online chat rooms that are not noticeably related to the PSB content (for example, ones that are moderated by private members with discussions on independent subjects). The same applies for online calculators or dating sites, as well as online games or links to offers of third parties, as these services are already offered by the market and, in principle do not demonstrate any link to the activities characteristic to public service broadcasters. The services are rather simple tools for the user, without any further shaping of the broadcaster itself. The aforesaid covers also information platforms similar to Wikipedia, where the content is primarily elaborated by the users. The assessment of online guides depends on the specific subject of the service.[367] As supplementary

Commission, Decision of 24.04.2007, State aid No E 3/2005, *Financing of public service broadcasters in Germany*, para. 229; *Schipanski*, K&R 2006, 217, 219.

364 Considering these requirements see above D. I. 1) b).

365 Regarding this argumentation cf. *Castendyk*, AfP 2008, 467, 468 et seq.; *Schipanski*, K&R 2006, 217, 219.

366 With reservations towards an exclusion of entertaining elements in online services: *Dörr*, in: *Detterbeck/Rozek/v. Coelln*, Recht als Medium der Staatlichkeit – Festschrift für Herbert Bethge zum 70. Geburtstag, pp. 451, 463.

367 In the same direction *Bravasso*, in: *Hancher/Ottervanger/Slot*, EU State Aids, para. 18–003, who explains that online information services *might* fall under a properly defined public service remit.

information to concrete PSB content, the required connection to the ordinary PSB services is given.[368] However, this does not count for independent online guides on various topics.

All services that have a clear relation to the existing programmes of the public service broadcaster or constitute original audio, audiovisual content on the internet, arranged by the broadcaster, may be part of the SGEI. This covers for example news-services, supplementary information regarding existing programs, videos and audio-podcasts (either new footage or repetitions of already presented programs), live-streams and archives of these products.

As a commercial service qualifies online selling (e-commerce), even if the goods are merchandise that relate to a specific TV or radio-format.[369] The same applies for media theme parks. One could argue that, through the distribution of articles with a logo or a reference to a specific broadcast, merchandising promotes the positive perception of the broadcaster and, therefore, facilitates his satisfaction of public needs; however, the primary intention behind merchandising is purely economic. The indirect advertising effects in merchandising are, therefore, irrelevant. At this point, the argument that the broadcaster has to convince through high-class broadcasting products and not through the best advertisement for itself or other activities with an effect on the public applies one more.

The obstacle to defining certain activities as part of the public service obligations does not mean that the public service broadcaster has no option to carry out specific performances. He is simply not entitled to finance the activity with public resources.[370] A division can be achieved for instance through the foundation of a subsidiary which carries out commercial activities. However, it has to be borne in mind that the financial means necessary to found the subsidiary may not lead to a favouring of the subsidiary, whenever public means are used.

(3) Pay-services

Issues have also been raised regarding services provided for remuneration. Such pay-services might, for instance, be pay-per-view, access to archives for a fee, online content against payment, near-video-on-demand,[371] etc. The Commission, in

---

368 The same applies for online riddles, as they might contain supplementary information to an existing service of the public service broadcaster.

369 Of same opinion: *Garzaniti*, Telecommunications, Broadcasting and the Internet: EU Competition Law and Regulation, para. 7–029; *Pelny*, ZUM 2005, 22, 28. Of other opinion regarding merchandising: *Schipanski*, K&R 2006, 217, 219. Of other opinion regarding e-commerce: *Ehricke*, Die EG-rechtliche Beurteilung der Rundfunkfinanzierung, p. 84.

370 Cf. also *Commission*, Decision of 24.04.2007, State aid No E 3/2005, *Financing of public service broadcasters in Germany*, para. 241.

371 This service allows a user access to platform on which a demanded movie is played in a repetitive loop. A movie therefore, in contrary to video-on-demand, will not be transmitted individually to a user.

its decision on the German broadcasting fees, declared payment-services to be primarily commercial services.[372] In its Communication, the Commission emphasises, however, that a 'remuneration element [...] does not necessarily mean that these services are manifestly not part of the public service remit provided that the pay element does not compromise the distinctive character of the public service'.[373] This statement is in accordance with the fundamental possibility of the public service broadcasters to use dual-funding-mechanisms[374] and the jurisdiction of the *CFI*[375]. Payment for the services, therefore, cannot bring into question the categorisation of these services as SGEI, provided that the service pursues a public interest in the sense of the Amsterdam Protocol and not a solely economic purpose.[376] An additional public value, depending on the case, may be seen in 'the objective of eliminating the influence of private interests over the content of the services offered'.[377]

(4) Digital channels/special-interest channels

Finally, the legality of special-interest channels, enabled through the introduction of digital television with a boundless number of channels, has been discussed. The Commission has decided that such special-interest channels can be qualified as SGEI.[378] A decisive factor, however, may well be, as in the case of sport and entertainment broadcasts, that the additional channel does not call the balanced overall programme concept into question.[379] This risk is not only hypothetical considering that a channel focusing on special interests, by definition, serves special needs. Consequently, such a channel might bring imbalance to the programme. As a new channel opens more capacities for the public service broadcaster, the channel must also be scrutinised upon the additional public value it provides in the sense of the Amsterdam Protocol.[380]

---

372 *Commission*, Decision of 24.04.2007, State aid No E 3/2005, *Financing of public service broadcasters in Germany*, para. 239.

373 *Commission*, Communication from the Commission on the application of State aid rules to public service broadcasting, (OJ C 257/1 of 27.10.2009), para. 83.

374 *Commission*, Communication from the Commission on the application of State aid rules to public service broadcasting, (OJ C 257/1 of 27.10.2009), para. 57. See also above C. III. 2).

375 *CFI*, 12 February 2008, Case T-289/03, *BUPA*, para. 189.

376 Of same opinion *Bartosch*, EuZW 2009, 684, 686 et seq.

377 *European Broadcasting Union*, Review of the Communication from the Commission on the application of State aid rules to public service broadcasting – EBU reply to the Commission's questionnaire, p. 20.

378 *Commission*, Decision of 14.12.1999, State aid No NN 88/98, *BBC News 24*, paras. 49 et seqq. Cf. also *Thyri/Jaeger*, wbl 2006, 197, 199.

379 Likewise: *Thyri/Jaeger*, wbl 2006, 197, 200.

380 Cf. *Commission*, Decision of 14.12.1999, State aid No NN 88/98, *BBC News 24*, paras. 49 et seqq.; Decision of 24.04.2007, State aid No E 3/2005, *Financing of public service broadcasters in Germany*, para. 227.

2) Clear definition (or 'precision of the definition')

The first *Altmark*-criterion requires the public service obligations to be *clearly defined.* Thus, the expounding of the obligations has to be as detailed as possible. Clarity is decisive in order to allow the adequacy of the compensation to be assessed.[381] It must be noted, moreover, that – according to the view taken here – the determination of the services falling under the public service remit (i.e. to define 'which activities can be part of the remit') has to be differentiated strictly from the question of the clarity of the definition (the 'precision of the definition').[382] Not all authors (including the Commission and part of the jurisprudence) have regard to this distinction, as displayed in the following.

a) 'Common' approach

The requirement of a 'clear' definition is admittedly rather vague. Consequently, the case-by-case application of this criterion can lead to varied outcomes.

The Commission explains in its Communication on PSB that the definition of the public service mandate falls within the competence of the Member States, whereas the Member States have to observe the general concept of SGEI.[383] According to the Commission, the public service mandate should be as precise as possible and it should leave no doubt as to whether a certain activity is intended to be included in the remit or not.[384] However, this does not necessarily mean that certain activities of the public service broadcaster have *to be named* as part of the public service obligations. The Commission, due to the need to safeguard the editorial independence of the public service broadcasters and the Member States' discretion to define the services, accepts instead a *qualitative* definition entrusting a given broadcaster with the obligation to provide a wide range of programming and a balanced and varied broadcasting service.[385]

Distinct criteria on how to formulate such a qualitative definition, however, are missing. It may solely be concluded from the wording that the definition does not have to include *quantitative* aspects considering the provision of PSB, e.g. how many minutes and hours may or have to be dedicated to certain programmes (for instance considering news, domestic or educational programmes), or how high the expenses

---

381 *Linke*, Die Gewährleistung des Daseinsvorsorgeauftrags im öffentlichen Personennahverkehr, p. 113.

382 Cf. *v. Wallenberg*, MMR 2004, 88, 90.

383 *Commission*, Communication from the Commission on the application of State aid rules to public service broadcasting, (OJ C 257/1 of 27.10.2009), para. 44. Although the paragraph concerns the definition of the public service remit in Art. 106(2) TFEU, there is no reason preventing it from an application to Art. 107(1) TFEU.

384 *Commission*, Communication from the Commission on the application of State aid rules to public service broadcasting, (OJ C 257/1 of 27.10.2009), para. 45.

385 *Commission*, Communication from the Commission on the application of State aid rules to public service broadcasting, (OJ C 257/1 of 27.10.2009), para. 47.

may be for specific broadcasts.[386] Nevertheless, it seems very doubtful whether it would be sufficient to solely reproduce or rephrase objectives for the programme like 'education', 'culture', 'entertainment' or the like, as the use of such specifications seems to clarify scarcely more than their absence.[387]

The aforementioned approach would leave the Member States with a wide discretion as to how to render the public service obligations. In its decision on the German broadcasting fees, however, the Commission displayed a more rigid *modus operandi*, though solely towards new media services. Regarding the traditional broadcasting activities of the German public service broadcasters, the Commission stated that a wide definition, comprising a varied and balanced programme, which is based on more qualitative than quantitative criteria, is acceptable.[388] In the assessment of the definition of new media services, the applied criteria were more restrictive. Although the public service remit may also comprise new services,[389] the *Commission* considered that a general authorisation of public service broadcasters to offer loose defined new media services and the resulting lack of predictability for third parties bears the risk that other market operators would be discouraged from developing and offering such services.[390] To get a clear view of what is covered from the definition, the *Commission* asked for generally applicable criteria that determine the link between a specific activity and the public service obligations, which would have to be laid down in a binding way that would guarantee a meaningful control.[391] Similarly, in its *RTP*-decision, the Commission assessed a definition as insufficient which solely imposed an obligation to provide 'other services to be specified on an ad hoc basis'.[392] These explanations seem to be more demanding than the requirements in the *Commission*'s Communication.

In its *BBC-Digital-Curriculum*-decision, the Commission had to assess a definition that was criticised by the applicant as being vague and not clearly described.[393]

---

386 Of same opinion *Grespan*, EStAL 2010, 79, 80: 'not qualitative requirements relating to objectively measurable aspects' but 'concept such as promotion of pluralism, respect of democratic values, and appropriate representation of different opinions and so on'.

387 Like that: *Thum*, Einfachgesetzliche Präzisierung des verfassungsrechtlichen Funktionsauftrags des öffentlich-rechtlichen Rundfunks, p. 178.

388 *Commission*, Decision of 24.04.2007, State aid No E 3/2005, *Financing of public service broadcasters in Germany*, para. 224.

389 *Commission*, Decision of 24.04.2007, State aid No E 3/2005, *Financing of public service broadcasters in Germany*, para. 229.

390 *Commission*, Decision of 24.04.2007, State aid No E 3/2005, *Financing of public service broadcasters in Germany*, para. 230.

391 *Commission*, Decision of 24.04.2007, State aid No E 3/2005, *Financing of public service broadcasters in Germany*, para. 235.

392 *Commission*, Decision of 15.10.2003, State aid No C 85/2001, *RTP* (ad-hoc payments), para. 171.

393 *Commission*, Decision of 01.10.2003, State aid No N 37/2003, *BBC Digital Curriculum*, para. 42.

Subsequently, the UK authorities modified the definition and recorded the intention to set up a plan at least fifteen months before the launch of the services. This plan would 'set out the subjects to be covered during the first five years of the service' and would 'be accompanied by explicit criteria for exclusion thus providing clarity for users and commercial providers of the subjects and/or learning outcomes that will not be provided by the BBC throughout the duration of the Plan'.[394] The Commission appreciated these modifications and finally considered the remit as adequately and sufficiently defined.[395]

The *CFI*, in contrast, seems to give the Member States a broader discretion regarding the definition of public service obligations. In its *TV2*-decision the court added the option to use broad terms to the possibility of defining the obligations solely in qualitative terms.[396] Herein the Danish law obliged a channel to provide a 'wide range of programmes and services comprising news coverage, general information, education, art and entertainment'. The provision could be effected through 'television, radio, Internet and the like'.[397] Additionally, the Danish law established certain qualitative guidelines the channel should follow, as it required that the broadcasting range should aim to provide 'quality, versatility and diversity'. Furthermore, in the planning of the programmes, freedom of information and expression should be a primary concern and particular emphasis should be placed on the Danish language and culture.[398] The *CFI* argued that, although the definition of the obligations is rather wide and essentially qualitative, it cannot be called imprecise.[399] Considering the clarity of the definition, the court puts specific emphasis on the clearly imposed aim 'to offer the entire Danish population varied television programming which aims to provide quality, versatility and diversity'.[400]

In summary, it may be concluded that the Member States have been granted not only a wide discretion in determining SGEI but also in relation to the degree of

---

394 *Commission*, Decision of 01.10.2003, State aid No N 37/2003, *BBC Digital Curriculum*, para. 43.

395 *Commission*, Decision of 01.10.2003, State aid No N 37/2003, *BBC Digital Curriculum*, para. 44.

396 *CFI*, 22. October 2008, joined Cases T-309/04, T-317/04, T-329/04 and T-336/04, *TV2*, para. 113.

397 *CFI*, 22. October 2008, joined Cases T-309/04, T-317/04, T-329/04 and T-336/04, *TV2*, para. 115.

398 *CFI*, 22. October 2008, joined Cases T-309/04, T-317/04, T-329/04 and T-336/04, *TV2*, para. 115.

399 *CFI*, 22. October 2008, joined Cases T-309/04, T-317/04, T-329/04 and T-336/04, *TV2*, para. 117.

400 *CFI*, 22. October 2008, joined Cases T-309/04, T-317/04, T-329/04 and T-336/04, *TV2*, para. 117.

precisions of the definition. Many authors also endorse this restricted competence of the Commission to check for manifest errors.[401]

b) *Criticism regarding the 'common' approach*

In this section, the sustainability of the wide approach to the definition of public service obligations is questioned. Moreover, the assessment of the arguments given might indicate possible criteria to be taken into account regarding the minimum content of a proper definition.

First of all, it might be illuminating to find out which objectives fall within the definition of public service obligations. The definition of the public service obligation marks the basis for a State aid assessment of public measurements. Within the assessment, the correct allocation of costs and revenues must be considered. Without a clear definition of the obligations, a proper allocation of costs and revenues is impossible. This affects especially the examination of the proportionality of a measure.[402] Furthermore, the beneficiary, as well as the State itself, have to know which specific activities are supported.[403] Otherwise, the proper implementation of the respective services is impeded, as well as the effective obligatory[404] control of the implementation of the services through the Member States. Moreover, according to the Commission, an opaque definition may lead to a disincentive for other market participants to develop new services.[405]

Indeed, competence for and oversight of the definition lies with the State. Nevertheless, according to the Amsterdam Protocol, this sovereignty is not just an option but an *obligation* for the State when entrusting an undertaking with public service obligations.[406] Hence, it can be argued that this obligation is not fulfilled through a meaningless definition. Moreover, *argumentum e contrario,* it cannot be an option

---

401 *Ehricke*, Die EG-rechtliche Beurteilung der Rundfunkfinanzierung, p. 73; *Schnaitter*, Möglichkeiten und Grenzen der Ausgestaltung des Programmauftrags der öffentlich-rechtlichen Rundfunkanstalten, p. 39. In inverse conclusion like that: *Donders*, Public Service Media and Policy in Europe, p. 77; *Stulz-Herrnstadt*, Nationale Rundfunkfinanzierung und europäische Beihilfenaufsicht im Lichte des Amsterdamer Rundfunkprotokolls, pp. 356 et seqq. In the same direction: *European Broadcasting Union*, Review of the Communication from the Commission on the application of State aid rules to public service broadcasting – EBU reply to the Commission's questionnaire, p. 16; *Eifert*, in: *Hahn/Vesting*, Beck'scher Kommentar zum Rundfunkrecht, § 11 RStV, para. 17.

402 Cf. also *Koenigs*, ZEuS 2006, 135, 165; *Storr*, K&R 2002, 464, 469.

403 See *ECJ*, 11 April 1989, Case T-66/86, *Ahmed Saeed*, para. 56.

404 *Grzeszick*, NVwZ 2008, 608, 614.

405 This was the concern of the Commission towards public service obligations in Germany comprising online services: *Commission*, Decision of 24.04.2007, State aid No E 3/2005, *Financing of public service broadcasters in Germany*, para. 230. Likewise: *Depypere/Tigchelaar*, Competition Policy Newsletter 2004 (2), 19, 22.

406 See above C. III. 2) a). See also *Degenhart*, AfP 2005, 493, 498.

for the *undertaking* itself to expand the obligations, as the definition solely falls within the competence of the Member State.[407] An insufficient definition of the public service obligations might eventually lead to a self-entrustment (so called 'mission creep').[408]

All these arguments indicate very strongly that the definition *must be as clear as possible*, especially for the ensuring of effective monitoring of the services.[409] Conversely, general descriptions and simple objectives without closer specifications should be avoided as far as possible. The objection that the Member States have a broad discretion not only in view of the selection of the services which are supposed to be part of the public service remit (the question of 'which activities can be part of the remit') but also regarding the precision of the definition is not compelling. In particular, it seems doubtful whether the Protocol covers more than the competence of the Member States to select the services which shall be part of the definition of the SGEI. Such a restraint would not broaden the Commission's competence to control for manifest errors in this respect, as the Member States' competence to determine the activities as such remains untouched. Solely the way to define the services (i.e. the precision) would be restricted. Therefore neither the principle of subsidiarity (Art. 5(2) TEU) nor the enabling of the services (Art. 14 TFEU) is violated. Consequently, the Member States do not enjoy discretion in this respect when an elaboration of a (more) clear(ly) formulation is possible.

Nevertheless, there might be reasons why a definition of the public service obligation cannot be described into the finest detail. A very important argument to support the possibility of a wide definition (to a certain extent) is the preservation or establishment of high editorial independence from any political authority whatsoever.[410] An environment in which the aim of a diverse programme offer can be pursued in the most objective way is only created through such independence.

---

407 That is an important intention behind the definition. See *Schweitzer*, in: *Cremona*, Market Integration and Public Services in the European Union, pp. 11, 35.

408 Considering the apprehension of a 'mission creep': *Depypere/Tigchelaar*, Competition Policy Newsletter 2004 (2), 19.

409 *Donders*, Public Service Media and Policy in Europe, p. 43; *Koenig/Haratsch*, EStAL 2003, 569, 573: 'definition needs to indicate whether or not the Member State wants to incorporate a particular activity of the respective organisation in the public remit'. Likewise moreover: *Degenhart*, AfP 2005, 493, 498; *Grzeszick*, NVwZ 2008, 608, 612 et seq.; *Koenigs*, ZEuS 2006, 135, 165; *Krone*, Gebührenfinanzierter Rundfunk und Beihilferecht, p. 133. A negative counterexample might be seen in the decision of the *Verwaltungsgericht Karlsruhe*, judgment of 28 September 2006, Case 1 K 559/06, 1 K 559/06a, para. 32, wherein the court was, due to the vague definition, not in the position to allocate costs and calculate a possible overcompensation.

410 See *CFI*, 22. October 2008, joined Cases T-309/04, T-317/04, T-329/04 and T-336/04, *TV2*, para. 118; *Eifert*, in: *Hahn/Vesting*, Beck'scher Kommentar zum Rundfunkrecht, § 11 RStV, para. 17; *Hesse*, AfP 2005, 499, 504.

Especially, given that the programme has to have the possibility to develop as extensive and quickly as the evolution in the country, if it wants to provide a realistic picture of the actual diversity. Therefore, editorial independence is fundamental for a pluralistic and democratic society.[411] Nonetheless, due to the given reasons, the definition should be more than an empty shell. Thus, when formulating the definition, the object of editorial independence should be taken into consideration, but only to the point where a possible infringement of this independence actually seems realistic.[412] The possibilities to define clearly under this premise will be the subject of the next section.

c) Scope to clarify the definition

A clear definition of the public service obligations has to be as precise as possible, yet formulated in a way that it does not infringe the editorial independence of the public service broadcaster.

Nevertheless, the argument of editorial independence cannot be brought into play concerning the type or number of the dissemination-media. The definition of the public service obligations should, therefore, comprise a specific enumeration of the media which the public service broadcaster is allowed to use to provide the services (e.g. radio, television, internet radio, online platforms, digital channels etc.). Such a definition does not infringe editorial independence as the independence to elaborate a programme within the respective supported medium would not be touched. A missing specification of the medium would empower the undertaking to extend its public service obligations without an explicit prior consent of the Member States. Consequently, a lack of precision regarding the definition of the dissemination-media is neither indicated nor acceptable within the first *Altmark*-criterion. Therefore, wording such as 'television, radio, Internet and the like' as contemplated in the *TV2*-decision[413] of the *CFI*, has to be seen as critical considering the adjunct of 'and the like'.

Another aspect to consider is the formulation of quantitative restrictions in the remit. This would comprise limitations regarding temporal and percentage standards. These restrictions, for instance, could comprise abstract proportionate determinations of the composition of the programme (e.g. 10% sports; 20% culture etc.), origin (e.g. 40% of the programme has to be produced in the domestic market), or

---

411 Therefore it is of little surprise that the independence of the media is also a fundamental principle in constitutions, e.g. in Germany (see). See also Art. 11(2) of the Charter of Fundamental Rights of the European Union and Art. 10 EHRC.

412 In the same direction: *Commission*, Decision of 24.04.2007, State aid No E 3/2005, *Financing of public service broadcasters in Germany*, para. 251; *Grzeszick*, NVwZ 2008, 608, 614.

413 *CFI*, 22. October 2008, joined Cases T-309/04, T-317/04, T-329/04 and T-336/04, *TV2*, para. 115.

self-production quotas,[414] a determination of the number of (digital) channels a broadcaster may provide, provisions regarding transmission times, or determinations considering the geographic territory the broadcaster is allowed to supply its services to. It would also be feasible to require a special focus on a specific type of programme (e.g. news) or a specific addressee (e.g. children, elderly, minorities) instead of setting certain figures, as such an approach would be less constraining.[415] The restrictions could be made for every single channel or dissemination-medium.

Still, all these quantitative restrictions bear (more or less) the problem that they might have an effect on the arrangement of the programme and, therefore, editorial independence.[416] Restrictions that influence the formation of the programme are therefore not indicated. However, provisions which directly leave the choices to the editors, leaving the programme unaffected, and only set the circumferential framework in which the programme may be developed, are still possible and desirable. Such a framework would leave the programme as such untouched, but would limit the 'playground' on which it may be performed. Examples would be a limitation of the number of channels or the geographic reception area for the broadcasting services. Here, only the extent of the programme is influenced, not the arrangement.[417] Such a provision may be demanded from the Member States in favour of State aid control.

More doubtful are mandatory quotas which set out general content standards for the programme. These provisions might not touch the specific formation of the programme, albeit they bind the freedom of the editor in view of the programme in an abstract way. A remedy in this context could be using abstract determinations regarding those types of broadcasts which could call a balanced programme concept into question (e.g. sport-shows or plain entertainment-broadcasts). Another possibility to attenuate the impact on editorial independence would be to formulate the provision as target-specifications.[418]

---

414 Whether or not such quotas are admissible under antitrust law, the fundamental freedoms or other any laws is no subject to this work.

415 *Thum*, Einfachgesetzliche Präzisierung des verfassungsrechtlichen Funktionsauftrags des öffentlich-rechtlichen Rundfunks, pp. 179 et seqq. Cf. also *Craufurd Smith*, LIEI 28 (1) [2001], 3, 4.

416 *Thum*, Einfachgesetzliche Präzisierung des verfassungsrechtlichen Funktionsauftrags des öffentlich-rechtlichen Rundfunks, p. 181. Less rigid: *Degenhart*, AfP 2005, 493, 498.

417 Cf. also *Degenhart*, AfP 2005, 493, 498.

418 Likewise: *Thum*, Einfachgesetzliche Präzisierung des verfassungsrechtlichen Funktionsauftrags des öffentlich-rechtlichen Rundfunks, p. 185. Such a target-specification has the characteristic to be in principle a mandatory limitation from which the broadcaster may derogate in justified individual instances. Not to be shared may be to suggestion of *Thum* (ibid.) to also use non-binding provisions, as such norms cannot give any information about the actual public service obligations.

Furthermore, quantitative restrictions may be formulated by the Member States considering all activities without a connection to editorial independence. In this context, the option of a negative-list, which outlines all the activities the public service broadcaster is not entitled to do, could be very valuable in clarifying the definition.[419] Such a list would give a clear overview of the activities that may not be financed through the granted means, as it can comprise activities which do not touch editorial independence and contributes significantly to a clearer definition. This could be seen as a mandatory element of the entrustment of the public service provider. Part of the list should comprise all activities the broadcaster might take on out which cannot, or should not, or may only under certain conditions, be part of the remit. Examples are especially online-services[420] or parts of them (e.g. calculators, chat-rooms, application-portals, single-portals, guides, betting services, music-download, games, route planners, e-commerce, etc.), further advertisement (to a certain extent), merchandising, printing activities (for example in view of the programme). Such negative-lists are only mandatory provided that the Member State does not want to finance such services or the services a broadcaster might provide cannot be qualified as SGEI due to their nature.

A negative-list has to be accompanied by a positive-list or a respective specification of the remit. In order to leave certain openness for minor developments and give latitude to the editorial arrangement it is expedient to formulate the tasks as interpretative examples instead of establishing them definitively.[421] The typical tasks of the broadcaster for fulfilling the remit should be named, for example production of programmes and purchase of rights, as well as the possibility of using new media services.

Due to the difficulties in objectively measuring the quality of broadcasts,[422] it appears to be hard to set qualitative objectives for the public service broadcasters.[423] Nevertheless, the objective of generating a higher value for the public with the services than the one provided by the market is a key attribute that distinguishes SGEI from other services. Therefore, the Member States should define how possible abstract objectives in this respect – especially for fulfilling democratic, social and cultural needs and the need to preserve media pluralism – are intended to be

419 Similar: *Thum*, NVwZ 2007, 521, 523.

420 Also pleading for a list of online services: *Dörr*, in: *Detterbeck/Rozek/v. Coelln*, Recht als Medium der Staatlichkeit – Festschrift für Herbert Bethge zum 70. Geburtstag, pp. 451, 462.

421 *Thum*, Einfachgesetzliche Präzisierung des verfassungsrechtlichen Funktionsauftrags des öffentlich-rechtlichen Rundfunks, p. 179.

422 *Craufurd Smith*, LIEI 28 (1) [2001], 3, 20; *Foster*, Public Broadcasters – Accountability and Efficiency, p. 31.

423 The quality itself is also not monitored through the Commission (see above C. I. 1) a) (2)). Nevertheless, the question of how quality is measured may indirectly play a role when the clarity of abstract objectives, which the broadcaster has to follow, is at stake.

achieved.[424] In other words, it is about the specification of terms like 'democratic, social and cultural needs'. Otherwise the definition remains unclear and abstract, thus making impossible the monitoring of the impact on the public value.[425] Possibilities of measuring quality could be seen for example in audience ratings, audience reach and surveys regarding specific broadcasts.[426]

It has to be borne in mind that, particularly in the context of specifying the objectives of services or setting up very specific lists of tasks and illegitimate activities, editorial independence is very vulnerable and the constraints could impede a quick reaction to new developments. A promising way of overcoming these issues, yet simultaneously defining sufficiently clear the task to be pursued, could be seen in an inductive concretisation within a procedural framework.[427] The Member States could create a national procedure in which the services are regularly monitored in view of their compliance with the abstract objectives. The introduction of new services would have to go through such an evaluation procedure, in which the additional public value would be assessed, and at the end of which the broadcaster is expressly entrusted with specific services. Due to the requirement of editorial independence, the valuation committee would have to be independent from the State (e.g. an independent broadcasting council).[428] A procedural solution regarding the evaluation of the viability of new services and significant changes to existing services does exist, for example, in the United Kingdom (so-called 'Public Value Test') and in Germany[429] (so-called 'Drei-Stufen-Test'; translated: 'Three-Step-Test').[430]

---

424 *Degenhart*, AfP 2005, 493, 498, strongly pleads for the usage of qualitative criteria.

425 Also critically: *Koenigs*, ZEuS 2006, 135, 165 et seq.

426 See also *Foster*, Public Broadcasters – Accountability and Efficiency, pp. 33 et seqq.

427 Cf. also *Thum*, Einfachgesetzliche Präzisierung des verfassungsrechtlichen Funktionsauftrags des öffentlich-rechtlichen Rundfunks, p. 188 et seqq.

428 *Thum*, Einfachgesetzliche Präzisierung des verfassungsrechtlichen Funktionsauftrags des öffentlich-rechtlichen Rundfunks, p. 189 et seq.

429 In Germany the test is only applied to online-services. Considering this test cf. *Dörr*, in: *Detterbeck/Rozek/v. Coelln*, Recht als Medium der Staatlichkeit – Festschrift für Herbert Bethge zum 70. Geburtstag, pp. 451, 464 et seqq.

430 This has been strongly promoted by the Commission regarding new media services: *Commission*, Communication from the Commission on the application of State aid rules to public service broadcasting, (OJ C 257/1 of 27.10.2009), paras. 84–91. See also *Repa/Tosics/Dias/Bacchiega*, Competition Policy Newsletter 2009 (3), 10, 14 et seqq. Critically: *European Broadcasting Union*, Review of the Communication from the Commission on the application of State aid rules to public service broadcasting – EBU reply to the Commission's questionnaire, p. 11. Considering other procedural suggestions, see for example *Donders*, Public Service Media and Policy in Europe, p. 35.

3) Entrustment

The first *Altmark*-criterion further demands that the recipient is actually 'required' to discharge public service obligations (entrustment). However, the *ECJ* did not specify within the *Altmark*-judgment the formal way in which the definition can be established. Regarding Art. 106(2) TFEU, an act of public authority is required.[431] This official act does not necessarily have to be an act of legislation or an individual regulatory act. Rather, any form is acceptable, for example, a contract or binding terms of reference.[432] This takes into account that the organisational structure in the Member States can be very diverse. The entrustment may take place at a national, regional or local level.[433] However, in view of the second *Altmark*-criterion, according to which the parameters on the basis of which the compensation is calculated must be established in an objective and transparent manner, it can be inferred that the definition has to be effected at least in text form. An oral entrustment is not sufficient. Otherwise, the definition – which is an integral part for the calculation of the compensation – would not be transparent.

The entrustment must indicate the specific beneficiary.[434] Moreover, the entrustment should also contain explanations about its duration of validity.[435] A limitation in time might also be used to evaluate the remit again.

---

431 *CFI*, 12 February 2008, Case T-289/03, *BUPA*, para. 181. Cf. also *Grespan*, EStAL 2010, 79, 83; *Quigley*, European State Aid Law And Policy, p. 163.

432 Cf. *Commission*, Communication from the Commission on the application of the European Union State aid rules to compensation granted for the provision of services of general economic interest (OJ C 8/4 of 11.01.2012), para. 50; *Krone*, Gebührenfinanzierter Rundfunk und Beihilferecht, p. 131; *Linke*, Die Gewährleistung des Daseinsvorsorgeauftrags im öffentlichen Personennahverkehr, p. 111; *Selmayr/Kamann*, K&R 2004, 49, 56. In *its* Decision of 22.05.2002, State aid No N 631/2001, *BBC license fee*, para. 35, the *Commission* considered a letter of the Secretary of State to be sufficient.

433 *Bravasso*, in: *Hancher/Ottervanger/Slot*, EU State Aids, para. 18–003.

434 *Krone*, Gebührenfinanzierter Rundfunk und Beihilferecht, p. 132; *Thum*, Einfachgesetzliche Präzisierung des verfassungsrechtlichen Funktionsauftrags des öffentlich-rechtlichen Rundfunks, p. 143. Cf. also *Commission*, Decision of 20 December 2011 on the application of Article 106(2) of the Treaty on the Functioning of the European Union to State aid in the form of public service compensation granted to certain undertakings entrusted with the operation of services of general economic interest (OJ L 7/3 of 11.01.2012), para. 14.

435 See for example *Commission*, Decision of 01.10.2003, State aid No N 37/2003, *BBC Digital Curriculum*, para. 42, wherein the applicant criticised the missing limitation in time. Cf. also *Commission*, Decision of 20 December 2011 on the application of Article 106(2) of the Treaty on the Functioning of the European Union to State aid in the form of public service compensation granted to certain undertakings entrusted with the operation of services of general economic interest (OJ L 7/3 of 11.01.2012), para. 14; *Linke*, Die Gewährleistung des Daseinsvorsorgeauftrags im öffentlichen Personennahverkehr, p. 113; *Thum*, Einfachgesetzliche Präzisierung

Questionable is whether the public service obligations have to be defined as strictly compulsory for the undertaking or whether it is sufficient to define the provision of certain services as an option. The Commission ascertained in its decision towards the German public broadcasting system that a plain authorisation to provide services cannot be seen as an adequate entrustment.[436] In contrast, an entrustment shall be considered sufficient when the specific scope and content of the services is fixed in a later formal act on the basis of the general authorisation clause.[437] According to these assumptions, the Member States have to specify the obligations in a formal act in any case. Additionally, the Member States have to define the services themselves and as exactly as possible. A general authorisation clause will not meet such a definition. However, a strong commitment of the provider to perform the services is not necessary in the opinion of the author. Although the term "public service obligation" might suggest that the tasks assigned to the undertaking are mandatory, the term 'obligation' might also refer to the requirements the undertaking would not assume or would not assume to the same extent in its own commercial interests. In this sense the obligation indicates the additional burden (e.g. transmission of cultural programmes or formation of a programme without consideration or focus on profit) the undertaking has to bear, *if* it decides to perform the services in question (e.g. broadcasting). Consequently, it is also sufficient to determine optional fields of activity; compulsory is solely the observance of the (defined) public interest while performing such an activity.[438] This approach complies with the intention behind the determination, namely to have the ability to monitor whether or not the undertaking was *actually entrusted* with the provision of these services *at the time it performs* them. The intention is also respected when the

---

des verfassungsrechtlichen Funktionsauftrags des öffentlich-rechtlichen Rundfunks, p. 143.

436 *Commission*, Decision of 24.04.2007, State aid No E 3/2005, *Financing of public service broadcasters in Germany*, para. 247. Cf. also *Commission*, Communication from the Commission on the application of State aid rules to public service broadcasting, (OJ C 257/1 of 27.10.2009), paras. 53 et seq.

437 *Commission*, Decision of 24.04.2007, State aid No E 3/2005, *Financing of public service broadcasters in Germany*, para. 247.

438 Of same opinion: *Grzeszick*, NVwZ 2008, 608, 612; *Schnaitter*, Möglichkeiten und Grenzen der Ausgestaltung des Programmauftrags der öffentlich-rechtlichen Rundfunkanstalten, pp. 45 et seq. Of other opinion: *Arhold*, in: *Montag/Säcker*, Münchener Kommentar zum Europäischen und Deutschen Wettbewerbsrecht (Kartellrecht) – Band 3, Art. 107 AEUV para. 230; *Hain*, MMR 2001, 219, 223; *Krone*, Gebührenfinanzierter Rundfunk und Beihilferecht, p. 132. Unclear: *CFI*, 12 February 2008, Case T-289/03, *BUPA*, para. 188 ('[...] must be understood as meaning that the operators entrusted with the SGEI mission [...] are, in principle, required to offer the service in question [...]') on the one hand and para. 189 ('In effect, the compulsory nature of the SGEI mission does not preclude a certain latitude being left to the operator on the market, including in relation to the content [...]') on the other.

performance of the services itself is optional. The contrary position would exclude concessions as possible acts of entrustment.[439]

It should be noted that the entrustment is imposed by the Member State on the broadcaster. It is not for the broadcaster to entrust himself. Consequently, provisions of a comprehensive-clause type are problematic as they put broadcasters in the position to determine the scope of the entrustment themselves. In practice, public service broadcasters occasionally use 'promises to the public' or 'self-commitments' to determine the specific scope of the entrustment when the explanations of the State were too broad. The Commission had to assess such self-commitments and criticised the lack of an additional official act supplementary to the self-commitments.[440] Self-commitments on their own, without at least an official approving act, were not enough. Although the Commission does not object to the possibility of the broadcasters proposing or elaborating new services, it is eventually for the State to certify that these proposals fall under the public service mission.[441] This position has the support of the author. 'Mission creep' caused by the broadcasters is something the first *Altmark*-criterion is specifically supposed to prevent. This conclusion stands in line with the provisions of the Amsterdam Protocol, which expects a definition of the public service obligation by the State and not by the broadcaster.[442] Therefore, the Member States have the final responsibility over the question whether certain activities are part of the remit or not.[443] Hence, self-commitments of the broadcaster to specify a broad remit are not sufficient without subsequent approval of the State.[444] Moreover, a public service remit formulated too broad (e.g. through comprehensive-clauses) infringes the required clarity of the definition and the necessary limitation through the Member State.[445]

---

439 Concessions, however, are viewed as appropriate acts of entrustment by the *ECJ*: 23 October 1997, Case C-159/94, *Commission/French Republic*, para. 66.

440 *Commission*, Decision of 24.04.2007, State aid No E 3/2005, *Financing of public service broadcasters in Germany*, paras. 248 et seqq.

441 *Commission*, Decision of 24.04.2007, State aid No E 3/2005, *Financing of public service broadcasters in Germany*, para. 312.

442 Of other opinion: *Ehricke*, Die EG-rechtliche Beurteilung der Rundfunkfinanzierung, p. 77.

443 Cf. *Dörr*, in: *Detterbeck/Rozek/v. Coelln*, Recht als Medium der Staatlichkeit – Festschrift für Herbert Bethge zum 70. Geburtstag, pp. 451, 462; *Krone*, Gebührenfinanzierter Rundfunk und Beihilferecht, p. 140.

444 *Degenhart*, K&R 2005, 295, 298. Of other opinion: *Ehricke*, Die EG-rechtliche Beurteilung der Rundfunkfinanzierung, pp. 76 et seqq.; *Hesse*, AfP 2005, 499, 504; *Krone*, Gebührenfinanzierter Rundfunk und Beihilferecht, pp. 121 et seqq.

445 *Degenhart*, AfP 2005, 493, 494.

II. 2nd Criterion: Objective and transparent establishment of compensation parameters

The second *Altmark*-criterion requires that the parameters on the basis of which the compensation is calculated are established beforehand in an objective and transparent manner. The feature was a novelty when the *ECJ* introduced it, as it has no counterpart in Art. 106(2) TFEU or other State aid rules.[446] Hence, its tenability in the system of State aid law is disputed.[447] Nevertheless, the Altmark-ruling is now established jurisprudence, which must be observed. When determining the compensation parameters, the Member States have a wide discretion, as this involves the assessment of complex economic facts.[448] The discretion, however, does not comprise the characteristics of objectiveness and transparency regarding the establishment of the parameters, as these are rigid requirements in the second *Altmark*-criterion.[449]

The intention behind the second criterion is to avoid compensation being determined in hindsight, based on the actual costs incurred *after* the performance of the service has started.[450] Therefore, the calculation method must be established *beforehand*. It should be based on a calculation-formula, albeit a full formula is not absolutely necessary.[451] Nevertheless, '[w]here the authority decides to compensate all cost items of the provider, it must determine at the outset how those costs will

---

446 *Bartosch*, EU-Beihilfenrecht, Art. 87 Abs. 1 EGV, para. 72; *Bovis*, CJEL 10 (3) [2004], 419, 441 et seq.; *Deuster*, Ausgleichszahlungen für Dienstleistungen von allgemeinem wirtschaftlichem Interesse, p. 159; *Koenigs*, ZEuS 2006, 135, 161; *Linke*, Die Gewährleistung des Daseinsvorsorgeauftrags im öffentlichen Personennahverkehr, p. 114 with further references; *Schwendinger*, Gemeinschaftsrechtliche Grenzen öffentlicher Rundfunkfinanzierung, p. 245.

447 Cf. *Linke*, Die Gewährleistung des Daseinsvorsorgeauftrags im öffentlichen Personennahverkehr, pp. 116 et seq. with further references.

448 *CFI*, 12 February 2008, Case T-289/03, *BUPA*, para. 214.

449 Cf. also *CFI*, 12 February 2008, Case T-289/03, *BUPA*, para. 214: 'It is precisely because the determination of the compensation is subject to only restricted control by the Community institutions, moreover, that the second *Altmark*-condition requires that those institutions must be in a position to verify the existence of objective and transparent parameters, which must be defined in such a way as to preclude any abusive recourse to the concept of an SGEI on the part of the Member State.'.

450 *Arhold*, in: *Montag/Säcker*, Münchener Kommentar zum Europäischen und Deutschen Wettbewerbsrecht (Kartellrecht) – Band 3, Art. 107 AEUV para. 233; *Ehricke*, Die EG-rechtliche Beurteilung der Rundfunkfinanzierung, p. 87; *Linke*, Die Gewährleistung des Daseinsvorsorgeauftrags im öffentlichen Personennahverkehr, p. 115; *Mortensen*, EStAL 2008, 239, 243; *Quigley*, European State Aid Law And Policy, p. 165.

451 *Commission*, Communication from the Commission on the application of the European Union State aid rules to compensation granted for the provision of services of general economic interest (OJ C 8/4 of 11.01.2012), para. 55.

be determined and calculated.'[452] Thus, the criterion encourages a determination of a 'price' for the provision of the services before the service has started.

The second criterion is a formal requirement. Therefore, the question whether the calculation might lead to an overcompensation is not measured against the second criterion but is part of the overcompensation-assessment of the third criterion, which is more specific in this respect.[453]

1) Parameters

The criterion only demands the prior establishment of parameters. The total amount of compensation needs neither to be definite nor does it have to be precisely calculable before the start of the services.[454] The term 'parameters' (i.e. mathematical variables that remain constant) indicates that only the relevant cost-factors and the calculation-formula have to be defined in order to allow a basic calculation with variables.[455]

2) Prior establishment

The parameters have to be established beforehand. 'Beforehand' refers to the performing of the services.[456] In favour of this interpretation is the fact that according to the *ECJ*, payments for the losses of an undertaking are considered State aid when the parameters of such compensation have not been established beforehand, and 'it turns out after the event that the operation of certain services in connection with the discharge of public service obligations was not economically viable'.[457]

Consequently, public service broadcasters that receive monies for losses incurring at a time when they are not covered by already established calculation-parameters are recipients of State aid. Particularly, when a broadcaster receives more financial means than planned and determined beforehand, the second criterion is not met.

---

452 *Commission*, Communication from the Commission on the application of the European Union State aid rules to compensation granted for the provision of services of general economic interest (OJ C 8/4 of 11.01.2012), para. 56.

453 Posing this question: *Travers*, EStAL 2003, 387, 391.

454 *Elste/Wiedemann*, WiVerw 2004, 9, 21; *Mortensen*, EStAL 2008, 239, 243; *v. Wallenberg*, MMR 2004, 88, 90.

455 *Elste/Wiedemann*, WiVerw 2004, 9, 21; *Kreße*, Gemeinwirtschaftliche Dienste im europäischen Beihilferecht, pp. 97 et seq.; *Linke*, Die Gewährleistung des Daseinsvorsorgeauftrags im öffentlichen Personennahverkehr, p. 115.

456 *Linke*, Die Gewährleistung des Daseinsvorsorgeauftrags im öffentlichen Personennahverkehr, p. 115 with further references.

457 *ECJ*, 24 July 2003, Case C-280/00, *Altmark Trans*, para. 91.

3) Objective manner

The establishment of the parameters has to be objective. This is the case when the calculation-parameters are based on coherent and objectively justifiable criteria.[458] Consequently, the calculation-formula must be comprehensible and based on realistic assumptions.[459] Arbitrarily set parameters are not considered objective.

In contrast, it is of little relevance how the procedure for setting the parameters was structured (e.g. parameters were adopted by several bodies), as only the objectiveness of the parameters themselves is relevant.[460] One possibility of establishing the parameters in an objective manner for a public service broadcaster would be an orientation on the deficit of the past years if applicable under consideration of indexed costs and revenues and adapting it, taking into account all forecasted developments.

4) Transparent manner

The requirement that the parameters are established in a transparent manner enables effective monitoring of the compensation system. In particular, competitors benefit from transparency as it allows them to gain information about the conditions under which SGEI are provided.[461] Consequently, for the monitoring procedure, the calculation must be publicly available[462] and comprehensible[463]. The establishment of the calculation-parameters, therefore, has to be conducted in a certain form, although it does not have to be a specific one. A solely oral establishment, however, cannot be regarded as transparent. Moreover, solely fixing *the amount of compensation* is not enough; rather, the *parameters* themselves, which are used to calculate the compensation, must be recorded in a document.[464] In other words, if it is already possible to calculate the compensation, the calculating-method has to be recognisable.

---

458 *Elste/Wiedemann*, WiVerw 2004, 9, 21; *Linke*, Die Gewährleistung des Daseinsvorsorgeauftrags im öffentlichen Personennahverkehr, p. 115.

459 *Elste/Wiedemann*, WiVerw 2004, 9, 21; *v. Wallenberg*, MMR 2004, 88, 90.

460 Cf. for example Decision of 26 November 2008 on State aid granted by Austria to the company *Postbus* in the *Lienz*-district, State aid No C 16/07 (OJ L 306/26 of 20.11.2009), paras. 72 et seqq., in which the *Commission* was solely scrutinizing the calculation of the agreed price. Of other opinion apparently *Schipanski*, K&R 2006, 217, 219 et seq.

461 *Arhold*, in: *Montag/Säcker*, Münchener Kommentar zum Europäischen und Deutschen Wettbewerbsrecht (Kartellrecht) – Band 3, Art. 107 AEUV para. 233.

462 Cf. *Commission*, Decision of 19.05.2004, State aid No C 2/2003, *TV2*, para. 71.

463 *Deuster*, Ausgleichszahlungen für Dienstleistungen von allgemeinem wirtschaftlichem Interesse, p. 159.

464 *Commission*, Decision of 20.04.2011, State aid No C 2/2003, *TV2*, para. 116. Cf. also *Commission*, Invitation to submit comments pursuant to Article 88(2) of the EC Treaty, State aid No C 16/07 (OJ C 162/19 of 14.07.2007), *Postbus Lienz*, para. 67.

The second criterion allows Member States to choose freely how to comply in practical terms even though the transparency-requirement demands a certain publicity of the compensation parameters.[465] The involvement of the States' parliament, for example, guarantees transparency, although it does not seem to be sufficient by itself.[466] Another possible way of reaching a higher transparency and objectivity would be to involve independent auditing firms.[467]

III. 3rd Criterion: Overcompensation

According to the third criterion, the compensation cannot exceed what is necessary to cover all or part of the costs incurred in the discharge of the public service obligations, taking into account the relevant receipts and a reasonable profit. The criterion broadly coincides with the proportionality-test carried out in the framework of the examination under Art. 106(2) TFEU and aims at preventing overcompensation.[468] To comply with the criterion, sufficient provisions have to be established by the Member States regarding the public service remit.[469]

By establishing the calculation-method of the compensation, the Member States enjoy a wide discretion. The Commission's control-competence in this respect is limited to manifest errors.[470] A manifest error, however, is reached, when the recipient is overcompensated. Nevertheless, the discretion does not give the Member States the competence to establish an incomprehensible calculation-system. Such a system would violate the second criterion.

465 *CFI*, 22 October 2008, joined Cases T-309/04, T-317/04, T-329/04 and T-336/04, *TV2*, para. 227. According to *Mortensen*, EStAL 2008, 239, 243, however, the establishment should comply with the transparency-directive.

466 Cf. *CFI*, 22 October 2008, joined Cases T-309/04, T-317/04, T-329/04 and T-336/04, *TV2*, para. 228, in which the involvement of the parliament was mentioned as a possibility of complying with the transparency-criterion, but only in conjunction with others. See also *Commission*, Decision of 20.04.2011, State aid No C 2/2003, *TV2*, para. 114.

467 See *CFI*, 22 October 2008, joined Cases T-309/04, T-317/04, T-329/04 and T-336/04, *TV2*, para. 228.

468 *Bartosch*, EU-Beihilfenrecht – Kommentar, Art. 87 Abs. 1 EGV, para. 72; *Ehricke*, Die EG-rechtliche Beurteilung der Rundfunkfinanzierung, p. 94; *Grespan*, EStAL 2010, 79, 88 et seq.; *Koenigs*, ZEuS 2006, 135, 161; *Krone*, Gebührenfinanzierter Rundfunk und Beihilferecht, pp. 156 et seq. But see also: *Harrison/Woods*, European Broadcasting Law and Policy, p. 307 ('distinction between the two must be made').

469 Cf. *Commission*, Decision of 24.04.2007, State aid No E 3/2005, *Financing of public service broadcasters in Germany*, paras. 264, 268.

470 *CFI*, 12 February 2008, Case T-289/03, *BUPA*, para. 220.

1) Net cost effect

The compensation cannot exceed what is necessary to cover all or part of the costs incurred in the discharge of the public service obligations. Thus, supporting means must solely cover the net cost effect of the burden imposed by the public service obligations.[471] This means that only the costs incurred by the provision of the public service obligations may be taken into consideration for the calculation.[472] Consequently, the costs of the *whole* service are *only* relevant when the whole service is a public service obligation.[473] The relevant costs are calculated by comparing the cost-revenue-situation of the provider carrying out the public service obligations with the hypothetical situation of the provider being relieved from these obligations (so-called Net-avoided-cost-methodology).[474]

Costs that do incur from public service obligations shall not be compensated. This comprises all costs for commercial services and all other costs solely related to activities outside the public service obligations.[475] In particular, investments in commercial activities are not part of the costs of the public service obligations.[476] The preclusion applies to costs that are connected to services which were inadmissibly named as public service obligations, too.[477]

a) Cross-subsidisation and separation of accounts

Where the public service broadcaster provides public service obligations and commercial services simultaneously, the hazard of cross-subsidisation occurs. Cross-subsidisation means that services that are not, or cannot be, part of the public service remit (i.e. commercial services) are (partly) financed through the compensation

---

471 *Commission*, Decision of 24.04.2007, State aid No E 3/2005, *Financing of public service broadcasters in Germany*, para. 263.

472 *Commission*, Communication from the Commission on the application of State aid rules to public service broadcasting, (OJ C 257/1 of 27.10.2009), para. 65; *Koenig*, BB 2003, 2185, 2186; *Koenig/Haratsch*, ZUM 2005, 275, 280.

473 Cf. *Koenig*, BB 2003, 2185, 2186.

474 Cf. the explanation of the method in *Commission*, Communication from the Commission – European Union framework for State aid in the form of public service compensation (2011) (OJ C 8/15 of 11.01.2012), paras. 25 et seqq. It has to be noted, however, that this Communication is not applicable to public service broadcasting (cf. para. 9 therein). Nevertheless, the calculation method has general validity. Cf. also *Koenig*, BB 2003, 2185, 2186; *Linke*, Die Gewährleistung des Daseinsvorsorgeauftrags im öffentlichen Personennahverkehr, p. 119.

475 *Commission*, Decision of 24.04.2007, State aid No E 3/2005, *Financing of public service broadcasters in Germany*, para. 270.

476 Cf. *Commission*, Decision of 24.04.2007, State aid No E 3/2005, *Financing of public service broadcasters in Germany*, paras. 275 et seqq.

477 Cf. *Commission*, Decision of 24.04.2007, State aid No E 3/2005, *Financing of public service broadcasters in Germany*, paras. 269 et eq.

payments. As commercial services are not to be compensated, cross-subsidisation inevitably leads to an overcompensation of the undertaking.

Consequently, the provision of commercial services and public service obligations at the same time requires a clear and appropriate separation of accounts between public service activities and commercial activities.[478] This obligation exists alongside eventual requirements arising from the Transparency Directive 2004/109/EC[479]. Appropriate measures to ensure this separation have to be established in the entrustment act.[480] Costs that are solely attributable to the public service as well as commercial activities have to be accounted accordingly.[481]

In PSB, however, the separate accounting of costs could be problematic as, for example, productions and programmes might be used for public service and commercial exploitation. The same accounts for resources and assets being used by both sides. According to the Commission, these costs, which are intended to serve the development of activities in the field of public and non-public services simultaneously, should be allocated proportionately, whenever possible in a meaningful way.[482] For example, according to the working hours used for one activity on the project or, if this is more relevant and quantifiable, another amount measuring the expenses (e.g. market-price of the usage, mileage regarding vehicles, etc.).[483]

When it comes to costs that benefit public services, as well as non-public services and that are not input costs which are intended to serve the development of activities (for example the commercial exploitation of self-productions would fall under these requirements), the Commission makes an exception from the aforementioned separation of costs in PSB. The Commission states in this respect that '[i]n other cases, whenever the same resources are used to perform public service and non-public service tasks, the common input costs should be allocated on the basis of the difference in the firm's total costs with and without non-public service

---

478 *Commission*, Communication from the Commission on the application of State aid rules to public service broadcasting, (OJ C 257/1 of 27.10.2009), para. 60; Decision of 24.04.2007, State aid No E 3/2005, *Financing of public service broadcasters in Germany*, para. 268.

479 Directive 2004/109/EC of the European Parliament and of the Council of 15 December 2004 on the harmonisation of transparency requirements in relation to information about issuers whose securities are admitted to trading on a regulated market and amending Directive 2001/34/EC (OJ L 390/38 of 31.12.2004). See in respect of the directive: *Koenig/Haratsch*, ZWeR 2004, 544.

480 *Commission*, Decision of 22.05.2002, State aid No N 631/2001, *BBC license fee*, para. 43.

481 *Commission*, Communication from the Commission on the application of State aid rules to public service broadcasting, (OJ C 257/1 of 27.10.2009), para. 66.

482 *Commission*, Communication from the Commission on the application of State aid rules to public service broadcasting, (OJ C 257/1 of 27.10.2009), para. 66.

483 From an economic point of view there is no compellingly applicable method of determining the share. Cf. *Nicolaides*, in: *Sánchez Rydelski*, The EC State Aid Regime – Distortive Effects of State Aid on Competition and Trade, p. 580.

activities [...]. In such cases, costs that are entirely attributable to public service activities, while benefiting also non-public service activities, need not be apportioned between the two and can be entirely allocated to the public service activity.'[484] The reason for this exception is that the net benefits of commercial activities have to be taken into account for the purpose of calculating the compensation.[485] The exception made by the Commission, however, is not convincing in the light of the third *Altmark*-criterion. The purpose behind the criterion is to prevent overcompensation. However, such overcompensation is not excluded when commercial services benefit from compensation intended for public service obligations, even if the benefits of commercial activities are taken into account during the calculation. One might think in this context of an entertainment channel outside the public service remit that fills its programme only with expensive productions out of the public service segment and is only able to transfer a small profit in return. This channel would eventually be financed by the financing means for the public services, although it is providing commercial activities in the open market. Thus, in conclusion, the general account-separation rules should apply in all situations in which both public services and non-public services are performed.

A clear way of separating accounts between commercial and public service activities could be seen in a functional and structural separation, especially through the funding of subsidiaries which perform the commercial services independently.[486] The subsidiaries would have to pay normal market remuneration for services, capital and assets provided to the (public service) parental company.[487]

b) Receipts

The net costs of the public service obligations have to be reduced by the amount of all relevant receipts. These receipts comprise all direct and indirect revenues and other benefits of the recipient that are caused by the public service obligations.[488] For deduction are also incorporeal advantages, as long as these benefits are measurable

484 *Commission*, Communication from the Commission on the application of State aid rules to public service broadcasting, (OJ C 257/1 of 27.10.2009), para. 67. The *Commission* uses the production of programmes as one example for the application of the exception (see para. 68 thereof).

485 *Commission*, Communication from the Commission on the application of State aid rules to public service broadcasting, (OJ C 257/1 of 27.10.2009), para. 67.

486 See *Commission*, Communication from the Commission on the application of State aid rules to public service broadcasting, (OJ C 257/1 of 27.10.2009), para. 69; Decision of 24.04.2007, State aid No E 3/2005, *Financing of public service broadcasters in Germany*, paras. 375 et seqq.; *Bartosch*, EU-Beihilfenrecht – Kommentar, Art. 86 Abs. 2 EGV, para. 26.

487 *Thyri/Jaeger*, wbl 2006, 197, 202.

488 Cf. *Commission*, Communication from the Commission on the application of State aid rules to public service broadcasting, (OJ C 257/1 of 27.10.2009), para. 71.

and quantifiable (e.g. higher revenues in commercial services because of a higher reputation effected by the public services).[489] PSB is usually marked by the fact that provision of the whole programme under certain conditions is qualified as a public service obligation. In this case, all revenues generated by the programme have to be subtracted from the costs of the public service obligations (e.g. advertising revenues, pay-per-view-revenues, subscriptions-revenues, etc.). Nevertheless, it does not seem precluded that a public service remit obliges the broadcaster to transmit solely a specific broadcast and not a whole programme. In this case, only the costs and revenues connected to this broadcast would have to be considered in order to calculate the legitimate compensation. Revenues from purely commercial activities, on the other hand, are not to be taken into account.

It is questionable how revenues that are formally part of a commercial activity, albeit their feasibility or success is based on the public service obligations, should be dealt with.[490] Here the public service obligations have an impact on the generation of the revenues. Even though the specific activity separated from other activities would be profitable, and therefore does not need any compensation, the cause for the revenues has its origin in the public service obligations. Consequently, the effected revenues must be taken into the account.[491] Profits generated through the commercial exploitation of the public service remit are therefore relevant receipts in the sense of the third criterion.[492]

c) *Reasonable profit*

The beneficiary can receive a reasonable profit for its services according to the third criterion. Such a profit may be granted by the Member State, albeit there is no obligation in European State aid law to grant such means.[493] The granting of a reasonable profit might prove not only necessary for private public service broadcasters, but also valuable for public ones, as the additional means could enable the undertaking to set aside reserves for future activities or (unexpected) costs not covered by the compensation-mechanism.[494]

---

489 Cf. *Koenig*, BB 2003, 2185, 2187.

490 E.g. a public service broadcaster generates merchandising-revenues through a commercially working subsidiary. In this case the profits through merchandising could not be generated (or at least not to the same extent) without the programme.

491 Regarding the example of revenues generated due to a higher reputation of the channel effected by the public services, the calculation could be complicated, as the question would have to be asked to which extent the revenues of the merchandising-subsidiary are caused by the public services.

492 Cf. *Commission*, Decision of 24.04.2007, State aid No E 3/2005, *Financing of public service broadcasters in Germany*, para. 273.

493 *Linke*, EWS 2011, 456, 457.

494 Cf. *European Broadcasting Union*, Review of the Communication from the Commission on the application of State aid rules to public service broadcasting – EBU

The option of granting a reasonable profit, however, does not (in any event) entitle the State to make the beneficiary itself profitable to a certain extent. Rather, the reasonable profit is another cost factor in the calculation of the compensation that can be taken into account, i.e. only an amount that the granting body pays additionally. Thus, in the case of a beneficiary that provides other (uneconomic) services, a reasonable profit in form of an additional compensation may only be granted for the investments used for the fulfilment of the public service obligations. If the recipient is already profitable in providing the public service obligations, but only to a minor extent (small profit), the third criterion entitles it to raise the profit to the magnitude of a reasonable profit.[495]

The *ECJ* did not specify in the *Altmark*-ruling how the reasonable profit is calculated, which makes the demarcation from an unreasonable profit exceedingly difficult.[496] However, if an undertaking is awarded a profit as part of the compensation, the calculation-scheme for the profit has to be established in the entrustment.[497]

It is not clear, which figures can be used to calculate the reasonable profit and how it is calculated after all. According to the Commission, a reasonable profit in PSB consists of a rate of return on own capital that takes account of the risk, or absence of risk, incurred by the undertaking.[498] Own capital can only be defined as own capital invested to provide the public service obligations, since the capital of commercial services cannot be funded. Despite the Commission's reference to own capital, it does not seem precluded to calculate the profit according to a different assessment base. This position is supported by the fact that the determination as to whether a profit is reasonable is always assessed based on a comparison between comparable entities. In this context, the return on own capital is not always the best benchmark, as structures of undertakings can be very different (e.g. an undertaking that is financed overly through borrowed capital). Therefore, for the sake of higher comparability, it is justified to use other methods to verify the reasonable profit, like,

---

reply to the Commission's questionnaire, p. 27. Partly of other opinion: *Commission*, Communication from the Commission on the application of State aid rules to public service broadcasting, (OJ C 257/1 of 27.10.2009), para. 72.

495 *Linke*, Die Gewährleistung des Daseinsvorsorgeauftrags im öffentlichen Personennahverkehr, p. 120.

496 Cf. *Schwendinger*, Gemeinschaftsrechtliche Grenzen öffentlicher Rundfunkfinanzierung, p. 246; *Travers*, EStAL 2003, 387, 391.

497 *Commission*, Communication from the Commission on the application of the European Union State aid rules to compensation granted for the provision of services of general economic interest (OJ C 8/4 of 11.01.2012), para. 57.

498 *Commission*, Communication from the Commission on the application of State aid rules to public service broadcasting, (OJ C 257/1 of 27.10.2009), para. 72. See also *Linke*, Die Gewährleistung des Daseinsvorsorgeauftrags im öffentlichen Personennahverkehr, p. 121.

for example, the EBITA (earnings before interest, tax and amortisation) margin, the return on sales, the return on assets or the return on capital employed.[499]

The reasonable profit must be determined based on a comparison. The most precise and preferable way would be using as a benchmark the recent years' average profit of those undertakings, comparable in structure and service portfolio and operating under competitive[500] conditions.[501] These undertakings should be from the same Member State and operate in the same sector; undertakings from other Member States or other sectors could alternatively be used, as long as the comparability is preserved.[502] In the case of no available comparable undertakings –a very likely scenario in PSB – the basis for calculation must be the profit on secure capital investment-options, eventually with a surcharge for the additional risk of the undertaking.[503]

'The level of risk depends on the sector concerned, the type of service and the characteristics of the compensation mechanism.'[504] Pursuant to Art. 5(7) of the Decision on the application of Art. 106(2) TFEU, in the case of a service that is not connected with a substantial commercial or contractual risk, particularly when the net cost incurred in providing the SGEI is essentially compensated in full ex-post, the reasonable profit may not exceed the relevant swap rate,[505] plus a premium of 100

---

499 *Commission*, Guide to the application of the European Union rules on state aid, public procurement and the internal market to services of general economic interest, and in particular to social services of general interest, SWD(2013) 53 final/2, 29.04.2013, p. 69; *Linke*, EWS 2011, 456, 458; *Niels/Jenkins/Kavanagh*, Economics for Competition Lawyers, p. 423.

500 Cf. *Commission*, Communication from the Commission on the application of the European Union State aid rules to compensation granted for the provision of services of general economic interest (OJ C 8/4 of 11.01.2012), para. 61; *Linke*, EWS 2011, 456, 458.

501 *Commission*, Guide to the application of the European Union rules on state aid, public procurement and the internal market to services of general economic interest, and in particular to social services of general interest, SEC(2010) 1545 final, 7.12.2010, pp. 50 et seqq.

502 *Linke*, Die Gewährleistung des Daseinsvorsorgeauftrags im öffentlichen Personennahverkehr, pp. 121 et seq.; *Linke*, EWS 2011, 456, 459; *Quigley*, European State Aid Law And Policy, p. 173.

503 *Elste/Wiedemann*, WiVerw 2004, 9, 18.

504 *Commission*, Communication from the Commission on the application of the European Union State aid rules to compensation granted for the provision of services of general economic interest (OJ C 8/4 of 11.01.2012), para. 61. See for examples for specific risk-factors *Linke*, EWS 2011, 456, 459.

505 Swap rates will soon be published on the Commission's DG Competition website (Guide to the application of the European Union rules on state aid, public procurement and the internal market to services of general economic interest, and in particular to social services of general interest, SWD(2013) 53 final/2, 29.04.2013, p. 69).

basis points.[506] In the case of public broadcasters, which are consistently sufficiently funded by their owners, there is usually no substantial risk to be recorded. Although the aforementioned decision is not necessarily applicable to PSB, the provisions may be seen as an indication of what would be acceptable under *Altmark*.

2) Control mechanisms

To guarantee the limitation of the compensation to the net costs of the public service obligations, the Member States must establish an effective control-mechanism regarding the financial situation after the services have been provided (ex-post-control-mechanism).[507] Otherwise, overcompensation in the sense of the third *Altmark*-criterion cannot be excluded.

Control mechanisms must guarantee that no possible overcompensation remains at the recipient's free disposal, but rather the means must be reimbursed to the State.[508] That is also the reason why an external body has to carry out the review.[509] Appropriate provisions have to be established in the entrustment,[510] including a claw-back-clause. The plain monitoring through auditing firms is not sufficient as the auditors cannot deprive the beneficiary from the means in the case of an overcompensation.[511]

It is not yet clear whether the control has to be conducted on a yearly basis or can be executed within longer intervals (e.g. once at the end of the entrustment). The Commission only claims a *preference* for yearly monitoring, while also stating that a four-year financing period should normally not be exceeded.[512] Regarding

506 *Commission*, Decision of 20 December 2011 on the application of Article 106(2) of the Treaty on the Functioning of the European Union to State aid in the form of public service compensation granted to certain undertakings entrusted with the operation of services of general economic interest (OJ L 7/3 of 11.01.2012), para.

507 *Commission*, Communication from the Commission on the application of State aid rules to public service broadcasting, (OJ C 257/1 of 27.10.2009), para. 77; Decision of 24.04.2007, State aid No E 3/2005, *Financing of public service broadcasters in Germany*, paras. 268, 279, 281.

508 *Commission*, Decision of 24.04.2007, State aid No E 3/2005, *Financing of public service broadcasters in Germany*, para. 281.

509 *Commission*, Communication from the Commission on the application of State aid rules to public service broadcasting, (OJ C 257/1 of 27.10.2009), para. 78.

510 *Commission*, Decision of 24.04.2007, State aid No E 3/2005, *Financing of public service broadcasters in Germany*, para. 282.

511 *Commission*, Decision of 24.04.2007, State aid No E 3/2005, *Financing of public service broadcasters in Germany*, para. 282.

512 *Commission*, Communication from the Commission on the application of State aid rules to public service broadcasting, (OJ C 257/1 of 27.10.2009), paras. 78 et seq. Speaking in favour of the possibility to control once at the end of the entrustment's duration: *Elste/Wiedemann*, WiVerw 2004, 9, 18.

the minimum three years control-obligation demanded in general State aid law,[513] it would not be surprising if the current time frame will be reduced in future.

3) Surplus

Overcompensation usually must be reimbursed. Due to the risk of cost and revenue fluctuations, the Commission makes an exception for an amount of up to 10% of the annual budgeted expenses of the public service mission.[514] The requirements for the retention of the surplus are as follows: the extent of the surplus is necessary for securing the financing of the public service obligations;[515] furthermore, the reserves must be established for a specific purpose and they must be regularised at fixed dates, when the determined overcompensation must be reimbursed.[516] These fixed dates at least equate to the interval after which the overall control has to be conducted.[517] If the operator is entitled to keep a surplus, appropriate rules must be expressively established in the entrustment.[518] Exceeding the 10% limit is only admissible in exceptional cases and only 'provided that this overcompensation is specifically earmarked in advance and in a binding way for the purpose of a non-recurring, major expense necessary for the fulfilment of the public service mission'.[519]

---

513 *Commission*, Guide to the application of the European Union rules on state aid, public procurement and the internal market to services of general economic interest, and in particular to social services of general interest, SWD(2013) 53 final/2, 29.04.2013, p. 70.

514 *Commission*, Communication from the Commission on the application of State aid rules to public service broadcasting, (OJ C 257/1 of 27.10.2009), para. 73; Decision of 19.05.2004, State aid No C 2/2003, TV2, para. 113; Decision of 24.04.2007, State aid No E 3/2005, *Financing of public service broadcasters in Germany*, para. 281. Cf. regarding possible reasons for such a leaving: *European Broadcasting Union*, Review of the Communication from the Commission on the application of State aid rules to public service broadcasting – EBU reply to the Commission's questionnaire, pp. 24 et seq.

515 *Commission*, Communication from the Commission on the application of State aid rules to public service broadcasting, (OJ C 257/1 of 27.10.2009), para. 73.

516 *Commission*, Decision of 19.05.2004, State aid No C 2/2003, TV2, para. 113; Decision of 22.06.2006, State aid No C 2/2004, *Ad-hoc financing measures of Dutch public service*, para. 148.

517 See above D. III. 2).

518 Cf. *Commission*, Decision of 24.04.2007, State aid No E 3/2005, *Financing of public service broadcasters in Germany*, para. 282.

519 *Commission*, Communication from the Commission on the application of State aid rules to public service broadcasting, (OJ C 257/1 of 27.10.2009), para. 74.

4) Anti-competitive practice

Specific market behaviour of the public service broadcaster might call into question the necessity of the compensation pursuant to the third *Altmark*-criterion. If the broadcaster displays anti-competitive market behaviour that leads to higher costs or lower revenues, the consequent compensation is no longer *necessary* to cover the provision of the public service obligations. Thus, the compensation has to be reduced to the necessary amount, which is equal to the amount the broadcaster would generate using normal market practices.[520]

Such an example is the acquisition of license rights. This accounts for the purchase of the rights as well us for their usage. A public service broadcaster that is consistently overbidding competitors for programme rights (e.g. football) in a way which either goes beyond the public service mandate or reasonable market behaviour (e.g. an unreasonable pricing level) uses the compensation in an unnecessary way to fulfil the public service obligations.[521] The same applies in the case of non-market-conform price undercutting that leads to decreased revenues, for example regarding the price of advertising.[522]

A further application is the usage of acquired rights. The characteristic aspect of 'necessity' demands the utilisation of those rights and/or the award of sub-licenses, if market conform behaviour would indicate it.[523] According to the Commission, in exceptional cases there might be objective (market conform) reasons for not using acquired rights. Nevertheless, the Member States have to establish a system in the remit, which clarifies under which circumstances the public service broadcaster does not have to use the acquired rights as well as a system that reveals the requirements for sub-licensing.[524]

To demonstrate behaviour that is in line with the market, public service broadcasters should adopt the conduct of a commercial undertaking in similar circumstances,

---

520 *Commission,* Decision of 15.10.2003, State aid No C 62/99, *RAI* (ad-hoc payments), para. 124; *Koenigs,* ZEuS 2006, 135, 161. It has to be noted that such a practice does also not comply with the behaviour of a well run undertaking in the sense of the fourth *Altmark*-criterion.

521 Cf. *Commission,* Communication from the Commission on the application of State aid rules to public service broadcasting, (OJ C 257/1 of 27.10.2009), para. 95.

522 Cf. *Commission,* Communication from the Commission on the application of State aid rules to public service broadcasting, (OJ C 257/1 of 27.10.2009), para. 94; Decision of 15.10.2003, State aid No C 62/99, *RAI* (ad-hoc payments), para. 124; Decision of 10.12.2003, State aid No C 60/99, *France 2 and 3* (ad-hoc payments), para. 90.

523 Cf. *Commission,* Decision of 24.04.2007, State aid No E 3/2005, *Financing of public service broadcasters in Germany,* paras. 299 et seqq.

524 Cf. *Commission,* Decision of 24.04.2007, State aid No E 3/2005, *Financing of public service broadcasters in Germany,* paras. 300 et seqq.

whereby it is anticipated to recover the costs normally associated with products or services of similar market value.[525]

IV. 4th Criterion: Efficiency

The fourth *Altmark*-criterion requires Member States either to choose the beneficiary through the implementation of a public procurement procedure, which would allow for the selection of the bidder who is capable of providing those services at the least cost to the community, or to limit the compensation to an amount an efficient undertaking would need to provide the services. In the latter case, the level of compensation must be determined based on an analysis of the costs which a typical undertaking, well run and adequately equipped so as to be able to meet the necessary public service requirements, would have incurred in discharging the obligations.

To date, looking at the existing decisions of the Commission and the European courts on PSB, no scrutinised undertaking has yet successfully complied with the fourth *Altmark*-criterion.[526]

1) Is the application of the fourth criterion necessary?

The challenging application of the fourth *Altmark*-criterion in relation to PSB led many authors to consider the question whether it is at all appropriate and necessary to utilise the fourth criterion when assessing whether a measure constitutes State aid. These concerns were especially driven forward by two decisions of the *ECJ* and the *CFI*. In the following discussion, the question as to whether the decisions of the European courts or the Commission actually justify a deviation from the standards of the fourth criterion is analysed.

a) Chronopost-ruling

In the *Chronopost*[527] decision, the *ECJ* ruled on a case of a French monopoly postal company (*La Poste*) providing logistic services for a subsidiary (*Chronopost*) at allegedly reduced prices. Examined under State aid law was solely the provision of the allegedly low-priced services itself, not the funding of the parent company or the subsidiary. Within the legal proceedings, the question was raised whether *La Poste* had received consideration for its services, which was comparable to that demanded by a private holding company or a private group of undertakings not operating in a

525 *Commission*, Decision of 22.05.2002, State aid No N 631/2001, *BBC license fee*, para. 50. Cf. also *Commission*, Decision of 15.10.2003, State aid No C 62/99, *RAI* (ad-hoc payments), para. 124. Propositions how to assess market-conform prices and behaviour are made below D. IV. 3) b).

526 *Donders*, Public Service Media and Policy in Europe, p. 64.

527 *ECJ*, 3 July 2003 – Joined Cases C-83/01 P, C-93/01 P and C-94/01 P, *Chronopost*.

reserved sector.[528] The court decided that the question raised need not be answered, as *La Poste* had been situated in completely different circumstances from that of a private undertaking acting under normal market conditions. The characteristics of *La Poste*'s services as well as the creation and maintenance of the necessary network were not in line with a purely commercial approach. Therefore such a network would never have been created by a private undertaking.[529] As a consequence, the court stated that 'in the absence of any possibility of comparing the situation of *La Poste* with that of a private group of undertakings not operating in a reserved sector, 'normal market conditions', which are necessarily hypothetical, must be assessed by reference to the objective and verifiable elements which are available'.[530] As a consequence, the *ECJ* accepted the costs borne by *La Poste* itself to assess the character of the measure under Art. 107(1) TFEU. In this context, a favouring should not be assumed, provided the following two conditions are met: 'first, it is established that the price charged properly covers all the additional, variable costs incurred in providing the logistical and commercial assistance, an appropriate contribution to the fixed costs arising from use of the postal network and an adequate return on the capital investment in so far as it is used for SFMI-Chronopost's competitive activity and if, second, there is nothing to suggest that those elements have been underestimated or fixed in an arbitrary fashion'.[531]

Due to the *Chronopost*-ruling, a significant number of authors have drawn the conclusion that, when an undertaking performing SGEI is not able to implement a benchmark-analysis required by the fourth criterion, a comparison with other undertakings may be omitted.[532] Rather the possibility of overcompensation might be assessed solely on the basis of the actual costs of the beneficiary, possibly in combination with the available objective and verifiable data. This view is likely to exempt most of the public service broadcasters from the application of the fourth criterion,

528 *ECJ*, 3 July 2003 – Joined Cases C-83/01 P, C-93/01 P and C-94/01 P, *Chronopost*, para. 32.

529 *ECJ*, 3 July 2003 – Joined Cases C-83/01 P, C-93/01 P and C-94/01 P, *Chronopost*, para. 36.

530 *ECJ*, 3 July 2003 – Joined Cases C-83/01 P, C-93/01 P and C-94/01 P, *Chronopost*, para. 38.

531 *ECJ*, 3 July 2003 – Joined Cases C-83/01 P, C-93/01 P and C-94/01 P, *Chronopost*, para. 40.

532 *Ehricke*, Die EG-rechtliche Beurteilung der Rundfunkfinanzierung, p. 96; *Koenigs*, ZEuS 2006, 135, 169; *Kreße*, Gemeinwirtschaftliche Dienste im europäischen Beihilferecht, p. 110; *Müller*, EStAL 2009, 39, 41 and 44; *Sinnaeve*, EStAL 2003, 351, 358. In the same direction *Bartosch*, EU-Beihilfenrecht – Kommentar, Art. 87 Abs. 1 EGV, para. 69; *Bartosch*, EStAL 2003, 375, 384 et seq.; *Grespan/Santamato*, in: *Mederer/Pesaresi/Van Hoof*, EU Competition Law – Volume IV – State Aid, para. 2.255.

as – due to the unique position of many broadcasters on the market – the implementation of a benchmark-analysis with other broadcasters is hardly possible.[533]

This position, however, cannot be agreed with.[534] The *Chronopost*-judgment targeted a very specific situation. It is neither applicable to the public funding of SGEI, nor open to generalisation. First of all, in the context of the judgment, solely the adequacy of the price paid by the subsidiary for certain services was doubtful. It was questioned whether the *provision of services* (for an inferior price) could be qualified as State aid and *not* whether the *price* paid for the services could have been illegal under State aid law. Hence, the *ECJ* found the calculation based on the parent undertaking's actual costs sufficient, because it was possible to exclude that the subsidiary had not underpaid for the services and therefore had not gained any favour. Therein, the question of a certain efficiency of the possible beneficiary (the subsidiary) would not have had any impact whatsoever on the assessment of the State aid situation. Moreover, a higher efficiency of the giving entity (the parent undertaking) would not have even been beneficial for the possible State aid recipient.[535]

Contrary to the situation in *Chronopost*, it is generally not possible to accurately assess whether a beneficiary receives a favour or only a compensation for the discharge of public service obligations in the sense of *Altmark*, when the basis for the assessment are solely the actual costs of the beneficiary and there is no proof that the undertaking is working efficiently.[536] However, this is the objective of the criterion in question.

Moreover, *Chronopost* was neither enacted in consideration of the *Altmark*-judgment nor was it mentioned in the ruling (due to the earlier adoption). Consequently, one could also argue that the *ECJ* has held the *Chronopost*-decision as being not relevant (any more) considering the financing of SGEI.[537]

---

533 Cf. *Ehricke*, Die EG-rechtliche Beurteilung der Rundfunkfinanzierung, p. 96; *Koenigs*, ZEuS 2006, 135, 169. This argument was also put forward by Denmark in the *TV2*-ruling, to convince the court not to apply the fourth criterion: *CFI*, 22 October 2008, joined Cases T-309/04, T-317/04, T-329/04 and T-336/04, *TV2*, para. 127.

534 Of same opinion: *Schwendinger*, Gemeinschaftsrechtliche Grenzen öffentlicher Rundfunkfinanzierung, p. 285; *Wolf*, in: *Montag/Säcker*, Münchener Kommentar zum Europäischen und Deutschen Wettbewerbsrecht (Kartellrecht) – Band 3, Art. 107 AEUV para. 787.

535 Though, an efficiency of the granting authority, anyway, is of no relevance in the context of the fourth *Altmark*-criterion.

536 *Wolf*, in: *Montag/Säcker*, Münchener Kommentar zum Europäischen und Deutschen Wettbewerbsrecht (Kartellrecht) – Band 3, Art. 107 AEUV para. 787. See also *Fuchs*, ZEuS 2007, 561, 590 et seq.

537 Arguing in favour of this position: *Schwendinger*, Gemeinschaftsrechtliche Grenzen öffentlicher Rundfunkfinanzierung, p. 248.

b) BUPA-ruling

In the *BUPA*-ruling,[538] the *CFI* had to consider a complaint from (several undertakings of) the *British United Provident Association* (*BUPA*) on the establishment of a so-called 'Risk Equalisation Scheme' (RES). The RES, according to the court, was 'a mechanism which provides for the payment of a charge to the HIA [Health Insurance Authority] by PMI [Private medical insurance] insurers whose risk profile is healthier than the average market risk profile and for a corresponding payment by the HIA to PMI insurers whose risk profile is less healthy than the average market risk profile.'[539] The payments in question were made through a fund specially established for the aforementioned purpose and administered by the HIA. The principle of calculation of the payments was that each PMI insurer had to bear the costs, which it would have had to bear if its own risk profile had been equivalent to the average market risk profile. In summary, the compensation granted to the insurers should only cover those payments of the insurers towards the insured (costs of the insurer) that exceeded the payments the insurer would have had, when he would have been exposed to an average market risk profile.

The *CFI* eventually made an exception from the formal requirements of the fourth *Altmark*-criterion and refrained from its application altogether.[540] The reason for resides in the special attribute of the costs that are compensated. The costs occur solely through the accrued insurance cases. All other costs (e.g. management costs, administrative or marketing costs), for which the insurer is directly responsible, are excluded from the calculation of the compensation.[541] As only claims of insurers are attributed to the remaining costs, 'the compensation provided for by the RES did not entail the possibility of offsetting any costs that might result from inefficiency on the part of the PMI insurers subject'.[542] A lack of efficiency of the operator is, therefore, excluded, whereby an application of the fourth criterion seemed solely formal and unnecessary.

It can be concluded from the decision that the fourth *Altmark*-criterion is not compulsory when the amount of compensation is (theoretically) in no way related to possible inefficiencies on the part of the undertaking's subject. However, this is not the case in PSB. The costs of the broadcasters result from their overall expenses. These costs are influenced by the providers, especially due to the type of management. An omission of the criterion according to the jurisprudence is therefore not possible.[543]

---

538 *CFI*, 12 February 2008, Case T-289/03, *BUPA*.

539 *CFI*, 12 February 2008, Case T-289/03, *BUPA*, para. 27.

540 *CFI*, 12 February 2008, Case T-289/03, *BUPA*, para. 248.

541 Cf. *CFI*, 12 February 2008, Case T-289/03, *BUPA*, para. 250.

542 *CFI*, 12 February 2008, Case T-289/03, *BUPA*, para. 250.

543 Of the same opinion: *Commission*, Decision of 20.04.2011, State aid No C 2/2003, *TV2*, para. 126. Denmark took the contrary position (ibid.). Cf. also *Grespan*, EStAL 2010, 79, 90.

c) *Decisions of the Commission*

In the following, decisions of the Commission will be examined, where it took the position that the fourth criterion did not have to be applied strictly.[544]

In a decision relating to the French Republic,[545] the Commission excluded (similarly to the *BUPA*-judgment) the existence of costs higher than those of a typical and well run undertaking. It was remarkable that the conclusion was not based on logical certainty (as in the *BUPA*-decision) but on a factual conviction of the Commission. The French authorities, although not implementing a public procurement procedure according to the fourth criterion, launched a similar public procedure that caught the interest of several bidders. According to the Commission, this procedure permitted a high grade of competition between the bidders.[546] The Commission therefore was convinced that the procedure in question would lead to a provision of the services with the least costs for the granting authority.[547] Additionally, a study was conducted that estimated the possible costs of the overall project and the potential amount of compensation needed beforehand.[548] These studies, previous to the contracting procedure, also suggested that the level of the compensation in this case did not exceed the costs arising from a well-managed undertaking.[549] The combination of the two aspects, the in-depth analysis of the likely costs and the subsequent negotiation-procedure with several undertakings, convinced the *Commission* that the chosen offer would reflect the most efficient provision.[550]

Although the decision shows that the proof of an efficient provision of the services in the sense of the fourth *Altmark*-criterion does not necessarily have to be implemented according to its formal requirements, it is questionable whether the decision significantly simplifies the efforts for the public service broadcasters to meet the criterion. Beside the fact that public service broadcasters are not usually chosen in a public procedure with other bidders, an in-depth analysis would not only have to prove the costs of the respective broadcaster, but also the costs any

544 It has to be noted that these kind of cases are rare exceptions. The assessment under the fourth criterion in principle is mandatory.

545 *Commission Europèene*, Décision Aide d'Etat n ° N 382/2004, C (2005)1170 fin, 03.05.2005, *DORSAL*.

546 *Commission Europèene*, Décision Aide d'Etat n ° N 382/2004, C (2005)1170 fin, 03.05.2005, *DORSAL*, para. 70.

547 *Commission Europèene*, Décision Aide d'Etat n ° N 382/2004, C (2005)1170 fin, 03.05.2005, *DORSAL*, para. 70: 'que celle retenue était bien la plus avantageuse économiquement' (translated: the chosen one [offer] was economically truly the most advantageous).

548 *Commission Europèene*, Décision Aide d'Etat n ° N 382/2004, C (2005)1170 fin, 03.05.2005, *DORSAL*, para. 72.

549 *Commission Europèene*, Décision Aide d'Etat n ° N 382/2004, C (2005)1170 fin, 03.05.2005, *DORSAL*, para. 78.

550 Cf. *Commission Europèene*, Décision Aide d'Etat n ° N 382/2004, C (2005)1170 fin, 03.05.2005, *DORSAL*, para. 79.

potential broadcaster would incur, when offering these services. Such a (market-) test would be very similar to the required analysis of the fourth criterion.

In a later case, regarding a State aid scheme in Slovenia, the Commission had to assess support for a power plant as compensation for the costs of a SGEI in the field of electricity supply.[551] Although the power plant was not chosen on the basis of a public procurement procedure, the Commission noted 'that Slovenia has demonstrated that [...] the choice of Trbovlje [the power plant] was the one that led to providing the SGEI at the least cost to the community, having regard to the specific factual and legal constraints prevailing in this case'.[552] The Commission drew this conclusion from the fact that 'in the current situation, no more than two power plants in Slovenia could in any event have fulfilled the public service obligation in question in their current state'.[553] One of the two power plants was already using its maximum capacity, therefore only one possibility was left. It is remarkable that the Commission only noted 'that there was *no indication* that the *Trbovlje* plant is not operated as a well run typical undertaking or is run in a particularly inefficient way'[554] instead of demanding a proof of the asserted fact.[555]

One might criticise the fact that, despite the power plant in question being the only option, this does not necessarily entail that the costs are the least possible for the community. Without an analysis of the costs incurred by the power plant, the efficiency remains doubtful. The Commission itself does not normally accept the legitimacy of a public procurement procedure if only one bid is submitted as a procedure meeting the fourth *Altmark*-criterion.[556] The situation therein is comparable to the situation when only one possible provider is capable of performing

551 *Commission*, Decision of 24 April 2007 on the State aid scheme implemented by Slovenia in the framework of its legislation on qualified energy producers – Case No C 7/2005 (OJ L 219/9 of 24.8.2007), para. 98.

552 *Commission*, Decision of 24 April 2007 on the State aid scheme implemented by Slovenia in the framework of its legislation on qualified energy producers – Case No C 7/2005 (OJ L 219/9 of 24.8.2007), para. 112.

553 *Commission*, Decision of 24 April 2007 on the State aid scheme implemented by Slovenia in the framework of its legislation on qualified energy producers – Case No C 7/2005 (OJ L 219/9 of 24.8.2007), para. 113.

554 *Commission*, Decision of 24 April 2007 on the State aid scheme implemented by Slovenia in the framework of its legislation on qualified energy producers – Case No C 7/2005 (OJ L 219/9 of 24.8.2007), para. 116. Accentuation by the author of the on hand work.

555 The Commission particularly took the restructuring of the power plant in the past and the fact that the remuneration for the services did not include any profits as indications for the efficiency (*Commission*, Decision of 24 April 2007 on the State aid scheme implemented by Slovenia in the framework of its legislation on qualified energy producers – Case No C 7/2005 (OJ L 219/9 of 24.8.2007), para. 116).

556 *Commission*, Communication from the Commission on the application of the European Union State aid rules to compensation granted for the provision of services of general economic interest (OJ C 8/4 of 11.01.2012), para. 68.

the services. A limitation of choice does not indicate anything about the efficiency of the chosen provider. It is, therefore, of little surprise that the Commission emphasised the grounding of the Decision on the particular factual background of the case, especially the fact that the obligation imposed was about to end in the near future.[557] Although the application of the decision to PSB appears attractive – due to the unique position and profile of such broadcasters compared to other market participants – the act may not be used as a general rule for public funding considering the aforementioned arguments.

In another case, namely the Italian *Poste Italiane,*[558] the universal postal service provider in Italy (which also offered financial products) was accused of receiving State aid through the remuneration paid by the *Cassa Depositi e Prestiti SpA* (a State controlled agency) for the placement of savings certificates. Although the fourth criterion was not formally fulfilled, the Commission did not object to the financing due to the fact that it was market conform.[559] According to the Commission, if the remuneration was market conform 'it would provide an appropriate estimate of the level of the costs that would be incurred by a typical well run undertaking'.[560] The market conformity was confirmed based on a benchmark analysis which examined whether the remuneration of similar financial instruments were comparable to the postal savings certificate. This decision shows that the fulfilment of the fourth *Altmark*-criterion can also be confirmed through an analysis of the market conformity regarding the prices paid. Nevertheless, regarding PSB, it can be difficult to implement an analysis on the market-conformity of the service, since actual benchmarks are missing.[561]

Summarising the decisions discussed above, it cannot be concluded that the fourth *Altmark*-criterion may be neglected in the case of PSB. However, the decisions show that it is possible to prove the efficiency demanded by the criterion in ways different from the formal conditions established there.

---

557 *Commission*, Decision of 24 April 2007 on the State aid scheme implemented by Slovenia in the framework of its legislation on qualified energy producers — Case No C 7/2005 (OJ L 219/9 of 24.8.2007), para. 120. See also para. 122 (ibid.): 'In the *specific legal and factual circumstances* of the case, the compensation does not appear to exceed what a typical, well run undertaking would have requested in order to carry it out' (accentuation by the author of the on hand work).

558 *Commission*, Decision of 21 October 2008 on a state aid scheme implemented by Italy to remunerate Poste Italiane for distributing postal savings certificates, C(2008) 5585 final, 21.10.2008, *Poste Italiane.*

559 *Commission*, Decision of 21 October 2008 on a state aid scheme implemented by Italy to remunerate Poste Italiane for distributing postal savings certificates, C(2008) 5585 final, 21.10.2008, *Poste Italiane*, paras. 170, 185.

560 *Commission*, Decision of 21 October 2008 on a state aid scheme implemented by Italy to remunerate Poste Italiane for distributing postal savings certificates, C(2008) 5585 final, 21.10.2008, *Poste Italiane*, para. 137.

561 See below D. IV. 3) b).

2) Public procurement procedure

Subsequently, a closer contemplation of the requirements of the fourth *Altmark*-criterion is indicated. One way of complying with the criterion is the implementation of a public procurement procedure, which would allow for the selection of the bidder capable of providing those services at the least cost to the community. The efficiency of an undertaking is in principle presumed when a procurement procedure has been implemented.[562] The *Altmark*-judgment itself gives no further explanations to the aspects of such a procedure.[563]

a) General requirements

A public procurement procedure according to the criterion could be considered similar to the procedures pursuant to the European public procurement directives. Regarding PSB Directive 2004/18/EC[564] (now: 2014/24/EC)[565] would apply.[566] The directive offers four types of procedures: open, restricted and negotiated procedure, as well as the competitive dialogue.[567] It is still unclear whether the application of all of these procedures complies with the fourth criterion.[568]

The Commission rightly demands an open, transparent and non-discriminatory procedure.[569] Otherwise, it cannot be excluded that the procedure allows for the selection of the bidder capable of providing those services at the least cost to the community. But, even then, the outcome of the procedure does not necessarily have to be equivalent with the least costs to the community.[570] The procedure rather

---

562 *Schwendinger*, Gemeinschaftsrechtliche Grenzen öffentlicher Rundfunkfinanzierung, p. 248.

563 See also Sinnaeve, EStAL 2003, 351, 357.

564 Directive 2004/18/EC of the European Parliament and of the Council of 31 March 2004 on the coordination of procedures for the award of public works contracts, public supply contracts and public service contracts (OJ L 134/114 of 30.04.2004).

565 Directive 2014/24/EU of the European Parliament and of the Council of 26 February 2014 on public procurement and repealing Directive 2004/18/EC (OJ L 94/65 of 28.03.2014).

566 That is also the opinion of the *Commission* (Communication from the Commission on the application of the European Union State aid rules to compensation granted for the provision of services of general economic interest (OJ C 8/4 of 11.01.2012), para. 63).

567 See Art. 28 et seqq. Directive 2004/18/EC.

568 Cf. *Arhold*, in: *Montag/Säcker*, Münchener Kommentar zum Europäischen und Deutschen Wettbewerbsrecht (Kartellrecht) – Band 3, Art. 107 AEUV para. 235.

569 *Commission*, Communication from the Commission on the application of the European Union State aid rules to compensation granted for the provision of services of general economic interest (OJ C 8/4 of 11.01.2012), para. 63. Of like opinion: *Dörr*, NZBau 2005, 617, 621.

570 *Commission*, Communication from the Commission on the application of the European Union State aid rules to compensation granted for the provision of

needs to determine the competitive market price through the comparison of several offers from market participants.[571] If this is not the case, the alternative benchmark-analysis demanded by the fourth criterion has to be applied, to ensure that the service is provided at least with certain efficiency. Particularly, when only one possible provider exists, the procedure is not eligible and capable of ensuring the provision with the least cost to the community. The main indication for the realization of the demanded procurement procedure therefore is that the procedure provides enough open and genuine competition.[572]

The minimum requirements for such a procedure, namely being open, transparent and non-discriminatory, are definitely met in the framework of an open procedure according to the Directive 2004/18/EC (now: 2014/24/EC). In every other procedure the assessment has to be carried out on a case-by-case basis.[573] Nevertheless, a prevention of a tender from an interested party without valid reason would counter the principle of openness.[574] A negotiated procedure and the competitive dialogue would give the authorities a wide discretion, whereby the procedure is only sufficient when it can be proved that it arranged a sufficiently open and genuine competition.[575] Therefore, publication of a contract notice and competition between several interested parties are minimum requirements. Mandatory publication of the contract notice follows especially from the transparency-requirement. When foreign undertakings could be interested in the provision of the services, only a

services of general economic interest (OJ C 8/4 of 11.01.2012), para. 68. See also *Travers*, EStAL 2003, 387, 391.

571 Also the *Commission* demands in regard of the fulfilment of the public procurement procedure in question that more than one undertaking submits a bit. Otherwise the procedure 'does not give rise to a sufficient open and genuine competition' (Communication from the Commission on the application of the European Union State aid rules to compensation granted for the provision of services of general economic interest (OJ C 8/4 of 11.01.2012), para. 68).

572 Cf. *Commission*, Communication from the Commission on the application of the European Union State aid rules to compensation granted for the provision of services of general economic interest (OJ C 8/4 of 11.01.2012), para. 68.

573 According to *Santamato*, in: *Mederer/Pesaresi/Van Hoof*, EU Competition Law – Volume IV – State Aid, para. 2.582, no procedure should be excluded categorically beforehand as a procedure in the sense of the fourth criterion (see also para. 2.578 therein).

574 Cf. *Commission*, Communication from the Commission on the application of the European Union State aid rules to compensation granted for the provision of services of general economic interest (OJ C 8/4 of 11.01.2012), para. 66. See also *Kühling*, in *Streinz*, EUV/AEUV, Art. 107 AEUV para. 38.

575 Cf. *Commission*, Communication from the Commission on the application of the European Union State aid rules to compensation granted for the provision of services of general economic interest (OJ C 8/4 of 11.01.2012), para. 66.

European-wide publication, with a list of the award criteria,[576] will comply with the condition.[577]

It is doubtful whether the least costs to the community are only achieved when the contract is awarded to the bidder with the lowest price. One might argue that the lowest price does not always depict the best offer. Therefore it seems more appropriate to see the least costs for the community in the economically most advantageous tender.[578] This allows taking environmental and social aspects of the offer into account.[579]

b) Public procurement procedures in the context of public service broadcasting

The possibility of implementing such a procurement procedure in the context of PSB is often disputed.[580] A significant issue is the finding of a single undertaking that could provide all the required services. Furthermore, it has to be noted that a commercial provider, which might get awarded the contract, does not have an interest in providing a(n expensive) high quality product when it is possible, according to its contract, to transmit inexpensive and, most likely, lower quality programmes. A very detailed contract, however, might limit the broadcaster's discretion in this respect, but also might infringe (aspired or required) editorial independence. Hence, the responsibility for the programme should not be shifted to a position that is

---

576 *Koenig/Haratsch*, ZUM 2005, 275, 281.

577 *Dörr*, NZBau 2005, 617, 622; *Kreße*, Gemeinwirtschaftliche Dienste im europäischen Beihilferecht, p. 96; *Linke*, Die Gewährleistung des Daseinsvorsorgeauftrags im öffentlichen Personennahverkehr, p. 123. Cf. also *Koenig/Kühling/Ritter*, EG-Beihilfenrecht, para. 101. Similar (but only *favouring* an European-wide publication): *Kühling*, in *Streinz*, EUV/AEUV, Art. 107 AEUV para. 38. See also *Hancher/Larouche*, in: *Craig/de Búrca*, The Evolution of EU Law, p. 763.

578 Of same opinion: *Commission*, Communication from the Commission on the application of the European Union State aid rules to compensation granted for the provision of services of general economic interest (OJ C 8/4 of 11.01.2012), para. 67; *Commission Européene*, Décision Aide d'Etat n ° N 382/2004, C (2005)1170 fin, 03.05.2005, *DORSAL*, para. 62; *Kreße*, Gemeinwirtschaftliche Dienste im europäischen Beihilferecht, p. 103; *Linke*, Die Gewährleistung des Daseinsvorsorgeauftrags im öffentlichen Personennahverkehr, p. 123. Both award criteria ('most economically advantageous' and 'lowest price') are also decisive in the framework of the Directive 2004/18/EC (see Art. 53(1) therein).

579 *Kreße*, Gemeinwirtschaftliche Dienste im europäischen Beihilferecht, pp. 102 et seq.; *Linke*, Die Gewährleistung des Daseinsvorsorgeauftrags im öffentlichen Personennahverkehr, p. 123.

580 For example: *Bartosch*, EuZW 2009, 684, 687; *Schipanski*, K&R 2006, 217, 221. According to *Bartosch* (ibid.) even the offices of the Commission itself acknowledge the lacking possibility of a public procurement procedure. Also sceptically: *Craufurd Smith*, LIEI 28 (1) [2001], 3, 11.

carried by commercial interests. This, indeed, makes it hard to tender the provision of all the services that public service broadcasters provide as a full package.

Nevertheless, it does not seem impossible to implement procurement procedures for certain parts of the business operation (outsourcing). This could include, for example, the production or purchasing of assets.[581] Competitive bidding for PSB funds has been implemented, for example, in New Zealand for the development and broadcasting of programmes that fulfil certain public service objectives.[582] This way, bids for public funding could also be submitted by commercial broadcasters.[583] Partly implemented public procurement procedures could, moreover, be a means to ensure purchasing at market prices. The latter might be of interest when examining the ways of proving the existence of a well run undertaking.[584]

In any case, it is not admissible to conclude solely from one potential factual obstacle in performing a public procurement procedure that the fourth *Altmark*-criterion should be operated less strictly.[585]

3) Efficiency-test

The alternative to a procurement procedure for proving that the services are provided efficiently is the determination of the admissible costs based on an analysis of the costs which a typical undertaking, well run and adequately equipped so as to be able to meet the necessary public service requirements, would have incurred in discharging the obligations. To date, neither the European courts nor the Commission have finally clarified on how to conduct the efficiency-test with legal certainty.[586] Thus, it is hardly surprising that the test raises various uncertainties as to its practical application.[587] In particular, it has to be noted that a plain price-cap-mechanism, in which the broadcaster receives a fixed amount which is adjusted

---

581 Likewise: *Armstrong/Weeds*, in: *Seabright/Hagen*, The Economic Regulation of Broadcasting Markets, pp. 81, 112; *Schipanski*, K&R 2006, 217, 222. See also *Krone*, Gebührenfinanzierter Rundfunk und Beihilferecht, p. 320; *Schwendinger*, Gemeinschaftsrechtliche Grenzen öffentlicher Rundfunkfinanzierung, pp. 77 et seq.

582 *Foster*, Public Broadcasters – Accountability and Efficiency, pp. 44 et seqq.

583 *Armstrong/Weeds*, in: *Seabright/Hagen*, The Economic Regulation of Broadcasting Markets, pp. 81, 112; *Peacock*, in: *Peacock*, Public Service Broadcasting Without the BBC?, p. 43.

584 See below D. IV. 3) a) (3).

585 *Gundel*, ZUM 2008, 758, 763 et seq.

586 Cf. *Arhold*, in: *Montag/Säcker*, Münchener Kommentar zum Europäischen und Deutschen Wettbewerbsrecht (Kartellrecht) – Band 3, Art. 107 AEUV para. 236; *Santamato*, in: *Mederer/Pesaresi/Van Hoof*, EU Competition Law – Volume IV – State Aid, para. 2.603.

587 See *Fuchs*, ZEuS 2007, 561, 585; *Jennert*, NVwZ 2004, 425, 427 et seq.; *Linke*, Die Gewährleistung des Daseinsvorsorgeauftrags im öffentlichen Personennahverkehr, p. 125.

yearly according to the retail-price-index, is insufficient, as this mechanism does not measure an efficient usage of resources.[588]

The requirement of an analysis of the costs which a typical undertaking would have incurred indicates the implementation of a benchmark-analysis.[589] Such a test might be very difficult to conduct, as public service broadcasters usually have a very unique cost structure and are, therefore, not readily comparable to other broadcasters. Not comparable are, especially, the public service obligations that cause significant costs, which private broadcasters working under market conditions would not accept (e.g. cost-intensive high-quality-productions). These practical issues have caused a significant number of authors and State organs to assert that use of the efficiency-test according to the fourth criterion is not possible in relation to PSB.[590]

On the other hand, there are also voices which deny a fundamental disqualification of the efficiency-test in view of PSB.[591] The Commission, in particular, does not share the view that it is impossible to determine the costs of a typical, well run undertaking as a benchmark.[592] However, it also must be noted that the Commission and the likeminded have yet to explain how such an analysis might be implemented in practice. Concrete clarifications are almost completely lacking. On the contrary, it is also not indicated to deny the possibility of examining public service broadcasters according to the fourth criterion, based on the assertion that the fourth criterion would not match to the situation of public service broadcasters.[593] The latter cannot be an argument, as even in public passenger transportation (which was actually the subject of the *Altmark*-judgment) the assessment according

588 Regarding this mechanism see *Foster*, Public Broadcasters – Accountability and Efficiency, pp. 40 et seqq.

589 Considering the requirements of the efficiency-test see below.

590 *Verwaltungsgericht Karlsruhe*, judgment of 28 September 2006, Case 1 K 559/06, 1 K 559/06a, para. 33; *Braum-Schleicher*, Daseinsvorsorge und service public durch den öffentlich-rechtlichen Rundfunk, p. 91; *Schipanski*, K&R 2006, 217, 221; *Schwendinger*, Gemeinschaftsrechtliche Grenzen öffentlicher Rundfunkfinanzierung, pp. 248 et seq.; *Streinz*, in: *Stern*, Die Bedeutung des Europäischen Rechts für den nationalen Rundfunk, pp. 59, 81; *v. Wallenberg*, MMR 2004, 88, 92. Cf. also *Gundel*, ZUM 2008, 758, 761 ICW fn. 54. Further the argument of Germany in the Commission's decision towards the German broadcasting fees: *Commission*, Decision of 24.04.2007, State aid No E 3/2005, *Financing of public service broadcasters in Germany*, para. 168. Similar the Argument of Denmark: *Commission*, Decision of 20.04.2011, State aid No C 2/2003, *TV2*, para. 127.

591 *Gundel*, ZUM 2008, 758, 761 ICW fn. 54; *Rengeling/Szczekalla*, Grundrechte in der Europäischen Union, § 18 Rn. 732 ICW fn. 150.

592 See in the decision towards the German broadcasting fees: *Commission*, Decision of 24.04.2007, State aid No E 3/2005, *Financing of public service broadcasters in Germany*, para. 168.

593 Of other opinion: *Donders*, Public Service Media and Policy in Europe, pp. 65, 87.

to the fourth criterion is more than difficult, as well.[594] In fact, the application was so problematic that the European authorities decided to adopt a comprehensive regulation,[595] which currently determines the public financing in public passenger transportation and comprises all *Altmark*-criteria apart from the fourth.[596] Despite the mentioned obstacles, the fourth *Altmark*-criterion was successfully applied in public passenger transportation before the adoption of the regulation. Therefore, possible obstacles are not necessarily a convincing argument regarding an omitted application of the fourth criterion.

In the following, the conditions laid down by the efficiency test in relation to the fourth criterion will be scrutinised. As a result, concrete suggestions will be given as to what the implementation of the test might look like in relation to PSB.

a) Analysis of the costs

The criterion demands a determination of the level of compensation necessary, based on an analysis of the costs which a typical undertaking, well run and adequately provided with means so as to be able to meet the necessary public service requirements, would have incurred in discharging those obligations, taking into account the relevant receipts and a reasonable profit for discharging the obligations. In the Commission's 2009 communication[597] on PSB, this analysis is not mentioned at all,[598] maybe due to the assumed challenges of the fourth criterion in this area.

---

594 Cf. for example the following statement of the *Commission*: '[...] for local transport it is very difficult to verify compliance with the "four Altmark criteria" since the assessment of the fourth criterion is particularly unsuited to the specific characteristics of the sector' (Revised proposal for a Regulation of the European Parliament and of the Council on public passenger transport services by rail and by road, COM(2005) 319 final, 20.7.2005, pp. 10 et seq.). The problem in public passenger transportation is that a variety of factors are responsible for incurring costs (e.g. region, form of transport, area, etc.). These factors and the corresponding different cost structures diminish comparability (cf. *Fuchs*, ZEuS 2007, 561, 589). Cf. generally also *Linke*, Die Gewährleistung des Daseinsvorsorgeauftrags im öffentlichen Personennahverkehr, pp. 128 et seq.; *Niels/Jenkins/Kavanagh*, Economics for Competition Lawyers, p. 41 with further references to the situation in the UK; *Sinnaeve*, EStAL 2003, 351, 358.

595 Regulation (EC) No 1370/2007 of the European Parliament and of the Council of 23 October 2007 on public passenger transport services by rail and by road and repealing Council Regulations (EEC) Nos 1191/69 and 1107/70 (OJ L 315/1 of 03.12.2007).

596 Cf. *Linke*, Die Gewährleistung des Daseinsvorsorgeauftrags im öffentlichen Personennahverkehr, pp. 178 et seqq.

597 *Commission*, Communication from the Commission on the application of the European Union State aid rules to compensation granted for the provision of services of general economic interest (OJ C 8/4 of 11.01.2012).

598 See also *Bartosch*, EuZW 2009, 684, 687.

Information about the application, however, can be found in the more abstract guidelines of the so called *Almunia*-package.[599]

(1) Benchmark comparison or analytical approach

The formulation of the fourth criterion implies that the assessment of a sufficient efficiency has to be based upon a benchmark comparison with the costs of other undertakings.[600] Such a benchmark analysis, however, appears not to be the only way of ensuring that the beneficiary's costs do not exceed the costs of a typical and well run undertaking. Another option might be seen in an analysis of the costs of the beneficiary itself, whenever benchmark undertakings are non-existing.[601] The individual costs of the broadcaster could be monitored to see whether they do not exceed average market prices (analysis of the costs of the undertaking).[602] Such an approach is admissible because a well run undertaking would also pay those market prices for services, assets or employees. However, regarding this approach, it is questionable whether a well run undertaking would also purchase these services, assets or hire employees to the same extent as the beneficiary. Whether this question could be answered within the framework of an analysis of the beneficiary shall be subject to the later presented possibilities to assess the efficiency of the undertaking receiving the means. Nevertheless, an analytical approach without a comparison with other broadcasters is another possible option to prove the acceptability of the costs in the sense of the fourth criterion. This is underpinned through decisions of the *CFI* and the Commission according to which the fourth criterion does not have to be applied in a formal way.[603]

---

599 Cf. *Commission*, Communication from the Commission on the application of the European Union State aid rules to compensation granted for the provision of services of general economic interest (OJ C 8/4 of 11.01.2012).

600 *Elste/Wiedemann*, WiVerw 2004, 9, 18 et seq.; *Fuchs*, ZEuS 2007, 561, 587; *Koenig*, BB 2003, 2185, 2187; Kühling, in *Streinz*, EUV/AEUV, Art. 107 AEUV para. 47; *Niels/Jenkins/Kavanagh*, Economics for Competition Lawyers, p. 417; *Tödtmann/Schauer*, NVwZ 2008, 1, 4.

601 *Koenig*, BB 2003, 2185, 2187 et seq.; *Koenig/Haratsch*, ZUM 2005, 275, 281; *Kreße*, Gemeinwirtschaftliche Dienste im europäischen Beihilferecht, p. 106; *Linke*, Die Gewährleistung des Daseinsvorsorgeauftrags im öffentlichen Personennahverkehr, p. 125 and 128; *Niels/Jenkins/Kavanagh*, Economics for Competition Lawyers, p. 418; *Thum*, Einfachgesetzliche Präzisierung des verfassungsrechtlichen Funktionsauftrags des öffentlich-rechtlichen Rundfunks, p. 136. Of other opinion: *Theobald*, IR 2004, 2, 4.

602 Of the same opinion: *Elste/Wiedemann*, WiVerw 2004, 9, 18 et seq. See also the *Poste Italiane* decision of the *Commission* above in D. IV. 1) c).

603 See above D. IV. 1) c).

(2) Typical undertaking

The efficiency test demands that the costs of the beneficiary do not exceed those of a typical undertaking. Therefore, the incurring costs of a broadcaster do not have to be outstandingly low in comparison to a similar undertaking, and neither does the husbandry have to be particularly efficient.[604] Rather, the criterion references an averagely-run business.[605] Consequently, the costs may not exceed the average costs of all comparable well run undertakings.

Whenever the efficiency test is conducted through a benchmark analysis on the basis of a comparison with other undertakings, the median of all comparable undertakings has to be determined.[606] Upon the investigation, several comparable undertakings have to be considered to ascertain the median,[607] although there is no explicit minimum amount. The undertakings do not necessarily have to be located in the same (Member) State or the same region.[608]

When determining the costs of a typical undertaking in the framework of an analytical approach – which considers basically only the costs of the beneficiary itself – the marketability of the prices paid by the undertaking has to be evaluated.[609] These costs do not necessarily have to reflect the best achievable market price, with respect to the standard of a typical undertaking, but at least have to be average in level. However, the broadcaster has to choose the most economically advantageous offer available in every situation. Otherwise, the beneficiary cannot be qualified as a well run undertaking.

(3) Well run undertaking

What has not yet been fully clarified is which requirements have to be met regarding the term 'well run undertaking'. In the framework of a comparison with other undertakings to determine the typical (average) undertaking, this condition demands

---

604 Cf. *Koenig*, BB 2003, 2185, 2187.

605 *Szyszczak*, in: *Szyszczak*, Research Handbook on European State Aid Law, p. 301.

606 *Deuster*, Ausgleichszahlungen für Dienstleistungen von allgemeinem wirtschaftlichem Interesse, p. 165; *Koenig/Kühling/Ritter*, EG-Beihilfenrecht, para. 89.

607 The *Commission* speaks about a 'sufficient number of undertakings whose costs may be taken into account' (*Commission*, Communication from the Commission on the application of the European Union State aid rules to compensation granted for the provision of services of general economic interest (OJ C 8/4 of 11.01.2012), para. 74). Of other opinion: *Schwendinger*, Gemeinschaftsrechtliche Grenzen öffentlicher Rundfunkfinanzierung, p. 248.

608 *Commission*, Communication from the Commission on the application of the European Union State aid rules to compensation granted for the provision of services of general economic interest (OJ C 8/4 of 11.01.2012), para. 74; *Niels/Jenkins/Kavanagh*, Economics for Competition Lawyers, p. 418.

609 Cf. also *Schwendinger*, Gemeinschaftsrechtliche Grenzen öffentlicher Rundfunkfinanzierung, p. 273; *Thum*, NVwZ 2007, 521, 523.

that solely well-run businesses are considered in the calculation.[610] Inefficient, not well-run companies must not be included in the computation. The efficiency may be approved, for example, 'on analytical ratios representative of productivity (such as turnover to capital employed, total cost to turnover, turnover per employee, value added per employee or staff costs to value added)'.[611] According to the Commission, the Member States may even apply all objective criteria available to prove the existence of a well run undertaking as long as the criteria 'are economically recognised as being representative of satisfactory management'.[612]

Some authors take the position that only private undertakings may be taken into account, because they are the only competing businesses, wherefore, regarding their success on the market, they are the only ones which can be held to be certainly well run.[613] However, the fact that an undertaking is owned by the state does not necessarily preclude a well-run undertaking.[614] Qualifying an enterprise as a 'well run undertaking' only remains dubious when the undertaking is receiving public funding. However, it can be ascertained that the business is well run when the fourth *Altmark*-criterion is met by the respective undertaking, too.[615] Ultimately, when the efficiency of a publicly funded benchmark company cannot be proven, only undertakings situated in competition may be considered.[616] This accounts for

---

610 *Deuster*, Ausgleichszahlungen für Dienstleistungen von allgemeinem wirtschaftlichem Interesse, p. 166. Cf. also *Commission*, Communication from the Commission on the application of the European Union State aid rules to compensation granted for the provision of services of general economic interest (OJ C 8/4 of 11.01.2012), paras. 71, 73.

611 *Commission*, Communication from the Commission on the application of the European Union State aid rules to compensation granted for the provision of services of general economic interest (OJ C 8/4 of 11.01.2012), para. 72.

612 *Commission*, Communication from the Commission on the application of the European Union State aid rules to compensation granted for the provision of services of general economic interest (OJ C 8/4 of 11.01.2012), para. 71. For methods see below D. IV. 3) b) (3).

613 *Schwendinger*, Gemeinschaftsrechtliche Grenzen öffentlicher Rundfunkfinanzierung, p. 273. Cf. also *Katsirea*, Public Broadcasting and European Law, p. 342.

614 Also taking into account public undertakings: *Schipanski*, K&R 2006, 217, 222.

615 In this case, both undertaking certainly must not validate their efficiency reciprocally (circular reasoning).

616 *Koenig*, BB 2003, 2185, 2187; *Linke*, Die Gewährleistung des Daseinsvorsorgeauftrags im öffentlichen Personennahverkehr, pp. 126 et seq.; *Niels/Jenkins/Kavanagh*, Economics for Competition Lawyers, pp. 417 et seq. More lenient seems to be the opinion of the Commission, as in inverse conclusion it only demands that if an undertaking receives public service compensation these means have to be granted on conditions that comply with Union law (cf. *Commission*, Communication from the Commission on the application of the European Union State aid rules to compensation granted for the provision of services of general economic interest (OJ C 8/4 of 11.01.2012), para. 74).

the determination of a merchantability of prices paid by an undertaking respectively. Comparable prices may only be used from a market with competition on it.[617]

The assumption that the costs of the beneficiary are equivalent to those of a well run undertaking is in question when cost-saving potentials have been discovered in the past and the concerned broadcaster did not exhaust these potentials in a reasonable period of time.[618] Due to the fact that every entrepreneur who is running his undertaking well would implement all possible and economically sensible means to exhaust cost-saving potential, one cannot qualify a beneficiary that neglects such facts as a well run undertaking.

Another point which might speak against the existence of a well run undertaking – and, therefore, against efficient costs in the sense of the fourth criterion *per se* – is the missing exploitation[619] of purchased (exclusive) rights (especially sports rights) within a reasonable timeframe.[620] A well run undertaking would only buy rights which it can harness. Thus, refraining from using the rights is an indication that the costs incurred are not the costs of a well run undertaking. This applies despite the fact that commercial broadcasters buy and retain specific rights to prevent new markets from developing, as the objective for the public service broadcaster is not to create a maximum of commercial success but the higher public value his services are supposed to achieve.

Eventually, according to the Commission 'the concept of a 'well run undertaking' entails compliance with the national, Union or international accounting standards in force'.[621] Moreover, the beneficiary must meet the qualitative criteria laid down by the Member State. Otherwise it cannot, again, be qualified as a well run undertaking.[622]

---

617 *Koenig*, BB 2003, 2185, 2187.

618 Cf. *Krone*, Gebührenfinanzierter Rundfunk und Beihilferecht, pp. 160 et seq.; *Thum*, NVwZ 2007, 521, 523 et seq.

619 Such exploitation may also be seen in a sublicensing of the rights if this usage has to be seen as the best way of creating the intended public value. Exploitation is also the usage in form of a summary (instead of a complete transmission) if this is the best way to achieve public value.

620 See also the similar view of the channel 'Premiere' in the Commission's State aid case against Germany: *Commission*, Decision of 24.04.2007, State aid No E 3/2005, *Financing of public service broadcasters in Germany*, paras. 139 et seq.

621 *Commission*, Communication from the Commission on the application of the European Union State aid rules to compensation granted for the provision of services of general economic interest (OJ C 8/4 of 11.01.2012), para. 72.

622 *Commission*, Communication from the Commission on the application of the European Union State aid rules to compensation granted for the provision of services of general economic interest (OJ C 8/4 of 11.01.2012), para. 72.

(4) *Adequately provided with necessary means*

Undertakings used for the benchmark have to be adequately provided with the means to be able to meet the necessary public service requirements. Part of the undertakings selected to calculate the cost-median may, therefore, only be undertakings that have the necessary resources to fulfil the beneficiary's public service obligations.[623] This requirement raises a significant obstacle regarding the implementation of a classical benchmark analysis. However, as already explained the conduct of an entire cost-comparison between undertakings is not the only possibility to comply with the fourth criterion.

b) *Possibilities of assessing the efficiency in public service broadcasting*

The term 'efficiency' is enigmatic and has been described in various ways in economic literature.[624] A common approach to characterise efficiency is through the concept 'to do things right' (in contrast to 'to do the right things' for effectiveness), whereas efficiency describes the relation between the services rendered and the factors utilised to perform the services.[625] Consequently, efficiency is to achieve a defined target (the public service obligations) with minimum means.[626]

The costs of the public service broadcaster must not exceed the costs of a hypothetical typical and well run broadcaster that would discharge the obligations. As already set out above, a well run undertaking would strive to perform at its maximum efficiency in its specific situation. In absolute comparison, however, the performance of the public service broadcaster does not have to be top notch, rather, a typical (average) performance is usually sufficient.

The question is whether this applies also for an assessment which does not rely solely on a benchmark analysis with other undertakings, but – as depicted above –[627] on an analysis of the costs of the undertaking itself. This analytical approach scrutinises and assesses mainly the husbandry of the beneficiary and, therefore, faces the problem that it might not be suitable for ascertaining whether the performance of the respective undertaking – especially the usage of resources – is (hypothetically) typical. However, whenever the feasibility of conducting an audit is limited by insufficient information, an assessment may also be based on the

---

623 *Commission*, Communication from the Commission on the application of the European Union State aid rules to compensation granted for the provision of services of general economic interest (OJ C 8/4 of 11.01.2012), para. 76; *Linke*, Die Gewährleistung des Daseinsvorsorgeauftrags im öffentlichen Personennahverkehr, p. 131.

624 Cf. *Keuper/Brösel*, ZögU 2005, 1, 5 et seq.

625 *Keuper/Brösel*, ZögU 2005, 1, 6.

626 The second economical principle (to achieve a maximum output with a fixed amount of means) would not be in line with the *Altmark*-criteria, as it contravenes the clear definition of the remit.

627 See D. IV. 3) a) (1).

second-best solution.[628] It is only essential that the approach, or the combination of various approaches, is eventually conclusive in the specific case. In this respect, the data for a performance audit can be gathered from many sources, such as surveys, interviews, observations and written documents.[629] In order to avoid doubts about the efficiency of a public service broadcaster, an analysis regarding solely the costs of the broadcaster itself ('analytical approach') has several options: for example, to ascertain that the performance of the beneficiary in the assessed area is *the best* a(n) (hypothetical) undertaking could perform while fulfilling the public service obligations, or conduct *punctual (benchmark) comparisons* regarding specific points in the analysis.[630]

Below, practical suggestions are offered as to how an efficiency-evaluation in the context of PSB could be conducted. It has to be noted, though, that usually the compliance with the fourth criterion will only be proven through an expert evaluation (commonly through an auditing firm).[631] Such a third party review has a higher persuasiveness in the context of a State aid procedure. Convincing auditing reports have to consider the *costs*[632] of the beneficiary and prove those to be equal with the costs of a typical, well run undertaking. A plain report of a national audit office that solely compares productivity between broadcasters is not sufficient when it is 'silent on the level of efficiency as such'[633].

(1) Market price

An analysis could be based on evaluating whether the undertaking paid for the necessary resources at the market price only, that is, economically the most advantageous price. Particularly, when 'a generally accepted market remuneration exists for a given service, that market remuneration provides the best benchmark for the

628 *International Organization of Supreme Audit Institutions* (INTOSAI), International Standards for Supreme Audit Institutions (ISSAI) 3000 – Standards and guidelines for performance auditing based on INTOSAI's Auditing Standards and practical experience, p. 54.

629 *International Organization of Supreme Audit Institutions* (INTOSAI), International Standards for Supreme Audit Institutions (ISSAI) 3000 – Standards and guidelines for performance auditing based on INTOSAI's Auditing Standards and practical experience, p. 54.

630 See in the following.

631 See *Schnieders*, NZV 2003, 518, 520. Cf. also *Koenig*, BB 2003, 2185, 2188.

632 In the *Commission*'s *TV2* decision Denmark fruitlessly intended to prove the compliance fourth criterion through an expert evaluation which did not consider the costs of *TV2*: *Commission*, Decision of 20 April 2011 on the measures implemented by Denmark (C 2/03) for TV2/Danmark (OJ L 340/1 of 21.12.2011), paras. 122, 124.

633 *Commission*, Decision of 20 April 2011 on the measures implemented by Denmark (C 2/03) for TV2/Danmark (OJ L 340/1 of 21.12.2011), paras. 130, 133.

compensation in the absence of a tender'.[634] This does not only apply for the service as a whole but also for parts of the services performed. A public service broadcaster that only pays market prices for its resources does not have undue costs, as long as the resources are used efficiently.

(a) Assessment of the prices

To confirm the market compatibility of the prices paid, the costs of the broadcaster have to be split and divided into categories. The classification depends on the available information about market prices. Costs can, for example, be production costs, costs for specific assets, personnel expenses, expenses for license and transmission fees, distribution costs (e.g. transmission, marketing and personnel expenses) or administrative costs (e.g. real estate costs, depreciation, expenses for IT and other personnel). The components of these costs may be combined for the market price contemplation solely if they are comparable (e.g. personnel expenses may be divided in the same category as long as position, occupation and other relevant salary factors are comparable from the perspective of the market). A combination on a more abstract level is possible whenever market prices for a comparable kind of category can be determined.

The existing costs within the formed cost categories (e.g. expenses for editors in a similar position, vehicles, expenses for specific IT-equipment or purchase costs for specific external services) have to be compared to the respective market price. There are various methods of concluding the market price whenever a recognised (market) price for a certain resource does not exist.[635] The market price, for example, might be determined through an open tender procedure (e.g. the broadcaster wants to purchase vehicles for the fleet).[636] The price could also be derived from a comparison with prices usually paid by other undertakings for the resource in question, or an evaluation of the existing available offers on the market. A prerequisite for a market price evaluation, however, is the accessibility to the relevant cost-data. Depending on the costs to assess, a working internal accounting system might be necessary.

(b) Usage of the resources

However, confirming the market price for the resources purchased can only be the first step towards an assessment under the fourth *Altmark*-criterion, since the market price does not give any information about whether the acquired resources

---

634 *Commission*, Communication from the Commission on the application of the European Union State aid rules to compensation granted for the provision of services of general economic interest (OJ C 8/4 of 11.01.2012), para. 69. See also above the *Commission*'s decision regarding *La Poste*.

635 Such a recognised market price might for example derive from collection agreements.

636 The method of an open tender procedure is a recognised method in State aid law to determine the market price.

are used efficiently. Again, there are various possibilities to measure efficient utilisation.

Regarding SGEI, the usage of resources *compellingly* connected to the public service obligations does not have to be assessed in respect of efficiency, as these resources are indispensable for fulfilling the public service obligations. Therefore, it cannot be asked whether an omission of these activities would have created more efficiency. For example, when the public service remit solely contains the clause that the broadcaster has the obligation to produce a high quality programme, one might question whether it is necessary to achieve the result through the establishment of more than one channel (as every channel might incur further costs). However, one might *not* question the usage of more than one channel when the remit expressly obliges the undertaking to set up four channels. In the latter case, all costs necessary to fulfil the public service obligation (e.g. incurred fees) are automatically the costs of a (typical) well run undertaking in the sense of the fourth criterion, as long as the price paid for the activity does not exceed the market price. This conclusion underpins the importance of clearly-defined public service obligations. The more specific the obligations, the better they can be used to justify expenses in the framework of the efficiency-test; that is because, whenever a remit clearly requires a certain expense, the efficiency of the use of the existing resources has to be seen as proven,[637] as the achievement of efficiency without effectiveness is useless[638] and, therefore, cannot be a legitimate activity of a well run undertaking. Thus, the first question after the determination of the market price of a resource is: Does the usage of the resource in question without any doubt meet an objective of the remit? Or, is it only a means among others to fulfil the remit? In the first case, paying the market price is enough to comply with the fourth *Altmark*-criterion.

In the latter, the following two questions have to be asked: firstly, whether the resources used served the fulfilment of the public service obligations and, secondly, whether there was an alternative approach that could have achieved the intermediate target using less resource. The first question clarifies the effectiveness of the measure (regarding the fulfilment of the public service obligations). Without being effective, the use of resources would be wasteful and inefficient. The second query directly targets the efficient usage of resources. To answer the second question, the generated output and the input used by the broadcaster are of interest. The challenge is to find sensible (sub-) categories to quantify both. The establishment of the categories depends on the data material accessible for an evaluation.

Primary outputs are the broadcasting services (programmes or broadcasts), which can be divided into genres (sports, entertainment, news, etc.) and subgenres (football, tennis, Olympics/ movies, movies with specific defined qualities/ afternoon

637 Another example would be that the remit requires the undertaking expressively to maintain a fleet of passenger cars in the amount of 20 vehicles. In this case purchasing 20 vehicles to market prices may not be seen as inefficient.

638 See *Keuper/Brösel*, ZögU 2005, 1, 6.

show, evening programme) defined by the auditor.[639] A further area for concentration could be secondary outputs, for example, procurement, production, administration performance, external services or achievement of main, auxiliary and supporting facilities (e.g. studios, technological operations, fleet).[640] The division of the output-factors should enable the establishment of more specific and, therefore, more assessable output-quantities (e.g. driven mileage/usage hours regarding fleet, usage of certain technical equipment, programme-minutes per editor instead of solely programme-minutes). The quantification of the output might allow statements regarding the capacity utilization (average usage hours of cars or technical equipment, average weekly working hours for staff). Consequently, a full or ordinary[641] utilisation can be proven, which, in turn, validates the necessity of incurring fixed costs.[642] Therefore, the results give an indication as to the subjective necessity of the resources' usage.

An additional second option to use the results to prove efficiency might be in combination with a supplementary punctual benchmark-comparison.[643] In this respect, the output-volumes have to be related to the input. Input might be expressed either in amounts (e.g. two employees), kinds (e.g. work-performance in hours) or price paid for the input (e.g. salaries for two employees: 80.000 £).[644] Primarily, the creation of input-output-relationships has to be implemented on the basis of the accessible information that is suitable for a punctual benchmark-comparison.

(2) Punctual benchmark-comparison

Based on the aforementioned figures regarding input-output-relationships and supplementary to the market-price-review, a punctual benchmark-comparison might be conducted. To understand the principle of a punctual benchmark-analysis, it has to be noted that benchmark-analyses are possible on various hierarchical and aggregational levels.[645] A punctual benchmark-comparison does not take into consideration

639 *Institut für Rundfunkökonomie an der Universität zu Köln*, Controlling für öffentlich-rechtliche Fernsehunternehmen, p. 49.

640 *Institut für Rundfunkökonomie an der Universität zu Köln*, Controlling für öffentlich-rechtliche Fernsehunternehmen, p. 49.

641 The proof of ordinary capacity utilization can be conducted on the basis of a punctual benchmark-comparison.

642 However, it does not prove that the actual usage of the resources is necessary from an objective point of view. Though, it alleviates doubts that the undertaking subjectively requires the resource. In combination with a punctual benchmark-comparison and a procedural assessment (see in the next sections) it might deliver evidence or at least a very strong indication that the undertaking operates efficiently.

643 See below next section.

644 Cf. *Institut für Rundfunkökonomie an der Universität zu Köln*, Controlling für öffentlich-rechtliche Fernsehunternehmen, p. 49.

645 *Grieble/Scheer*, Grundlagen des Benchmarkings öffentlicher Dienstleistungen, p. 13.

the undertaking's cost as a whole, but only selected parts of the costs, and compares them with the respective costs of a comparable undertaking. Punctual benchmarks are, for example, suitable for proving the efficient usage of resources, of which the market-compatibility of the prices paid has been verified already. For example, the working hours of a specific editorial department could be compared with the working hours of similar departments of other broadcasters with comparable output and conditions. This way, not only the salaries of the staff (market price) but also their performance could be evaluated.[646]

Apart from an application supplementary to the above-mentioned market price test, punctual benchmarking might also be used *solely* to verify the efficient performance of larger components of the broadcaster's activities.[647] Benchmark-objects in this respect are for example processes, products and product-groups, product-areas and organisation of the undertaking.[648] In particular, it might be feasible to compare (part of) the broadcaster's organisational structure to those of other undertakings with a comparable output volume (e.g. same amount of people to be in charge of comparable tasks and procedures). Consideration might also be given to whether certain productions are comparable to those of other well run broadcasters with a view to their costs.[649] Regarding broadcasts, at least a division of broadcast-productions in self- and coproduction as well as procured productions might be sensible, as self-production might usually be more expensive than external services (due to supply of capacities and their less intensive usage; more rigid compliance with working time arrangements etc.).[650]

As the fourth criterion only requires a benchmark-comparison with a hypothetical undertaking ('typical'), it is acceptable to define parts of this undertaking from data of companies not operating in broadcasting, as long as the secondary output of the consulted companies is comparable. Such comparable secondary performances may especially be found in 'neutral' activities, such as organisation, fleet[651] or personnel department. Also, companies from other Member States may be used.[652] Even if costs for certain resources are generally different in different Member States, a comparison is not excluded as long as it is possible to adjust the figures on the basis of statistically substantiated data (for example, with the help of figures from the countries' statistical offices).

---

646 Combined with capacity-utilization evaluations the conclusion might even be more substantial.

647 *Schipanski*, K&R 2006, 217, 222.

648 *Grieble/Scheer*, Grundlagen des Benchmarkings öffentlicher Dienstleistungen, p. 14.

649 See also *Schipanski*, K&R 2006, 217, 222.

650 A compellingly additional question in the case of higher costs of self-productions would then be whether self-productions instead of external services are necessary to fulfil the public service remit.

651 Though, this point depends on the composition of the fleet.

652 See above D. IV. 3) a) (2).

(3) Analysis of the processes

Strong indicators for a well run undertaking are the establishment of rationalised processes, as well as clear and functioning efficiency-focused company-structures.[653] An undertaking that has no potential to improve its processes compared to a state-of-the-art managed undertaking, or whose potential for improvement only mirrors the ordinary situation of a typical, well run undertaking, compellingly complies with the fourth *Altmark*-criterion. The product and business processes are directly linked to the incurring of costs. Therefore, it can be argued that a fully-rationalised undertaking with a clear philosophy towards efficiency and without any latitude for further improvement is *even more efficient* than a typical undertaking carrying the same public service obligations. Thus, another possibility to indicate that the input used to achieve the respective output has been held to the minimum might be seen in an analysis of the beneficiary's processes, structures and implemented code of conduct, potentially also entailing a study concerning possible rationalisations within the undertaking.[654]

(a) Is such an assessment possible?

The conduct of such an analysis is possible in various ways. For example, an extensive study of the working processes of the undertaking, taking all possible rationalisation actions into account, might provide a valuable proof of compliance with the fourth *Altmark*-criterion. The persuasiveness increases where the procedures have been reviewed to ensure best practice and, hence, ascertain the 'best price' for the provision of a service. The processes, structures and lived philosophies of the undertaking indirectly give valuable information about its efficiency. An analysis of the company-processes might also be used to check the plausibility of the results from a market-price-analysis in combination with a punctual-benchmark, or supplement these methods in parts of the undertaking where no relevant data was available to conduct the investigation.[655]

---

653 According to the *Commission* 'in the absence of any official definition, the Member States should apply objective criteria that are economically recognised as being representative of satisfactory management' to prove the existence of a well run undertaking (Communication from the Commission on the application of the European Union State aid rules to compensation granted for the provision of services of general economic interest (OJ C 8/4 of 11.01.2012), para. 71).

654 See below the next section.

655 For example when prices are confirmed as market-prices and the capacity-usage is very high there is still no undeniable proof that the capacity-usage is objectively necessary to fulfil the remit efficiently. An analysis of the processes, however, might underpin the conclusion of an undertaking in the sense of the fourth criterion.

An evaluation of the beneficiary's processes,[656] structures and implemented philosophies should focus on all efficiency-relevant areas of the company. This concerns, particularly, company management, strategy and company politics, staff and employee orientation, partnerships, resources, processes and the exploited potential of the substitution of outcome through alternatives.[657] According to INTOSAI, the auditor measuring the performance in the public sector typically might ask the following questions:

- 'Is there a clear structure of performance goals and have the appropriate priorities and instruments been chosen for the use of public funds?
- Is there a clear distribution of responsibility between the different levels of authority, bearing in mind the principle of subsidiarity?
- Is there a general cost awareness and an orientation towards production of services, putting citizens' needs in focus?
- Is there an adequate emphasis on management controls and reporting requirements?'[658]

Particularly, policies and priorities have to be defined by the management and their achievement has to be inspected frequently. This follows from the finding that only what is measured is prioritized, while everything else receives lesser attention.[659]

The aforementioned questions might be complemented by others which give an explanation of the efficiency of the processes. However, all questions asked have to lead to meaningful answers regarding efficiency of structures and processes of an undertaking applying economic state-of-the-art-standards. Although the focus of questioning is always set case-by-case with regard to the specific structure of the undertaking in question, the catalogue of questions should at least aim at corporate strategy, structure and organisation of the undertaking, as well as controls and reporting.[660]

(b) Practical conduct

The analysis might be based on checklists, which are recommended to be elaborated not only for the undertaking as a whole, but for specific areas of the undertaking in

---

656 Processes in this respect are sequences of production-steps towards the end product (cf. *Grieble/Scheer*, Grundlagen des Benchmarkings öffentlicher Dienstleistungen, p. 17).

657 Cf. *Grieble/Scheer*, Grundlagen des Benchmarkings öffentlicher Dienstleistungen, pp. 29 et seqq.

658 *International Organization of Supreme Audit Institutions* (INTOSAI), International Standards for Supreme Audit Institutions (ISSAI) 3000 – Standards and guidelines for performance auditing based on INTOSAI's Auditing Standards and practical experience, pp. 20 et seq.

659 Cf. *Andersen/Henriksen/Spjelkavik*, BIJ 2008, 723, 731 with further references.

660 See straightway.

order to assess the particularities of the different structures and processes. Different parts of the undertaking, in which different questions are asked in the framework of such a checklist, could be finance/controlling, purchasing, logistic, production (here, eventually diverted into production of material and editorial work), personnel, properties, marketing/distribution, etc.[661] The division depends on the differences or similarities in processes and structure. The examination, for example, can be conducted based on interviews (especially with heads of departments and managing staff), the evaluation of documents regarding structure and processes, and monitoring of the processes.

A very important part of an efficient undertaking is a clear corporate strategy and its realisation within the undertaking. Confrontation with vision, goals and strategy to achieve objectives are self-evident in private companies, whereas public service broadcasters do not necessarily engage in such objectives due to the fact that broadcasting fees do not create an incentive to improve efficiency.[662] Corporate strategy depicts the plan of how to build and maintain potentials for success, which is needed to achieve effectivity and efficiency.[663] Potentials for success in PSB are a more cost-efficient, qualitatively higher and/or faster fulfilment of the public service remit.[664] The public service broadcasters, therefore, should lay down performance goals to achieve decreasing broadcasting fees without any change of quality in the programme from the perspective of the recipient.[665] The checklist could comprise questions such as whether a corporate strategy has been clearly formulated for the whole undertaking, and whether individual objectives for different corporate areas have clearly been set, which are derived from the overall corporate strategy. It is crucial that these strategies are embraced by the employees, i.e. that they have a significant impact on the everyday decisions of the employees.[666] An auditor's report at this point, in particular, could be based on interviews and sample checks on processes of the recent past.

The corporate strategy should also comprise performance goals regarding the structuring of corporate areas. The actual structure of the areas could be monitored in relation to the overall objective. This section demands questions with a view to functions and responsibilities, governance and reporting lines, capacities and capacity-utilization, allocation of resources as well as interfaces within the company area and to others. With regards to the latter having a sensible structure might prevent

661 Considering the separation of controlling areas see also *Schneider*, Möglichkeiten und Grenzen von finanzwirtschaftlichen Kennzahlen im Rahmen einer rundfunkspezifischen Controlling-Konzeption für öffentlich-rechtliche Rundfunkanstalten, p. 26.

662 *Keuper/Brösel*, ZögU 2005, 1, 3 et seq.

663 *Keuper/Brösel*, ZögU 2005, 1, 4.

664 *Keuper/Brösel*, ZögU 2005, 1, 5.

665 *Keuper/Brösel*, ZögU 2005, 1, 5.

666 *Grieble/Scheer*, Grundlagen des Benchmarkings öffentlicher Dienstleistungen, p. 22.

duplication of work and waste of resources. A typical negative-example in broadcasting would be granting various editorial offices a fixed amount of resources per year to work independently.[667] Such an approach could not be seen as best practice since, without a loss of quality, it would be more efficient to establish an exchange between editorial offices (to prevent duplication) and allocate means based on the projects intended to be conducted by the editors. Moreover, complex organisations with opaque governance and responsibilities might hinder efficient operating results as well. Valid questions in this case might be: are functions clearly separated within the specific company area; is sufficient communicative exchange within the area and with other company departments ensured; are resources being allocated in the best way possible (especially considering capacity-utilisation); has the area a clear governance structure and is this structure known by the employees; etc.

Furthermore, as already indicated by INTOSAI (see above), management controls and reporting are decisive factors when recognising and creating potentials for higher efficiency and should therefore not be neglected. In particular, internal accounting has the function to reveal decision-relevant information for the management to maximise public value using the most cost-efficient possibilities.[668] Questions asked in this section would relate to the installation of sensible control and reporting structures that a well-run enterprise would have undertaken to achieve and maintain efficiency. Particularly, considering the significant costs of programme productions it is important to be able to calculate precise budgets based on causation for different programmes, including proportionate operating expenses (activity-based-accounting).[669] Beside the possibilities of conducting internal and external benchmarking, this kind of reporting would allow monitoring the costs of a specific format and setting it in relationship to the targeted public value. As indicated before, usage statistics could also be relevant.[670]

---

667 Considering this approach in public service broadcasting see *Institut für Rundfunkökonomie an der Universität zu Köln*, Controlling für öffentlich-rechtliche Fernsehunternehmen, p. 10.

668 Cf. *Institut für Rundfunkökonomie an der Universität zu Köln*, Controlling für öffentlich-rechtliche Fernsehunternehmen, pp. 46 et seqq. See also *Schneider*, Möglichkeiten und Grenzen von finanzwirtschaftlichen Kennzahlen im Rahmen einer rundfunkspezifischen Controlling-Konzeption für öffentlich-rechtliche Rundfunkanstalten, p. 26.

669 Cf. *Schneider*, Möglichkeiten und Grenzen von finanzwirtschaftlichen Kennzahlen im Rahmen einer rundfunkspezifischen Controlling-Konzeption für öffentlich-rechtliche Rundfunkanstalten, p. 43.

670 *Schneider*, Möglichkeiten und Grenzen von finanzwirtschaftlichen Kennzahlen im Rahmen einer rundfunkspezifischen Controlling-Konzeption für öffentlich-rechtliche Rundfunkanstalten, p. 44.

(4) The possibility of additional rationalisation

The aforementioned options could be further supported by an auditor's report regarding possible options for rationalisation. Such a report would monitor the broadcaster with the goal to determine latitudes for restructuring and optimising processes to achieve a higher efficiency. Nevertheless, conducting such a monitoring without implementing the necessary measures is insufficient. This accounts especially when the examination is only based on a simple assessment of the means necessary for the undertaking to fulfil the services and the imposition of various rationalisation obligations.[671] A potential for rationalisation rather indicates that the undertaking is not well run in the sense of the fourth criterion, wherefore the assessment is not enough to prove efficiency.

The report would assess not only the beneficiary's established structures and processes, under the standard of a well run undertaking, but also involve a targeted search for possibilities for improvement. A (mainly) fruitless examination in this respect would help to validate positive results arising from an analysis on preceding lines.

Possibilities for rationalisation reside especially in production activities, as long as the alternatives serve the public service obligations in the *same* way as the present activity.[672] In this respect, co-productions and the purchasing of productions are usually less expensive than in-house-productions.[673] The establishment of a number of channels might also be reconsidered when the additional channels do not add significant public value to the programme of the broadcaster (e.g. not only repetitions of entertainment programmes with minor public recognition). Interesting might be the bundling and dovetailing of tasks, especially when editorial offices work on similar programmes independently without being in contact with each other (hazard of duplication or neglect of essential information). Particularly, when there is a great variation of independently working editorial offices one might review whether these tasks could be fulfilled more efficiently and in the same quality (including editorial independence) within one integrated editorial office.[674] At least the usage of the same administration (back-office functions) to minimise and share overhead costs could be an option. Cost-saving-latitude might also be found in the overhead costs, which do not directly affect the programme-outcome of the broadcaster.

---

671 Probably of other opinion: *Hesse*, AfP 2005, 499, 506.

672 In this respect a substitution of self-productions through purchased productions would not be possible, when the remit obliges the beneficiary to produce himself.

673 *Institut für Rundfunkökonomie an der Universität zu Köln*, Controlling für öffentlich-rechtliche Fernsehunternehmen, p. 8; *Schneider*, Möglichkeiten und Grenzen von finanzwirtschaftlichen Kennzahlen im Rahmen einer rundfunkspezifischen Controlling-Konzeption für öffentlich-rechtliche Rundfunkanstalten, p. 7.

674 This way for example fix costs could be minimised (e.g. for additional premises, separate facilities).

(5) *Monitoring of quality?*

It is debatable whether the efficiency-test pursuant to the fourth *Altmark*-criterion has to involve monitoring of the quality of the undertaking's output. Since the criterion solely asks for the compliance with certain cost-restrictions, quality-evaluations are usually *superfluous.*

Nevertheless, a certain quality of the output (especially the programme) could be relevant whenever a service obviously does not achieve the public service objective it is based on. Thus, according to the Commission an 'undertaking entrusted with the operation of an SGEI that does not meet the qualitative criteria laid down by the Member State concerned does not constitute a well run undertaking even if its costs are low'[675]. This applies in particular when a programme's sole reason is to draw the viewers' attention[676] to the broadcaster (i.e. pure entertainment programmes without any other intentional public value behind them). As the transmission of such programmes does not have another purpose but being appealing to the viewer, they are lacking any foundation if they do not reach the target of mass appeal. A well run undertaking would supersede such broadcasts in the medium term. The perpetuation of such a programme could therefore be an indicator that the related expenses are not those of a well run undertaking. Whenever entertainment-programmes exist, with the sole purpose to entertain, an assessment according to the fourth *Altmark*-criterion should therefore encompass an analysis of the success of these programs. A measurable benchmark in this respect could be audience ratings.

(6) *Heuristic*

Despite the possibilities for assessing PSB discussed above, it has to be noted that it is impossible to quantify a market price for the *final* outcome of PSB,[677] as the intention behind the services is not a monetary one but to create a higher public value for the population. A measurable and quantifiable unit for this (additional) value is lacking. Therefore, auxiliary methods such as the previously mentioned have to be consulted.

However, due to the complexity of the processes in major companies, as well as the contestability regarding the methods of managerial accounting and relevant benchmark figures, absolutely precise assessments regarding the efficiency of an undertaking are impossible to state. In particular, the practicability of monitoring

---

675 *Commission*, Communication from the Commission on the application of the European Union State aid rules to compensation granted for the provision of services of general economic interest (OJ C 8/4 of 11.01.2012), para. 72.

676 Considering this goal in the framework of public service obligations see above D. I. 1) c) (1).

677 *Institut für Rundfunkökonomie an der Universität zu Köln*, Controlling für öffentlich-rechtliche Fernsehunternehmen, p. 7; *Schneider*, Möglichkeiten und Grenzen von finanzwirtschaftlichen Kennzahlen im Rahmen einer rundfunkspezifischen Controlling-Konzeption für öffentlich-rechtliche Rundfunkanstalten, p. 8.

has to be ensured (e.g. not every single paper sheet used can be assigned to a cost centre), whereby any assessment, also regarding benchmark comparisons, relies to a certain extent on an element of judgment.[678] In other words, when conducting a study about the efficiency of a public service broadcaster, the Member States have to exploit all means possible to evaluate whether this is a typical, well run undertaking or not. However, whenever this is carried out, the assessment does not have to treat every single cost-relevant detail exhaustively, but rather provide a conclusive examination of the broadcaster as a whole without abnormalities regarding economic efficiency. Investigations into relatively inessential parts of the undertaking regarding cost efficiency may be of limited assistance for the sake of feasibility.

This view is underpinned by the spirit of the interpretative rule in Art. 14 TFEU which highlights the feasibility of SGEI. In this respect the aforesaid would enable the services to comply with the *Altmark*-criteria on a practically feasible way. Eventually, although the services have to be efficient regarding the fourth *Altmark*-criterion, efficiency is not the primary goal of the services as they are intended to ensure better-quality performances for the population, which may often conflict with a restrictive handling of resources.[679] Hence, the examination of undertakings according to the fourth *Altmark*-criterion should not be handled in an unduly rigid way.[680]

(7) Intermediate conclusion

The depicted options to confirm the efficiency of the beneficiary should best be used in combination. Nevertheless, '[p]erformance auditing should not be streamlined'[681], for which reason there might even be more possibilities to judge the efficiency of public service broadcasters apart from a public procurement procedure or a benchmark comparison involving the broadcaster as a whole. Undertaking an analysis might require the change of auditing methods and approaches with further

---

678 Cf. *Linke*, Die Gewährleistung des Daseinsvorsorgeauftrags im öffentlichen Personennahverkehr, p. 128; *Rinken/Kellmer*, Verw 39 [2006], 1, 10 et seqq.

679 For example the recording of a rarely displayed animal-behaviour for a nature-documentary might require the employment of a lot of working hours. An efficiently thinking undertaking would probably record the documentary without the behaviour in question if the increase of the working hours would be disproportionate. A quality-orientated producer would probably accept the additional expenses for the sake of the viewers which get to see something extraordinary.

680 Cf. *Linke*, Die Gewährleistung des Daseinsvorsorgeauftrags im öffentlichen Personennahverkehr, p. 128; *Rinken/Kellmer*, Verw 39 [2006], 1, 10 et seqq.

681 *International Organization of Supreme Audit Institutions* (INTOSAI), International Standards for Supreme Audit Institutions (ISSAI) 3000 – Standards and guidelines for performance auditing based on INTOSAI's Auditing Standards and practical experience, p. 29.

inside knowledge on the monitoring object and the available data.[682] It is necessary to emphasise again that a clear definition of the remit, expressly comprising the usage of specific resources, can justify utilisation in the review under the fourth *Altmark*-criterion.

Paying market prices in combination with punctual benchmark-comparisons – or, alternatively, an in-depth-analysis of the processes of the undertaking – are convincing methods to prove that the beneficiary is a well run undertaking using all means to be efficient. A report on the possibilities for further rationalisation would help to validate the plausibility of the found results. It is important that the public service broadcasters are able to raise the relevant information, which might bring necessary adjustments to the accounting system.[683] The anchoring of a meaningful control might lead to a higher acceptance of broadcasting fees throughout the population, too. Nevertheless, the broadcasters have to eventually ask themselves sincerely whether they use all opportunities an efficiency-minded company would take to achieve the goal (the public service obligations) reaching the best quality with the least costs.

682 Cf. *International Organization of Supreme Audit Institutions* (INTOSAI), International Standards for Supreme Audit Institutions (ISSAI) 3000 – Standards and guidelines for performance auditing based on INTOSAI's Auditing Standards and practical experience, p. 50.

683 The requirement was already raised by *Foster*, Public Broadcasters – Accountability and Efficiency, pp. 26 et seq.

E. Conclusion

The presented analysis indicates that public funding in PSB has to be essentially qualified as State aid, if the financing does not comply with the four criteria of the *Altmark Trans* Jurisprudence. In particular, the argument that broadcasting fees are not granted by a Member State or through State resources is immaterial in most cases. However, meeting the *Altmark*-criteria does not appear to be impossible, contrary to common belief.

In this respect, the Member States have to act thoroughly when defining public service obligations. Especially, the often cited discretion of the Member States regarding the definition of SGEI does not apply in view of the clarity of the definition, as the competence to control the definition stays with the Commission. In that matter the presented analysis takes a different view from the commonly represented positions. In particular, the Amsterdam Protocol does not change this conclusion. This issue is often ignored. The definition, rather, has to be as clear as possible and should comprise a precise catalogue of those activities the broadcaster is entitled and not entitled to do. Abstract terms should be used as rarely as possible. Regarding new developments and to make the definition less restraining, the Member States might establish an evaluation procedure (as a number of States have done; e.g. the Public Value Test) through which the admissibility of new activities under the public service obligations is ascertained *ad hoc* and eventually (at least indirectly) endorsed by the Member State.

To comply with the *Altmark*-ruling, the establishment of the definition and the calculation scheme for the compensation payments resulting from it have to be done before the start of the services. Moreover, the Member States are not authorised to compensate public service broadcasters with more than what is necessary to fulfil the public service obligations, which applies under *Altmark* as well as under Art. 106(2) TFEU. In order to give the broadcaster broader financial latitude in their operations, Member States might consider granting the broadcaster an additionally reasonable profit. According to the view presented here, a reasonable profit does not infringe State aid law even if the public service broadcaster is also a broadcaster owned by the State.

Concrete instructions towards how to conduct an analysis according to the fourth *Altmark*-criterion are – as far as can be seen – completely lacking. The commonly disputed possibility of public service broadcasters complying with the fourth criterion, however, is not necessarily excluded according to the presented analysis. In particular, the Commission's decision-making practice demonstrated the possibility of proving the efficiency of a beneficiary through means other than a pure benchmark analysis. Especially, the assessment of the structures, processes and organisation of the company in question is a practical approach by which to validate that the beneficiary expends only the costs of a typical well run undertaking. Such an analysis can be combined with a punctual benchmark analysis regarding areas where comparative data from companies operating under market conditions can be obtained. The conduct of such an evaluation, however, would not be solely relevant in the framework of Art. 107(1) TFEU, but could also help to improve the perception of PSB in the eyes of the eventual payers of the services, namely the general public. The proof of an efficient handling of public resources could mitigate the often raised accusation of a waste of public funds and create a higher acceptance and, therefore, legitimacy of broadcasting fees.[684]

However, even though such an analytic approach seems feasible, the efforts to evaluate a large company are significant. To dissolve the existing evaluation problems, it might be possible for the European Institutions to elaborate a regulation that takes the difficulties of the PSB market into account and declares public funding under the fulfilment of certain requirements compatible with the common market. A similar regulation has been adopted, for example, in the area of public transportation, to overcome the difficulties of the application of the fourth *Altmark*-criterion through the eventual non-application of it and the introduction of a practicable system superseding the requirement.[685] Through the declaration that the funding is compatible with the common market, the regulation would relieve the Member States from the procedure of Art. 108(3) TFEU. At the same time, the act could specify the first three *Altmark*-criteria with regard to PSB. Such a regulation could be a convenient solution by which to combine the required legal certainty with an awareness of the specific policy and practical implications of PSB.

684 See also *Foster*, Public Broadcasters – Accountability and Efficiency, p. 31.

685 Regulation (EC) No 1370/2007 of the European Parliament and of the Council of 23 October 2007 on public passenger transport services by rail and by road and repealing Council Regulations (EEC) Nos 1191/69 and 1107/70 (OJ L 315/1 of 03.12.2007). Cf. Art. 9(1) therein.

Appendices

Abbreviations

Art.	Article
cf.	confer (lat.)
CFI	Court of First Instance
e.g.	exempli gratia (lat.)
EC	Treaty Establishing the European Community
ECJ	European Court of Justice
EGC	General Court
et al.	et alia (lat.)
et seq. / et seqq.	et sequens / et sequentes (lat.)
fn.	footnote
ibid.	ibidem (lat.)
ICW	in conjunction with
i.e.	id est (lat.)
OJ	Official Journal of the European Union
p. / pp.	page / pages
para. / paras.	paragraph / paragraphs
PSB	PSB
SGEI	Service(s) of General Economic Interest
TFEU	Treaty on the Functioning of the European Union
TEU	Treaty on European Union

Bibliography

A

Amato, Giuliano and Ehlermann, Claus-Dieter (eds.) (2007) *EC Competition Law – A Critical Assessment.* Oxford et al.: Hart Publishing.

Andersen, Bjørn and Henriksen, Bjørnar and Spjelkavik, Ingrid (2008) Benchmarking applications in public sector principal-agent relationships, *Benchmarking: An International Journal*, 15 (6), pp. 723–741.

Arbeitsgemeinschaft der öffentlich-rechtlichen Rundfunkanstalten der Bundesrepublik Deutschland (ARD) (eds.) (2008) *ARD-Jahrbuch 08–40. Jahrgang.*

Arhold, Christoph (2007) The Case Law of the European Court of Justice and the Court of First Instance on State Aids in 2006/2007 (Part 1), *European State Aid Law Quarterly*, pp. 151–214.

Armstrong, Mark and Weeds, Helen (2007) Public service broadcasting in the digital world, pp. 81–149, in: Seabright, Paul and Hagen, Jürgen von (eds.) *The Economic Regulation of Broadcasting Markets – Evolving Technology and the Challenges for Policy.* Cambridge et al.: Cambridge University Press.

B

Bacon, Kelyn (ed.) (2009) *European Community Law of State Aid.* Oxford et al.: Oxford University Press.

Bartosch, Andreas (1999) Öffentlichrechtliche Rundfunkfinanzierung und EG-Beihilfenrecht - eine Zwischenbilanz, *Europäische Zeitschrift für Wirtschaftsrecht*, pp. 176–180.

Bartosch, Andreas (2001) Neues zum Tatbestandsmerkmal der „Belastung des Staatshaushalts" i.S. des Art. 87 I EG, *Neue Zeitschrift für Verwaltungsrecht*, pp. 643–645.

Bartosch, Andreas (2003) Clarification or Confusion? – How to Reconcile the ECJ's Rulings in Altmark and Chronopost, *European State Aid Law Quarterly*, pp. 375–386.

Bartosch, Andreas (2009) *EU-Beihilfenrecht – Kommentar.* München: C.H. Beck.

Bartosch, Andreas (2009) Öffentlichrechtliche Rundfunkfinanzierung und EG-Beihilfenrecht – Zehn Jahre später, *Europäische Zeitschrift für Wirtschaftsrecht*, pp. 684–688.

Bosman, Wieland (2012) Paradigmenwechsel in der Rundfunkfinanzierung: Von der Rundfunkgebühr zum Rundfunkbeitrag, *Kommunikation & Recht*, pp. 5–11.

Bovis, Christopher (2004), Financing Services of General Economic Interest, Public Procurement and State Aid: The Delineation Between Market Forces and Protection, *The Columbia Law Journal of European Law*, 10 (3), pp. 419–443.

Boysen, Sigrid and Neukirchen, Mathias (2007) *Europäisches Beihilferecht und mitgliedstaatliche Daseinsvorsorge.* Baden-Baden: Nomos.

Braum-Schleicher, Tanja (2006) *Daseinsvorsorge und service public durch den öffentlich-rechtlichen Rundfunk – Eine Analyse im Lichte der Dienstleistungsfreiheit und des europäischen Beihilfesystems.* Frankfurt a. M.: Peter Lang.

Bullinger, Martin (1985) Rundfunkordnung im Bundesstaat und in der Europäischen Gemeinschaft – Aktuelle rechtliche Probleme –, *AfP – Zeitschrift für Medien- und Kommunikationsrecht,* 4, pp. 257–265.

C

Castendyk, Oliver (2008) Das Angebot der Rundfunkanstalten im Internet – was müssen sie dürfen?, *AfP – Zeitschrift für Medien- und Kommunikationsrecht,* pp. 467–473.

Castendyk, Oliver and Dommering, Egbert and Scheuer, Alexander (eds.) (2008) *European Media Law.* Alphen a/d Rijn: Kluwer Law International.

Craig, Paul and de Búrca, Gráinne (eds.) (2011) *The Evolution of EU Law.* Second edition. Oxford et al.: Oxford University Press.

Craufurd Smith, Rachael (2001) State Support For Public Service Broadcasting: The Position Under European Community Law, *Legal Issues of Economic Integration,* 28 (1), pp. 3–22.

Craufurd Smith, Rachael and Böttcher B. (2002) Football and Fundamental Rights: Regulating Access to Major Sporting Events on Television, *European Public Law,* 8 (1), pp. 107–133.

D

Damm, Andreas (1998) *Gebührenprivileg und Beihilferecht – Zur Vereinbarkeit der Finanzierung des öffentlich-rechtlichen Rundfunks in Deutschland mit Art. 92 EGV.* Berlin et al.: Springer.

Degenhart, Christoph (2005) Finanzierung des öffentlich-rechtlichen Rundfunks aus nationaler und internationaler Sicht: Der Rundfunkauftrag als Grundlage und Grenze, *AfP – Zeitschrift für Medien- und Kommunikationsrecht,* pp. 493–499.

Degenhart, Christoph (2005) Öffentlich-rechtlicher Rundfunkauftrag und Rundfunkgebühr nach dem siebten und achten Rundfunkänderungsstaatsvertrag, *Kommunikation & Recht,* pp. 295–302.

Degenhart, Christoph (2008) Rundfunkrecht in der Entwicklung – Ein Rechtsprechungsbericht, *Kommunikation & Recht,* pp. 214–223.

Depypere, Stefaan and Broche, Jérôme and Tigchelaar, Nynke (2004) State aid and broadcasting: state of play, *Competition Policy Newsletter,* 1, pp. 71–73.

Depypere, Stefaan and Tigchelaar, Nynke (2004) The commission's state aid policy on activities of public service broadcasters in neighbouring markets, *Competition Policy Newsletter,* 2, pp. 19–22.

Deuster, Jan (2007) *Ausgleichszahlungen für Dienstleistungen von allgemeinem wirtschaftlichem Interesse – Das Verhältnis von Art. 87 Abs. 1 EG zu Art. 86 Abs. 2 EG nach der Altmark Trans-Rechtsprechung unter besonderer Berücksichtigung der öffentlichen Finanzierung des Luftverkehrs.* Münster et al.: LIT.

Donders, Karen (2012) *Public Service Media and Policy in Europe.* Houndmills et al.: Palgrave Macmillan.

Döpkens, Harm-Randolf (2009) Anmerkung zu EuGH, Urteil vom 22. Oktober 2008 – T-309/04, T-317/04, T-329/04 und T-336/04, *Zeitschrift für Urheber- und Medienrecht,* pp. 214–216.

Dörr, Dieter (1998) *Die öffentlich-rechtliche Rundfunkfinanzierung und die Vorgaben des EG-Vertrages.* Reihe Arbeitspapiere des Institut für Rundfunkökonomie an der Universität zu Köln – Heft 94 [Online]. Available at: http://www.rundfunk-institut.uni-koeln.de/institut/pdfs/9498.pdf [Accessed: 20 July 2013].

Dörr, Dieter (2009) Die Finanzierung des öffentlich-rechtlichen Rundfunks zwischen den Vorgaben aus Karlsruhe und den Anforderungen aus Brüssel, pp. 451–467, in: Detterbeck, Steffen and Rozek, Jochen and Coelln, Christian von (eds.) *Recht als Medium der Staatlichkeit – Festschrift für Herbert Bethge zum 70. Geburtstag.* Berlin: Duncker & Humblot.

Dörr, Oliver (2005) Infrastrukturförderung (nur) nach Ausschreibung?, *Neue Zeitschrift für Baurecht und Vergaberecht,* pp. 617–623.

E

Eberle, Carl-Eugen (2001) Die Rundfunkgebühr auf dem EU-Prüfstand, *AfP – Zeitschrift für Medien- und Kommunikationsrecht,* pp. 477–481.

Eberle, Carl-Eugen (2006) Gestaltung der deutschen Rundfunkordnung durch die europäische Beihilfenaufsicht?, pp. 497–506, in: Geiss, Karlmann and Gerstenmaier, Klaus-A. and Winkler, Rolf M. and Mailänder, Peter (eds.), *Festschrift für Karl Peter Mailänder zum 70. Geburtstag am 23. Oktober 2006.* Berlin: de Gruyter.

Ehricke, Ulrich (2006) *Die EG-rechtliche Beurteilung der Rundfunkfinanzierung.* Baden-Baden: Nomos.

Elste, Günter and Wiedemann, Torsten (2004) Auswirkungen des EuGH-Urteils in der Rechtssache Altmark Trans auf die Konzessionierung und Finanzierung im ÖPNV, *Wirtschaft und Verwaltung,* pp. 9–26.

Erkens, Andre (2009) *Der öffentlich-rechtliche Rundfunk und exklusive Sportberichterstattung – Geben ist öffentlich-rechtlicher denn Nehmen – Darf und/oder muss der öffentlich-rechtliche Rundfunk exklusive Sportberichterstattung anbieten?.* Hamburg: Kovac.

European Broadcasting Union (2008) *Review of the Communication from the Commission on the application of State aid rules to public service broadcasting – EBU reply to the Commission's questionnaire* [Online]. Available at: http://ec.europa.eu/competition/state_aid/reform/ comments_broadcasting/ebu_en.pdf [Accessed: 20 July 2013].

F

Fairbairn, Carolyn (2004) Commentary: why broadcasting is still special, pp. 58–70, in: Peacock, Alan (ed.) *Public Service Broadcasting Without the BBC?*. London: The Institute of Economic Affairs.

Fechner, Frank (2013) *Medienrecht.* 14th edition. Tübingen: Mohr Siebeck.

Foster, Robin (1992) *Public Broadcasters – Accountability and Efficiency.* Edinburgh: Edinburgh University Press.

Frenz, Walter and Götzkes, Vera (2010) Öffentlich-rechtliche Rundfunkanstalten als Beihilfeempfänger, *Zeitschrift für Urheber- und Medienrecht*, pp. 563–567.

Frey, Dieter (1999) Das öffentlich-rechtliche Fernsehen im Wettbewerbsrecht der EG, *Zeitschrift für Urheber- und Medienrecht*, pp. 528–542.

Fuchs, Eileen (2007) Was ist ein „durchschnittliches, gut geführtes Unternehmen? – Zum Urteil des EuGH in der Rs. „Altmark Trans", *Zeitschrift für Europarechtliche Studien*, pp. 561–608.

G

Garzaniti, Laurent (2003) *Telecommunications, Broadcasting and the Internet: EU Competition Law and Regulation.* 2nd edition. London: Sweet & Maxwell.

Geuer, Ermano (2013) Der neue Rundfunkbeitrag aus europarechtlicher Sicht – Wann eine staatliche Beihilfe der Notifizierungspflicht gegenüber der EU-Kommission unterfällt, *Computer und Recht*, pp. 156–160.

Goerlich, Helmut and Meier, Anne-Kristin (2007) Selbstverpflichtungen und Autonomie am Beispiel des öffentlich-rechtlichen Rundfunks – Zugleich zur »Neuen Steuerung« und ihren Verfahren, *Zeitschrift für Urheber- und Medienrecht*, pp. 889–898.

Greissinger, Christian (2001) *Vorgaben des EG-Vertrages für nationales Rundfunk- und Multimediarecht.* Baden-Baden: Nomos.

Grespan, Davide (2010) A Busy Year for State Aid Control in the Field of Public Service Broadcasting, *European State Aid Law Quarterly*, pp. 79–98.

Grieble, O. and Scheer, A.-W. (2000) *Grundlagen des Benchmarkings öffentlicher Dienstleistungen.* Veröffentlichungen des Instituts für Wirtschaftsinformatik – Heft 166 [Online]. Available at: http://www.uni-saarland.de/fileadmin/user_upload/Fachrichtungen/fr13_BWL/professuren/PDF/heft166.pdf [Accessed: 20 July 2013].

Grzeszick, Bernd (2008) Der Telemedien-Auftrag des öffentlich-rechtlichen Rundfunks zwischen Verfassungs- und Gemeinschaftsrecht, *Neue Zeitschrift für Verwaltungsrecht*, pp. 608–615.

Gundel, Jörg (2008) Nationale Rundfunkfinanzierung, Art. 86 EGV und das EG-Beihilfenrecht: Die Position der Gemeinschaftsgerichte, *Zeitschrift für Urheber- und Medienrecht*, pp. 758–765.

H

Hahn, Werner and Vesting, Thomas (2012) *Beck'scher Kommentar zum Rundfunkrecht.* 3rd edition. München: C.H. Beck.

Hain, Karl-E. (2001) Die Europäische Transparenz-Richtlinie und der öffentlich-rechtliche Rundfunk in Deutschland, *MultiMedia und Recht*, pp. 219–224.

Hancher, Leigh (2003) Towards a New Definition of a State Aid under European Law: Is there a New Concept of State Aid Emerging?, *European State Aid Law Quarterly*, pp. 365–373.

Hancher, Leigh and Ottervanger, Tom and Slot, Piet Jan (2012) *EU State Aids.* Fourth Edition. London: Sweet & Maxwell.

Harrison, Jackie and Woods, Lorna (2007) *European Broadcasting Law and Policy.* Cambridge: Cambridge University Press.

Heidenhain, Martin (2010) *European State Aid Law.* München: C.H. Beck.

Hesse, Albrecht (2005) Die Finanzierung des öffentlich-rechtlichen Rundfunks aus europäischer und nationaler Sicht – Der dynamische Auftrag des öffentlich-rechtlichen Rundfunks, *AfP – Zeitschrift für Medien- und Kommunikationsrecht*, pp. 499–507.

High Level Group on Media Freedom and Pluralism (2013) *A free and pluralistic media to sustain European democracy.* The Report of the High Level Group on Media Freedom and Pluralism.

I

Institut für Rundfunkökonomie an der Universität zu Köln (ed.) (1993) *Controlling für öffentlich-rechtliche Fernsehunternehmen.* Reihe Arbeitspapiere des Institut für Rundfunkökonomie an der Universität zu Köln – Heft 7/1993 [Online]. Available at: http://rundfunkoek.uni-koeln.de/institut/pdfs/0793.pdf [Accessed: 20 July 2013].

International Organization of Supreme Audit Institutions (INTOSAI), *International Standards for Supreme Audit Institutions (ISSAI) 3000 – Standards and guidelines for performance auditing based on INTOSAI's Auditing Standards and practical experience* [Online]. Available at: http://www.issai.org/media/13517/perfor mance_audit_ guidelines_e.pdf [Accessed: 20 July 2013].

J

Jennert, Carsten (2003) Staatliche Daseinsvorsorge zwischen Beihilferecht und Vergaberecht, *Wettbewerb in Recht und Praxis*, pp. 459–468.

Jennert, Carsten (2004) Finanzierung und Wettbewerb in der Daseinsvorsorge nach Altmark Trans, *Neue Zeitschrift für Verwaltungsrecht*, pp. 425–431.

K

Katsirea, Irini (2008) *Public Broadcasting and European Law – A Comparative Examination of Public Service Obligations in Six Member States.* Alphen Aan Den Rijn: Kluwer Law International.

Keuper, Frank and Brösel, Gerrit (2005) Zum Effektivitäts-Effizienz-Dilemma des öffentlichrechtlichen Rundfunks, *Zeitschrift für öffentliche und gemeinwirtschaftliche Unternehmen*, pp. 1–18.

Kirchhof, Paul (2010) *Die Finanzierung des öffentlich-rechtlichen Rundfunks.* Baden-Baden: Nomos.

Koenig, Christian (2001) Funktionen des Bietverfahrens im EG-Beihilfenrecht, *Europäische Zeitschrift für Wirtschaftsrecht*, pp. 741–747.

Koenig, Christian (2003) Die neuen EG-beihilfenrechtlichen Kompensationsmaßstäbe in der Daseinsvorsorge – das Altmark Trans-Urteil in der Praxis, *Betriebs-Berater*, pp. 2185–2188.

Koenig, Christian and Bartosch, Andreas and Braun, Jens-Daniel (2002) *EC Competition and Telecommunications Law.* The Hague et al.: Kluwer Law International.

Koenig, Christian and Busch, Martin (2011) Quersubventionierung im kommunalen Konzern – EU-beihilfenrechtliche Grenzen, *Das Gewerbearchiv*, pp. 181–186.

Koenig, Christian and Haratsch, Andreas (2001) How to cut a long story short: Das PreussenElektra-Urteil des EuGH und die EG-Beihilfenkontrolle über das deutsche Rundfunkgebührensystem, *Zeitschrift für Urheber- und Medienrecht*, pp. 537–547.

Koenig, Christian and Haratsch, Andreas (2003) The Licence-Fee-Based Financing of Public Service Broadcasting in Germany after the Altmark Trans Judgment, *European State Aid Law Quarterly*, pp. 569–578.

Koenig, Christian and Haratsch, Andreas (2004) Der Anwendungsbereich der EG-Transparenzrichtlinie im Lichte der jüngsten Rechtsprechung des EuGH, *Zeitschrift für Wettbewerbsrecht*, pp. 544–567.

Koenig, Christian and Haratsch, Andreas (2005) Ring frei im DVB-T-Beihilfenstreit vor der Europäischen Kommission – Terrestrischer digitaler Rundfunk vor dem Aus?, *Zeitschrift für Urheber- und Medienrecht*, pp. 275–283.

Koenig, Christian and Kühling, Jürgen (2000) Mitgliedstaatliche Kulturförderung und gemeinschaftliche Beihilfekontrolle durch die EG-Kommission, *Europäische Zeitschrift für Wirtschaftsrecht*, pp. 197–203.

Koenig, Christian and Kühling, Jürgen and Ritter, Nicolai (2005) *EG-Beihilfenrecht.* 2nd edition. Frankfurt a. M.: Verlag Recht und Wirtschaft.

Koenigs, Kirsten (2006) Die deutsche Rundfunkgebühr und das Europäische Beihilferecht, *Zeitschrift für Europarechtliche Studien*, pp. 135–176.

Krausnick, Daniel (2005) *Das deutsche Rundfunksystem unter dem Einfluss des Europarechts.* Berlin: Duncker & Humblot.

Kraussnick, Daniel (2007) Gebührenfinanzierung unter dem Damoklesschwert – Zur Entscheidung der Europäischen Kommission vom 24. April 2007, *Zeitschrift für Urheber- und Medienrecht*, pp. 806–813.

Kreße, Bernhard (2006) *Gemeinwirtschaftliche Dienste im europäischen Beihilferecht.* Köln et al.: Heymann.

Kroeber, Alfred L./ Kluckhohn, Clyde (1978) *Culture: a critical review of concepts and definitions.* Millwood, New York: Kraus Reprint Co.

Krone, Daniel (2010) *Gebührenfinanzierter Rundfunk und Beihilferecht – Gemeinschaftsrechtliche Analyse der deutschen Rundfunkgebühr und Optionen für eine Anpassung des nationalen Ordnungsrahmens.* Hamburg: Kovac.

Kruse, Eberhard (2001) Das Merkmal der „Staatlichkeit" der Beihilfe nach Art. 87 Abs. 1 EG – Nach dem EuGH-Urteil zum deutschen Stromeinspeisungsgesetz, *Zeitschrift für das gesamte Handelsrecht und Wirtschaftsrecht*, 165, pp. 567–592.

Kübler, Friedrich (2004) Europäisches Beihilferecht, Transparenzrichtlinie und Rundfunkgebühr, pp. 231–241, in: Fuchs, Andreas and Schwintowski, Hans-Peter and Zimmer, Daniel (eds.) *Wirtschafts- und Privatrecht im Spannungsfeld von Privatautonomie, Wettbewerb und Regulierung – Festschrift für Ulrich Immenga zum 70. Geburtstag.* München: C.H. Beck.

L

Laitenberger, Johannes (2003) Perspektiven für die EG-rechtliche Entwicklung im audiovisuellen Bereich, pp. 31–37, in: Stern, Klaus and Prütting, Hanns (eds.) *Nationaler Rundfunk und Europäisches Gemeinschaftsrecht zwischen Kommunikationsfreiheit und Regulierung.* München: C.H. Beck.

Linke, Benjamin (2010) *Die Gewährleistung des Daseinsvorsorgeauftrags im öffentlichen Personennahverkehr.* Baden-Baden: Nomos.

Linke, Benjamin (2011) Der Begriff des „angemessenen Gewinns" bei Ausgleichsleistungen für DAWI im europäischen Beihilferecht am Beispiel des öffentlichen Personenverkehrs, *Europäisches Wirtschafts- und Steuerrecht*, pp. 456–460.

M

Mederer, Wolfgang and Pesaresi, Nicola and Van Hoof, Marc (eds.) (2008) *EU Competition Law – Volume IV – State Aid.* Leuven, Belgium: Claeys & Casteels.

Michel, Eva-Maria (2005) Konvergenz der Medien – Auswirkungen auf das Amsterdamer Protokoll und das Europäische Beihilferecht, *MultiMedia und Recht*, pp. 284–287.

Montag, Frank and Säcker, Franz Jürgen (eds.) (2011) *Münchener Kommentar zum Europäischen und Deutschen Wettbewerbsrecht (Kartellrecht) – Band 3 – Beihilfen- und Vergaberecht.* München: C.H. Beck.

Mortensen, Frands (2008) Altmark, Article 86(2) and Public Service Broadcasting, *European State Aid Law Quarterly*, pp. 239–249.

Müller, Thomas (2009) Efficiency Control in State aid and the Power of Member States to define SGEIs, *European State Aid Law Quarterly*, pp. 39–46.

N

Neun, Andreas (2002) Öffentlich-rechtlicher Rundfunk: Grenzen des *Wachtums – Programm- und Angebotsdiversifizierung der Rundfunkanstalten der Bundesrepublik Deutschland.* Berlin: Duncker & Humblot.

Niels, Gunnar and Jenkins, Helen and Kavanagh, James (2011) *Economics for Competition Lawyers.* Oxford: Oxford University Press.

Nitsche, Ingrid (2001) *Broadcasting in the European Union: The Role of Public Interest in Competition Analysis.* The Hague: Kluwer Law International.

O

Oppermann, Thomas (1997) *Deutsche Rundfunkgebühren und europäisches Beihilferecht.* Berlin: Duncker & Humblot.

P

Peacock, Alan (2004) Public service broadcasting without the BBC?, pp. 33–53, in: Peacock, Alan (ed.) *Public Service Broadcasting Without the BBC?.* London: The Institute of Economic Affairs.

Pelny, Stefan (2005) Das Verfahren der EU-Kommission gegen Dänemark: Ein Menetekel für die Länderregierungschefs in Deutschland?, *Zeitschrift für Urheber- und Medienrecht*, pp. 22–30.

Q

Quigley, Conor (2009) *European State Aid Law And Policy.* Second edition. Oxford: Hart.

R

Reese, Stephanie (2006) *Der Funktionsauftrag des öffentlich-rechtlichen Rundfunks vor dem Hintergrund der Digitalisierung – Zur Konkretisierung des Funktionsauftrages in § 11 Rundfunkstaatsvertrag.* Frankfurt a. M. et al.: Peter Lang.

Rengeling, Hans-Werner and Szczekalla, Peter (2004) *Grundrechte in der Europäischen Union – Charta der Grundrechte und Allgemeine Rechtsgrundsätze.* Köln et al.: Heymann.

Repa, Lukas and Tosics, Nóra and Dias, Pedro and Bacchiega, Alberto (2009) The 2009 Broadcasting Communication, *Competition Policy Newsletter*, 3, pp. 10–16.

Ruttig, Markus (2001) *Der Einfluß des EG-Beihilferechts auf die Gebührenfinanzierung der öffentlich-rechtlichen Rundfunkanstalten.* Frankfurt a. M. et al.: Peter Lang.

Rinken, Alfred and Kellmer, Oliver (2006) Kommunale Krankenhäuser als Instrumente sozialstaatlich-kommunaler Daseinsvorsorge im europäischen Verfassungsverbund, *Die Verwaltung*, 39, pp. 1–28.

Ritter, Lennart and Braun, W. David (2004) *European Competition Law – A Practitioner's Guide.* Third edition. The Hague: Kluwer Law International.

S

Sánchez Rydelski, Michael (ed.) (2006) *The EC State Aid Regime – Distortive Effects of State Aid on Competition and Trade.* London: CMP Publishing.

Santa Maria, Alberto (2007) *Competition and State Aid – An Analysis of the EC Practice.* Alphen aan den Rijn: Kluwer Law International.

Santamato, Sandro and Pesaresi, Nicola (2004) Compensation for services of general economic interest: some thoughts on the Altmark ruling, *Competition Policy Newsletter*, 1, pp. 17–21.

Schipanski, Tankred (2006) Jüngste Entwicklungslinien eines eventuellen Beihilfecharakters der Gebührenfinanzierung des öffentlich-rechtlichen Rundfunks, *Kommunikation & Recht*, pp. 217–223.

Schnaitter, Marcus (2008) *Möglichkeiten und Grenzen der Ausgestaltung des Programmauftrags der öffentlich-rechtlichen Rundfunkanstalten.* Münster: LIT.

Schneider, Sabine (1996) *Möglichkeiten und Grenzen von finanzwirtschaftlichen Kennzahlen im Rahmen einer rundfunkspezifischen Controlling-Konzeption für öffentlich-rechtliche Rundfunkanstalten.* Reihe Arbeitspapiere des Institut für Rundfunkökonomie an der Universität zu Köln – Heft 63/1996 [Online]. Available at: http://www.rundfunk-institut.uni-koeln.de/institut/pdfs/6396.pdf [Accessed: 20 July 2013].

Schnieders, Ralf (2003) Comment on ECJ-judgement Urteil of 24.7.2003, Case C-280/00 (Altmark Trans), *Neue Zeitschrift für Verkehrsrecht*, pp. 518–520.

Schwarze, Jürgen (2000) Medienfreiheit und Medienvielfalt im Europäischen Gemeinschaftsrecht, *Zeitschrift für Urheber- und Medienrecht*, pp. 779–801.

Schweitzer, Heike (2011) Services of General Economic Interest: European Law's Impact on the Role of Markets and of Member States, pp. 11–62, in: Cremona, Marise (ed.) *Market Integration and Public Services in the European Union.* Oxford: Oxford University Press.

Schwendinger, Gerd (2007) *Gemeinschaftsrechtliche Grenzen öffentlicher Rundfunkfinanzierung – Audiovisuelle Daseinsvorsorge und Pluralismus-sicherung im Lichte von EG-Beihilferecht und Dienstleistungsfreiheit.* Baden-Baden: Nomos.

Selmayr, Martin and Kamann, Hans-Georg (2004) Public Broadcasting and the EC State Aid Law: No „Carte Blanche" after Altmark Trans, *Kommunikation & Recht*, pp. 49–58.

Selmer, Peter and Gersdorf, Hubertus (1994) *Die Finanzierung des Rundfunks in der Bundesrepublik Deutschland auf dem* Prüfstand des EG-Beihilferegimes. Berlin: Duncker & Humblot.

Sinnaeve, Adinda (2003) State Financing of Public Services: The Court's Dilemma in the Altmark Case, *European State Aid Law Quarterly*, pp. 351–363.

Soltész, Ulrich (2012) Ryanair und Tierkörperbeseitigung – Wendepunkt für beihilferechtliche Konkurrentenklagen, *Europarecht*, pp. 60–68.

Storr, Stefan (2002) Grundversorgung in Rundfunk und Binnenmarkt – Unterschiede und Perspektiven, *Kommunikation & Recht*, pp. 464–473.

Streinz, Rudolf (2007) Die Bedeutung des Amsterdamer Protokolls für den öffentlich-rechtlichen Rundfunk in Deutschland, pp. 59–92, in: Stern, Klaus (ed.): *Die Bedeutung des Europäischen Rechts für den nationalen Rundfunk*. München: C.H. Beck.

Streinz, Rudolf (2012) *EUV/AEUV – Vertrag über die Europäische Union und Vertrag über die Arbeitsweise der Europäischen Union*. 2nd Edition. München: C.H. Beck.

Stulz-Herrnstadt, Michael (2004) *Nationale Rundfunkfinanzierung und europäische Beihilfenaufsicht im Lichte des Amsterdamer Rundfunkprotokolls*, Berlin: Duncker & Humblot.

Sumrada, Nana and Nohlen, Nicolas (2005) Control of State Aid for Public Service Broadcasting: Analysis of the European Commission's Recent Policy, *European State Aid Law Quarterly*, pp. 609–620.

Szyszczak, Erika (2011) *Research Handbook on European State Aid Law*. Cheltenham: Edward Elgar.

T

Theobald, Christian (2004) Aktuelles aus dem Infrastrukturrecht: Wechselwirkungen zwischen Energie- Verkehrs- und Telekommunikationswirtschaft, *Infrastruktur-Recht*, pp. 2–4.

Thum, Kai (2007) *Einfachgesetzliche Präzisierung des verfassungsrechtlichen Funktionsauftrags des öffentlich-rechtlichen Rundfunks*. Frankfurt a. M. et al.: Peter Lang.

Thum, Kai (2007) Vereinbarkeit der Gebührenfinanzierung des öffentlich-rechtlichen Rundfunks mit EG-Beihilferecht, *Neue Zeitschrift für Verwaltungsrecht*, pp. 521–527.

Thyri, Peter and Jaeger, Thomas (2006) Sportfernsehen und EG-Wettbewerbsrecht, *wirtschaftsrechtliche blätter*, pp. 197–206.

Tigchelaar, Nynke (2003) State Aid to Public Broadcasting – Revisited – An Overview of the Commission's Practise, *European State Aid Law Quarterly*, pp. 169–182.

Tödtmann, Ulrich and Schauer, Michael (2008) Aktuelle Rechtsfragen zum öffentlichen Personennahverkehr – Nationale und europäische Rechtsentwicklung sowie Konsequenzen für die Praxis, *Neue Zeitschrift für Verwaltungsrecht*, pp. 1–7.

Travers, Noel (2003) Public Service Obligations and State Aid: Is all really clear after Altmark?, *European State Aid Law Quarterly*, pp. 387–392.

V

Vesterdorf, Peter L. and Nielsen, Mogens Uhd (2008) *State Aid Law of the European Union*. London: Sweet & Maxwell.

W

Wallenberg, Gabriela von (2004) Anmerkung zu EuGH, Urteil vom 27.11.2003 – verb. Rs. C-34/01 bis C-38/01, *MultiMedia und Recht*, pp. 88–92.

Wiedemann, Verena (2004) Public Service Broadcasting, State Aid, and the Internet: Emerging EU Law, *European State Aid Law Quarterly*, pp. 595–603.

Winter, Jan A. (2004) Re(de)fining the Notion of State Aid in Article 87(1) of the EC Treaty, *Common Market Law Review*, 41, pp. 475–504.

Wittig-Terhardt, Margret (2001) Zur Situation des öffentlich-rechtlichen Rundfunks im Lichte des Amsterdamer Protokolls Nr. 23 – Unter besonderer Berücksichtigung der Entscheidungen der Europäischen Kommission zu den Spartenprogrammen Kinderkanal und Phoenix von ARD und ZDF, pp. 727–755, in: Classen, Claus Dieter and Dittmann, Armin and Fechner, Frank and Gassner, Ulrich M. and Kilian, Michael (eds.) *„In einem vereinten Europa dem Frieden der Welt zu dienen ..." – Liber amicorum Thomas Oppermann*. Berlin: Duncker & Humblot.

Table of Commission's State-aid decisions regarding PSB

Decision of 02.10.1996, State aid No NN 141/95, *RTP*
Decision of 24.02.1999, State aid No NN 70/1998, *Kinderkanal/Phoenix*
Decision of 14.12.1999, State aid No NN 88/98, *BBC News 24*
Decision of 03.04.2002, State aid No NN 2/2002, *ZDF Medienpark*
Decision of 22.05.2002, State aid No N 631/2001, *BBC license fee*
Decision of 01.10.2003, State aid No N 37/2003, *BBC Digital Curriculum*
Decision of 15.10.2003, State aid No C 62/99, *RAI* (ad-hoc payments)
Decision of 15.10.2003, State aid No C 85/2001, *RTP* (ad-hoc payments)
Decision of 10.12.2003, State aid No C 60/99, *France 2 and 3* (ad-hoc payments)
Decision of 19.05.2004, State aid No C 2/2003, *TV2*
Decision of 06.10.2004, State aid No N 313/2004, *TV2* (recapitalisation)
Decision of 20.04.2005, State aid No E 8/2005, *RTVE*
Decision of 20.04.2005, State aid No E 10/2005, *France 2 and 3*
Decision of 20.04.2005, State aid No E 9/2005, *RAI*
Decision of 07.06.2005, State aid No N 54/2005, *Chaine française d'information international*
Decision of 22.03.2006, State aid No E 14/2005, *RTP*
Decision of 22.03.2006, State aid No N 638/2005, *Aide à la création de la chaîne corse Via Stella*
Decision of 22.06.2006, State aid No C 2/2004, *Ad-hoc financing measures of Dutch public service*
Decision of 04.07.2006, State aid No NN 31/2006, *RTP*
Decision of 07.03.2007, State aid No NN 8/2007, *RTVE*
Decision of 24.04.2007, State aid No E 3/2005, *Financing of public service broadcasters in Germany*
Decision of 27.02.2008, State aid No E 4/2005, *RTE* and *TNAG (TG4)*
Decision of 27.02.2008, State aid No E 8/2006, *VRT*
Decision of 16.07.2008, State aid No N 279/2008, *France Télévisions*
Decision of 04.08.2008, State aid No N287/08, *TV2/Denmark A/S* (rescue aid)
Decision of 01.09.2009, State aid No C 27/2009, *France Télévisions*
Decision of 28.10.2009, State aid No E 2/2008, *ORF*
Decision of 03.12.2009, State aid No C 38/2009, *RTVE*
Decision of 26.01.2010, State aid No E5/2005, *Dutch public broadcasters*
Decision of 20.04.2011, State aid No C 2/2003, *TV2*
Decision of 20.04.2011, State aid No C 19/2009, *TV2* (restructuring)
Decision of 20.12.2011, State aid No SA.33294, *RTP* (amendment of decision NN 31/2006)
Decision of 20.12.2011, State aid No C 85/2001, *RTP* (years 1992–1998)
Decision of 08.11.2013, State aid No SA.37136, *Financement de la station de radio locale France*

www.ingramcontent.com/pod-product-compliance
Ingram Content Group UK Ltd.
Pitfield, Milton Keynes, MK11 3LW, UK
UKHW021902290926
8980IPUK00015B/1008

9 783631 665688